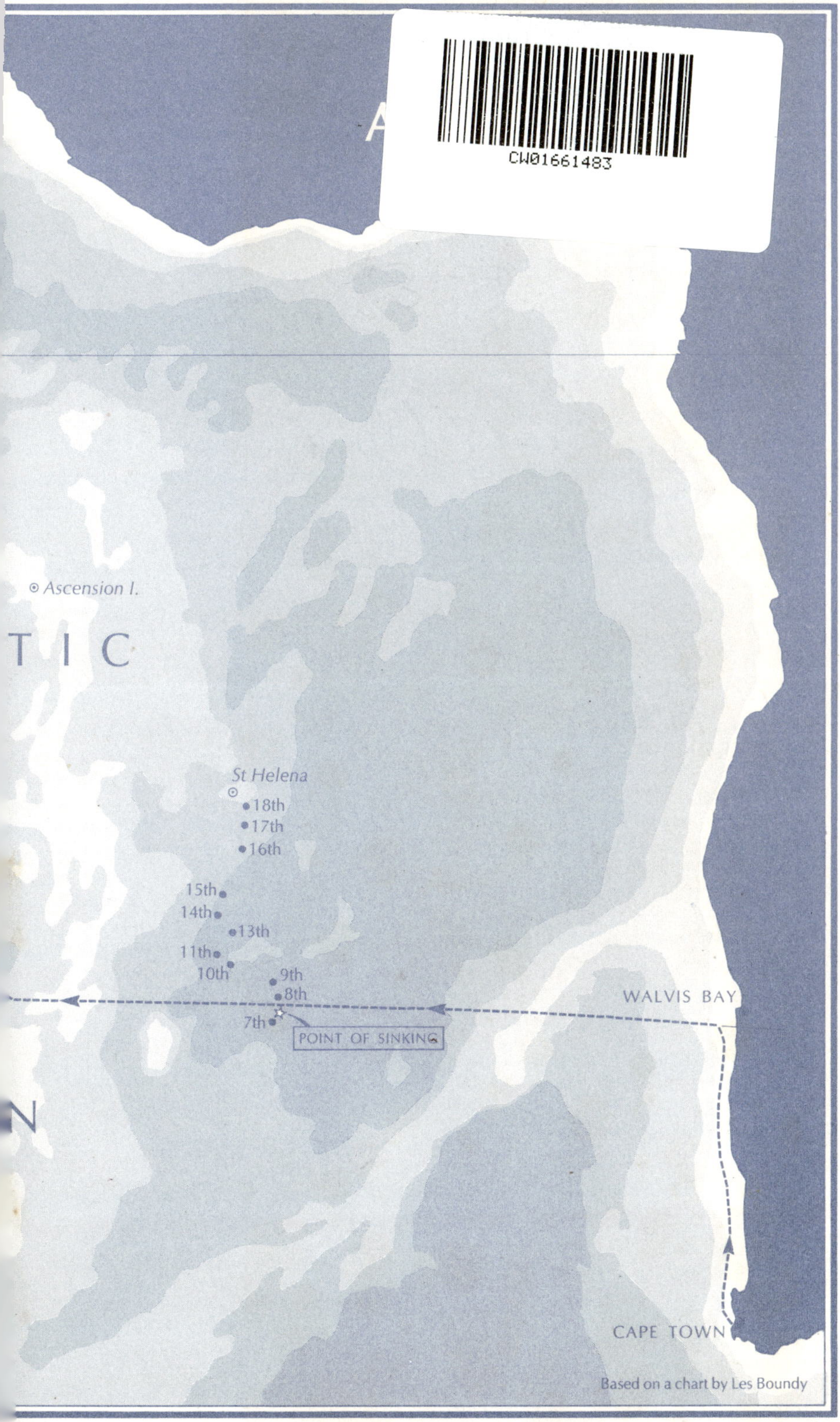

A
Ascension I.
T I C
N
St Helena
18th
17th
16th
15th
14th
13th
11th
10th
9th
8th
7th
POINT OF SINKING
WALVIS BAY
CAPE TOWN
Based on a chart by Les Boundy

L. Skea

Dulcie Kup (Kendall)

J.R. Davies

D. J. Mustons

Douglas Quenlien

Ann King. (Davies)

Donald Miller

E L Rogerson (Mrs)

GOODNIGHT, SORRY FOR SINKING YOU

Elsie Rogerson

with sincere good wishes

Ralph Barker

David Reid (Punk)

Esther Simms

Basil Almond

Violet Williams

David Simms

Susan Nagle (Almond)

David Almond

Francis Almond

George Nutter

Janet Evans (Davies)

Ron Stubbs (4th Officer)

by the same author

Down in the Drink
The Ship-Busters
Strike Hard, Strike Sure
The Thousand Plan
Great Mysteries of the Air
Aviator Extraordinary
Verdict on a Lost Flyer
The Schneider Trophy Races
Against the Sea
Survival in the Sky
The Blockade Busters
The Hurricats
The RAF at War

The Last Blue Mountain
One Man's Jungle
Not Here, But in Another Place

Ten Great Innings
Ten Great Bowlers
Test Cricket: England v Australia
(with Irving Rosenwater)
The Cricketing Family Edrich
Innings of a Lifetime

GOODNIGHT, SORRY FOR SINKING YOU

The Story of the S.S. *City of Cairo*

RALPH BARKER

Ralph Barker

COLLINS
8 Grafton Street, London W1
1984

William Collins Sons and Co. Ltd
London · Glasgow · Sydney · Auckland
Toronto · Johannesburg

First published 1984
© Ralph Barker 1984

ISBN 0 00 216464 7

Maps by Brian Dear
Photoset in Linotron Ehrhardt by
Rowland Phototypesetting Ltd
Bury St Edmunds, Suffolk
Made and printed in Great Britain by
William Collins Sons and Co. Ltd, Glasgow

CONTENTS

ILLUSTRATIONS

CHAPTER 1

Premonitions and Superstitions

Gazing apprehensively at the grimy, grey-camouflaged hull of the antiquated coal-burner *City of Cairo*, 78-year-old Kate Richardson, arriving on the Bombay dockside, turned aggressively to her daughter and son-in-law and enquired, with the scornful incredulity of the aged, 'Are we going home in *that* ship?' Told that indeed they were, she delivered herself of the kind of forthright prediction she felt her seniority demanded. '*That ship will never get to England.*'

In spite of themselves the middle-aged couple thus addressed felt a doleful ache in the solar plexus as they savoured the prophecy. Even the name of the vessel had been painted over, as though, on embarkation, all identity and individualism were to be surrendered.

Had they been right to choose this moment to travel? Perhaps the old girl did have some presentiment of impending doom. Was it significant that she had often expressed a wish to be buried at sea?

The date was 1st October 1942, a time when baleful premonitions and timorous apprehensions were by no means exclusive to the aged or the middle-aged. For Victor Chambers, fighting fit at 22 but debarred from military service as a skilled aircraft tradesman, being bombed out of a Spitfire factory, which he had recently experienced, was not his idea of wartime adventure. In search of it, he volunteered to help build troop-carrying gliders in India. The outward voyage, in a 20,000-ton liner with naval escort, had been exciting and memorable; but climate and labour difficulties had caused the glider project to be abandoned, and he had resigned himself to going back to building Spitfires. When he heard a rumour that the return crossing of the Indian Ocean, at least as far as Durban, was to be attempted alone, he wondered what he had got himself into. Now, delivered by taxi to the gang-plank, his instinctive reaction when he sighted the minuscule – as it seemed to him – *City of Cairo*, 8,024 tons, was to get back in the taxi and wait for another ship. Seeing women boarding ahead of him, however, his cowardice failed him and he paid off the taxi and looked for his cabin. He had wanted adventure, but he wouldn't have chosen this.

For many of the passengers, however, the voyage offered escape from traumatic experiences in the retreat from the Japanese to a haven that even in wartime seemed infinitely desirable. Among the numerous widows there could have been no more ostensibly tragic figure than the 21-year-old Diana Jarman. Falling in love with a young subaltern in her father's regiment named John Jarman, Diana had been told that marriage must wait. But when the regiment was posted from India to Malaya her parents relented. There was just time for a brief honeymoon before the regiment left.

Fourteen months later, in December 1941, the Japanese invaded Malaya. Captain Jarman, as he had become, was killed in action on February 12th 1942 in the defence of Singapore. Diana's father survived but was taken prisoner.

Diana boarded the *City of Cairo* two years all but a day after her wedding. Too high-spirited to be melancholy for long, and boasting that she would 'try anything once', she was nevertheless a loving and sensitive person. As a child she had shown patience and understanding with a younger sister deaf from birth (her mother had contracted German measles during the pregnancy), which revealed and perhaps helped to form her character. Blonde and vivacious, she had shed the puppy-fat that had accompanied her back to India when she left school at 17, and, more recently, the glasses she had worn as a temporary corrective. On that outward voyage she had entered enthusiastically into all the shipboard entertainments and surrounded herself with lovesick subalterns. Now, tiring of being first a grass widow and then a real one, and untrained for any worthwhile employment in India, she had rebelled against what she saw as a futile existence and opted to go back to England to join one of the women's services. Meanwhile, if there was any fun to be had, she was resolved not to miss it.

This was Diana Jarman, a girl alternately earnest and frivolous, whose staunchness and pluck in adversity were soon to be tested. Inside her wedding ring she had had the first three words of her favourite quotation minutely engraved: 'One crowded hour. . . .' When reproduced in full the quotation, from a very much earlier war, aptly summarized her philosophy: 'One crowded hour of glorious life is worth an age without a name.'

Diana's crowded hour was to come.

Equally poignant was the departure from India of Dulcie Kendall and her three-year-old son Colin. Four years earlier, at 20, and perhaps more sophisticated than Diana at that age, Dulcie had married an engineer with Burma Railways. When the Japanese advanced on Rangoon, Dulcie and the child were evacuated to India, but her husband remained in the extreme north of Burma, working on an extension of the railway through to China. As the Japanese penetrated farther into Burma he was forced to flee, and during the crossing of the great jungle-covered mountain barrier that separates Burma from India he contracted cerebral malaria. Dulcie was in Calcutta, about to visit him in hospital, when she was told of his death. Stunned by the news, she headed for Bombay and home.

Even now, with her fair hair and blue eyes and impeccable taste and dress sense, she did not appear an object of sympathy, nor did she wish to. But when she went to buy clothes for the voyage an intuitive Indian girl in a Bombay dress shop saw through her façade. 'Will you have my St Christopher medal?' she asked.

'I *couldn't* do that,' said Dulcie, with the characteristic accent and accentuation of her kind. 'That's *yours.*'

'No – you must take it. You're going on a journey, a dangerous journey. I can get another.' And Dulcie Kendall was wearing the charm when she boarded the *City of Cairo.*

*

The wives of two eminent men in the Indian Civil Service, each in her forties and each with four children, had also chosen this moment to brave the sea trip home. They were Lady Almond, wife of Sir James Almond, Judicial Commissioner, North-West Frontier Province, and Eileen Simms, of Co. Donegal, whose husband was Collector of Sholapur in Bombay Province. Born on Empire Day 1893, Lady Almond had been christened May Victoria, the latter, too, proving not inappropriate, since she was of similarly small stature and indomitable spirit. After much anxious thought, she and her husband had concluded that, if they didn't get the three boys – Basil, 16, Francis, 13, and David, 12 – back to England soon to complete their education, it would be too late. Susan, aged 10, would naturally accompany them, keeping the family together.

Belonging to a generation which took British supremacy for granted, with the public school as the essential preparation, they judged the attendant risk to be worth the taking. If they also suspected that the hazards of the voyage might be no greater, in the face of the Japanese advance, than the hazards of staying in India, they kept such craven thoughts to themselves.

The motivation for the Simms family – Mary, 12, David, 10, Lisa, 7, and Esther, 3 – was much the same. Additionally, Eileen Simms's father had died three months earlier and she wanted to be home in Donegal with her mother. Other factors were civil unrest in India and the Japanese threat. Neither family appreciated quite how precarious the journey might be.

The youngest and perhaps the least mature of the women with children was the dark-haired Joan Redl, who clung somewhat awkwardly to her two-year-old son David, nicknamed 'Qunk' by his father. A restless, fretful child, Qunk was the youngest of the nineteen children on board, and Joan, deprived of the domestic support she had enjoyed in India, found him a handful. Foreseeing this, her soldier husband, posted with his regiment to the Middle East, took them aboard and introduced himself to the young ship's surgeon, Douglas Quantrill, and asked if he would look after them during the voyage. Quantrill was pleased enough to have such a strikingly attractive girl at his table.

After showing Joan Redl and Qunk to their cabin on the promenade deck, Quantrill strolled down to the after well-deck, where he watched the derricks being swung out to haul up the nets carrying the cargo, mostly cotton and manganese ore, though he noticed one incongruous item dangling and pirouetting grotesquely from the cables – a brand-new bicycle. The shouts of coolies, the tooting of horns as the taxis sought to deliver their human cargo, and the shrill sirens of the multiplicity of ships mingled with myriad unidentified sounds to orchestrate a cacophonous dockside symphony. The smells, too, were hybrid. Yet Quantrill only had to incline his gaze to enjoy a contrasting landscape: the magnificent arch that symbolised Bombay as the gateway to India, and the houses and gardens of the wealthy on Malabar Hill.

Suddenly his attention was captured by a new sound – the whine of heavy-duty tyres on tarmacadam. He looked round to see a convoy of trucks slowing to a halt, escorted by an Army patrol and a posse of policemen. From the rear of the trucks the coolies lifted a consignment of rectangular black boxes which they proceeded to stack just below him in No. 4 Hold. He wondered idly what they contained. Something pretty valuable, apparently, to warrant an armed security guard. He made a mental note to find out what was in them.

Among the childless couples on board the most intriguing were the Gordons, Crawford and Margaret. Margaret Gordon was an Australian, married to a Scots engineer thirteen years her senior. She had met him when visiting friends in Quetta from her home in the Melbourne suburb of Sandringham. Her features were too strong for stereotyped feminine beauty, but she was a handsome woman, while he had the orthodox good looks of the ascetic Scot. They were married in Bombay in 1937 when Margaret was 29; before that, following graduation at Melbourne University, she had taught at a boarding school on the outskirts of Geelong.

Crawford Gordon (she always called him Gordon) was deputy chief engineer of Bengal Railways, and, when the Japanese chased the British out of Rangoon, he hurried to the Himalayan foothills by river-boat during the monsoon to help with the retreat, only to find the narrow-gauge railway that served the area flooded after torrential rain. It was on this heart-breaking mission that he contracted dengue fever, an eruptive and infectious disease causing excruciating pains in the joints accompanied by acute prostration and debility. Margaret contracted it too while nursing him, but her strong constitution and mental stability were proof against the post-sickness depression that afflicted Gordon. Never very robust, he suffered a nervous breakdown and fell victim to a virulent persecution mania, a condition from which recovery was slow. 'The only remedy', pronounced his doctor, 'is to get him out of India.' So the Gordons, too, were refugees.

It would be Margaret Gordon's destiny, like Diana Jarman's, to have her resilience tested far beyond any preconceived standards of endurance.

Among other families on the run from the Japanese, and putting their trust in British sea power, were a Dutchman and his wife and son and a Belgian and his wife and son. Both were on their way to join their respective freedom forces based in England. The Dutchman, W. Ferdinand Dieckhaus, was a self-made man who had established himself in Rangoon with a Dutch import-export firm in the thirties and married an attractive part-Goanese girl whose father had been Chief Justice of Burma. After sending his family ahead to Calcutta, Dieckhaus had a gruelling experience as one of the last European civilians to escape from Rangoon, and neither his physique (he was over six feet tall and well built) nor his nervous system had fully recovered. His son Ferdinand junior ('Ferdy') was a lusty infant of two years and three months. In contrast, the Belgian Pierre Jaspar, had been president of two international companies in Bombay and was a member of one of his country's most distinguished and aristocratic families, dating back to 1465. His wife Janine was a delicate beauty, but his six-year-old son Michel, although sturdy enough, lacked the robustness of young Ferdy.

Of the unmarried women on board, several were missionaries who were putting their trust elsewhere. They included Gladys Usher, of the Council for World Mission, aged 52, an energetic and warm-hearted woman whose work in teacher training and in the service of women and girls in Bengal had proved her a selfless friend of India; and two other spinsters, Evelyn Ashdown (54) and Cecilia Norris (61) from the St Stephen's Community of the Cambridge Mission in Delhi, who coupled an unobtrusive faith with another characteristic of their kind, a keen and often irreverent sense of humour. These two ladies were being repatriated at the end of their service, but Gladys Usher, sent home for a rest after a long period of overwork, expected to return to Bengal. Whatever might befall, it seemed safe to assume that all three could be relied upon in emergency for an example of Christian forbearance and self-sacrifice.

The most formidable character among the women missionaries – and for that matter among the missionary men – was the auburn-haired Dr Marjorie Miller, as perhaps befitted a medical specialist who had been working at the Leprosy Mission at Purulia, near the Bengal border, for 20 years. She had gone out there in 1921, and in doing so had inadvertently renewed a childhood friendship with someone who had meanwhile become an administrator at the Mission. Dominating, even regal in appearance, she was a benevolent authoritarian, as no doubt she needed to be in her job.

Her husband, lay missionary A. Donald Miller, was the son of a parson in Lincoln. Less self-assertive than his wife, he was not without courage, and he had welcomed the arrival of what he saw as both a general and a personal reinforcement of strength. Eventually he had the temerity to invite her to marry him, and she had the wisdom to accept; perhaps her arrival in Purulia had not been so inadvertent after all. Now, coming home for the husband to take up the appointment of General Secretary of the Leprosy Mission in London, the Millers had all their worldly possessions, packed into twenty-seven crates, in the hold. Chided by Evelyn Ashdown and Cecilia Norris, the two spinsters from Delhi, for laying up so many treasures on earth, Donald Miller quoted the Indian poet Rabindranath Tagore: 'Renunciation is not for me. . . .'

Dedicated as these worthy crusaders were, and confident in the last instance of salvation, they were not immune from the apprehensions inseparable from wartime travel. But they were immensely reassured on boarding the vessel.

The *City of Cairo* was built at Hull in 1915 for Ellerman Lines and was sailing under the management and in the colours of the Hall Line under requisition. She was in reasonable shape for her twenty-seven years, having undergone a Special Survey at Port Natal only two months earlier and passed as eligible to retain her classification after necessary repairs had been completed. She was a single-screw steamship, with two decks and two masts, schooner rigged and with a cruiser stern; her length was 465 feet and her beam 55 feet 8 inches, and her two 386 hp engines gave her a cruising speed of 12½ knots. Her crew was a mixed one, totalling 155, of whom less than a third were European. The remainder were Lascars, the term applied to Indian and other Asian crews employed on European ships; communication was by means of a simplified form of Hindi.

The deck Lascar crews were professional sailors, but by far the majority were engine room, galley and saloon personnel who were not strictly sailors at all; thus they were liable to find themselves at a disadvantage in times of crisis. But as a group they were sober, docile, disciplined and hard-working, and they had long since proved themselves under wartime pressures, serving with honour in World War I. On routes to India and the Far East they were preferred to Europeans partly because they were cheaper and partly because of their inherent tropical acclimatization, filling a gap in areas for which British seamen showed little enthusiasm. But there was another side of the same coin: they were reckoned to be about two-thirds as efficient as Europeans in northern climes and still less so in conditions of extreme cold.

In addition to her normal muster the *Cairo* was carrying two spare Lascar crews, recruited in India for ships under construction in the United Kingdom. This, with 98 passengers, brought her total complement to just under 300.

The vessel's appearance, in her wartime camouflage, with the inevitable streaks of rust on her drab grey hull, might be unprepossessing, and her structure and fittings were oppressively Edwardian, but the passenger cabins, apart from one area where ants had intruded, were clean and comfortable, the air was circulated by electric fans, and the public rooms, which included a dining saloon, a lounge/music-room, and a smoking room, were well appointed. Stepping on to freshly scrubbed decks, and dazzled by newly polished brass, the passengers were welcomed aboard by immaculately dressed officers, for some of whom the arrival of a bevy of unaccompanied ladies, whether widows or not, was an added excitement. Douglas Quantrill, the ship's doctor, who had already acquired Joan Redl – whom he dubbed Joan Crawford, there being a likeness – as a table companion, was quick to enlist the young war widow Diana Jarman as well.

The master, Captain William Rogerson, was a Liverpudlian. At 46 he was one of the company's senior captains, marked down as a future commodore of Ellerman Lines. A rugged man of no more than medium height, with a glint in his eye, he was well built in proportion, and partial to exercising on deck with a medicine ball with any of his crew whom he could cajole into co-operating. The consensus was that 'when you got the ball from the Old Man you felt it'. But he had his artistic side, revealed in his hobby of painting, and demonstrated in the canvases that hung on the walls of his cabin, mostly of marine subjects. Blunt and direct without being in any way discourteous, he was not a showman, and his crew knew exactly where they stood with him. They respected him as a seaman and backed their opinion by sailing with him, as many of them had done, throughout the war so far. The sense of being a valued member of a team stimulated an atmosphere on board that, although strictly regulated and disciplined, was relaxed and friendly.

No one contributed to this atmosphere more enthusiastically than the dynamic chief officer, 41-year-old Sidney Britt. Sociable and self-assured (some thought him cocksure), dapper and clean-shaven, he too was a master mariner, with experience in sail, justly proud of his rank and achievements; he had recently been decorated with the M.B.E. For him, as for Captain Rogerson, there was only one question-mark against future promotion: the luck to survive. An extrovert, autocratic yet happy-go-lucky, he was adaptable and gregarious, and his ability to put passengers at their ease was an important factor in the reputation the *Cairo* enjoyed of being a happy ship.

Before meeting Britt, however, most of the passengers had had an opportunity to judge the quality of their reception – and rated it highly – through the personalities of the purser, Francis McQuone, 47, and his assistant, writer (clerk) and third steward Jack Edmead, ten years his junior. These two men were in striking physical contrast: McQuone, a man of substance in more ways than one, was burly and rotund; Edmead was tall, angular, and flat-footed. Both had experience as hoteliers, and indeed McQuone and his wife had almost completed negotiations for the purchase of an hotel in Chester, and McQuone was 'swallowing the anchor' – going ashore for good – after this trip. McQuone combined a strict probity with a bland sense of humour; he didn't mind having his leg pulled, and Edmead was ready to oblige. Like all officers of the ship they were well turned out, and no one cut quite the dash that Edmead achieved when he went ashore in foreign ports, dressed in whites and topee, to prosecute the ship's business. 'Mr Edmead,' Captain Rogerson would say on these occasions, 'you're a credit to the *City of Cairo*.'

If McQuone's urbanity ever faltered it could usually be traced to his abhorrence of missionaries and ministers of the Church, with whom, on this particular voyage, the ship seemed to him infested. He shared the seafarer's popular superstition that it was unlucky to have them on board, and his position as purser exposed him to the assumption they made – as he believed – that he and his staff owed them special attention. Edmead taunted him into laughing about it, but with a dozen missionaries and missionary helpers aboard, McQuone was pessimistic.

The lofty figure of Jack Edmead became especially familiar with the passengers because of the part he played in organizing their leisure activities. Another of McQuone's staff who became a favourite, with passengers and crew alike, was stewardess Annie Crouch from Liverpool. Sixty-four years old, she had gone back to sea to escape the bombing. Annie Crouch was renowned for her answer to offers of a drink: 'Oh dear – would a brandy and ginger be too expensive?'

That evening the adult passengers were assembled in the lounge, issued with lifejackets, and addressed by Chief Officer Britt. 'We'll be sailing at six o'clock in the morning,' he told them, 'and there'll be a boat drill soon after we sail.' Passengers would find details of their boat station, with instructions in the use of lifejackets, posted on the wall of their cabins. There were eight lifeboats, Britt told them, all mounted on the boat deck, securely lashed but slung out ready for lowering to the boat stations on the promenade deck. Of these lifeboats, six were 27 feet 6 inches long and had a rated capacity of 48, though this would be to fill them to the point of discomfort. Two were smaller boats, 21 feet long, with a much lower freeboard and a capacity of 25. They were little more than jolly-boats, and in peacetime they had been mounted astern, but to make room for a 4.7″ gun they had been moved to the boat deck, where space for them existed. They were numbered 3 and 4.

Boats 1, 3, 5 and 7 were on the starboard side, Boat 1 being the farthest forward and Boat 7 the farthest aft. Boats 2, 4, 6 and 8 were on the port side. 'Odd numbers to starboard, even numbers to port,' recited Britt. They must all make themselves thoroughly familiar with their boat stations.

Britt then listed the ship's defensive armament, which included the 4.7″ gun, two twin Marlins and two anti-aircraft Oerlikons, backed up by four machine guns. 'We have six Navy and four Army gunners,' he added, 'DEMS gunners, they're called, for Defensively Equipped Merchant Ships.' All gun mountings were out of bounds. There would be a practice shoot next day, for which due warning would be given.

Finally Britt asked passengers with the necessary qualifications to come forward and offer themselves as boat wardens. They would not normally be expected to help with the actual lowering of boats, merely to superintend loading from the promenade deck in the event of orders to abandon ship. They would be given a list of occupants for each boat, and through frequent boat drills they would get to know their charges.

Amongst the passengers there was a leavening of deck officers from other companies, some going home on leave and some reporting back for duty after other assignments, or after being sunk. Volunteers who stepped forward included the jovial, rubicund Tommy Green from Bristol, a chief officer in the British India Steamship Navigation Company and a master mariner; the shrewd, Orkney-born Bob Skea, second officer on a tanker recently taken over by the Navy, also a master mariner – and a master of irony too; and the steadfast and reliable George Nutter, a fair-skinned Lancastrian with Roman nose and straw-coloured hair, chief radio officer on a Bibby Line troopship. Nutter, who was going home for his first leave of the war, had a Board of Trade lifeboat certificate. Another recruit, although not a seaman, was the Dutchman Dieckhaus, welcomed because of his experience as a St John's Ambulance Brigade volunteer during the bombing of Rangoon. All four were active men in their thirties who were glad of something to do.

One other traveller, not on the passenger list, had padded his way stealthily aboard and was ready to sail. The stowaway was a ginger cat, a huge, scruffy, untameable tom, denizen of the Bombay dockside. Flushed from his land-based haunts, he had found refuge in the labyrinthine passageways of the *City of Cairo.* He was not present to hear Britt's address, but he would not have been daunted by the prospect of danger. For a cat from his dubious background, it was an inimical world.

CHAPTER 2

Bound for Old Blighty Shore

The 4,500-mile voyage from Bombay south-south-west to Durban took 20 days, too long for Captain Rogerson's liking. If the old tub couldn't do better than that she would lose her passenger licence. The weather was fair and no one was seasick, but most of the passengers took some time to get their sea legs, and few indulged in deck games. The ship steered a zig-zag course in daylight and was blacked out at night, and the closed port-holes made the cabins unpleasantly stuffy. Some passengers slept on deck at first, but the nights turned so cold and damp that they were all sleeping in their cabins by the time they reached Durban. Apart from one or two submarine scares the voyage was uneventful, but lifejackets were ordered to be carried at all times. Lifeboat drills, however – held twice weekly – tended to be casual, and so far as possible a peacetime cruise routine was maintained.

Friendships were in some cases encouraged, in others rebuffed: at such close quarters, attachments once formed were not easy to sever. There were the inevitable shipboard flirtations, romances, and *affaires*. Kindred spirits, and those with comparable experience, found a sympathetic hearing. Dulcie Kendall gave welcome support to another Burma widow, Freda Bullen, and felt supported in return. Freda had gone to Burma in 1937 to visit a brother and see a new country, and there she had met and married an engineer; in 1940 she gave birth to twin boys. Freda escaped from Burma by transport plane with the children, but her husband was yet another victim of the debilitating trek across the mountains: he reached Calcutta safely, then contracted malaria and died. For this gentle, reserved young woman, burdened by grief and two lively twin boys, there was no alternative but to go home to her parents in Shropshire. The self-assured Dulcie Kendall was the best possible cure for her melancholy.

Another pair who teamed up and became almost inseparable were Diana Jarman (promptly dubbed the 'convoy cutie' by the puckish Bob Skea) and the attractive brunette Joan Redl. Of much the same age, they liked the same things and the same people.

Sunbathing, and a dip in the canvas pool, were the limit of physical effort for the majority. Reading was popular, although the library on board was a disappointment. One man who found a good book was the Rev. Robert Waddell, a 33-year-old Church of Scotland educational missionary: he was in the middle of Margaret Stein's *The Sun is my Undoing.* It was the darkness, though, in these U-boat-infested seas, that he felt was more likely to undo him. Waddell had got special home leave to help his sister settle business affairs following the death of his father and brother, the latter killed in the R.A.F.

Including Bert Waddell there were four fully-fledged 'padres' on board, a quartet of 'Jonahs' that others besides Purser McQuone viewed with superstitious disquiet. These four took turns, during the crossing to Durban, to hold Sunday-morning service in the lounge, when they did their best to atone for their unwelcome presence by their prayers. All too often the lesson, or the text of the sermon, was taken from the story of the shipwreck of St Paul, a choice which even the lay missionaries found overdone.

There was more variety in the evenings, when concerts, horse-racing, roulette, and tombola (bingo) were inter-changed. Lady Almond organized a bridge four. Among those who formed a poker school were the Belgian Pierre Jaspar, the Dutchman Ferdinand Dieckhaus, the ship's surgeon Douglas Quantrill, and the second officer, a down-to-earth Devonian named Les Boundy.

A disappointment for the younger element was that the public rooms were too small for dancing. Some form of musical diversion, however, was usually forthcoming, from gramophone or live performer. The Second Engineer, Bob Gerner, who had earned a commendation for brave conduct on a previous voyage, could sometimes be persuaded, by popular request, to exercise his resonant baritone in the music room: brave conduct indeed. Accompanying him at the upright piano would be the versatile chief officer, Sidney Britt: Britt also played for the Church Services on Sundays. A repatriated BP engineer from Abadan played the violin, and a ship's engineer travelling as a 'distressed British seaman', as men who had lost their ships were labelled, assuaged his distress by playing the piano in ragtime style.

Third Officer James Allister Whyte, standing on the monkey island above the music-room on the eight-to-midnight watch, would often hear muted strains of familiar melodies rising through the ventilation shaft. Those amateur concert artists were at it again! Soon, he knew, would come Bob Gerner's and everyone else's favourite, 'A Nightingale Sang in Berkeley Square'.

Everyone took to the 25-year-old Jimmy 'Knocker' Whyte, whose distinctive, infectious laugh could be heard all over the ship.[1] 'We'll soon cure him of that laugh!' promised his fellow officers. But they did not succeed. Stocky and pipe-smoking, with twinkling eyes that disappeared when he smiled, he had a reputation for tenacity: if he set out to do something he generally did it, and a ruthless streak dared anyone to stand in his way. On his last leave he had taken his mate's certificate, and on his next he planned to sit for his master's ticket. No one doubted that he would get it. Formerly a Sea Scout, from Erith in Kent, he had been brought up on the Thames in small boats. Described by his scoutmaster as 'just about the toughest lad I've had through my hands', his tenacity and toughness were going to be needed.

A man with a keen eye for the foibles of others was Orkney-born Bob Skea. He was sitting at the Gordons' table, and he admired them as an affectionate couple while realizing that Crawford Gordon was a man of moods. In one of his rare talkative moments Gordon related how he had consulted an Indian seer about his future and been disillusioned by the result. 'It's all foolishness,' he said, and he repeated one of the guru's forecasts

[1] In the Royal and Merchant Navies, just as all Wilsons are 'Tug' and all Harrises are 'Bert', so all Whites (or Whytes) are 'Knocker'.

with relish. One thing he could be sure of, the guru had told him, was that he would never go home. 'And here I am on the ship!'

Skea, whose humour, though never malicious, could often be mischievous, wanted to say 'Careful! You're not home yet!' But catching Margaret Gordon's eye he held his peace.

Gordon was being treated for post-illness depression by Douglas Quantrill, who held a surgery daily on the poop deck. This was next to the firemen's cookhouse, where the curry, Quantrill believed, judging from the aroma, was prepared not for European stomachs but for connoisseurs. Quantrill was worried about Crawford Gordon, and he warned Margaret not to let her husband loose on deck at night lest he jump overboard.

Another of Quantrill's patients was Ada Taggart, an Ellerman Line stewardess from Montrose whom the company were repatriating after illness; 50 years old, she had worked for the company for 14 years. The illness – Quantrill diagnosed it as rheumatoid arthritis – had left her with extreme weakness in the hands and feet, and Purser McQuone looked for someone who would be prepared to wash, dress and undress her during the voyage, for which some financial concession would be made. Sybil Chapman, 42, wife of a recently retired military bandsman, had run her own school in India and had nursing experience, and she enjoyed helping the appreciative Ada Taggart.

Physically, the wonder of the voyage was Sybil Chapman's mother, Kate Richardson; she had forgotten about her sepulchral forecast on the Bombay dockside and was enjoying herself. Her dark brown hair, without a trace of discoloration, was in bizarre contrast to her daughter's premature grey. Most people took the two women for sisters and were greatly diverted when the grey-haired lady addressed her companion as 'Mother'.

The average speed achieved on the leg from Bombay to Durban was less than 10 knots, and the ship seemed likely to be required to shed her passengers from Cape Town on. This was an outcome which did not appeal to the crew or anyone else, and Captain Rogerson, although blaming inferior coal for the sluggish crossing of the Indian Ocean, and for the tell-tale trail of smoke they sometimes emitted, had his engines checked over while the ship was bunkering at Durban. Unless the ship could do the regulation 10 knots necessary for carrying passengers he could not transport them beyond Cape Town. He had every expectation, though, that on the 900-mile run from Durban to Cape Town his advertised cruising speed of 12½ knots would be achieved without making smoke, and that the *Cairo* was fully capable of joining a fast convoy if one was available or of continuing with passengers on her own.

The matter was of some consequence. Up until the previous month, the waters around Cape Town had been undisturbed by U-boats, but in September and early October a new threat had developed. Shifting the centre of U-boat operations from the Caribbean after heavy losses, Admiral Dönitz, Flag Officer Submarines, with the approval of Admiral Raeder, C-in-C German Navy, had ordered *Gruppe Eisbar*, the Polar Bear Group, consisting of four submarines, U68, U156, U172 and U504, all Type IXc boats of 1250 tons, to make a surprise foray against Allied shipping off Cape Town. A U-tanker, U459, was to accompany the group, refuelling the boats somewhere south of St Helena, the tiny island in the middle of the South Atlantic where Napoleon had been exiled.

Dönitz's order was dated 1st August 1942, and the British Admiralty, through their intercept service, knew that a U-boat flotilla with a refuelling unit was likely to begin operating in the South Atlantic in September. Lacking reserve anti-submarine units, however, they could do little about it.

The four U-boats sailed from Lorient independently between 15th and 20th August; meanwhile U459, crammed with fuel and torpedoes, set course from Bordeaux. The four commanders were: Karl-Friedrich Merten (U68); Werner Hartenstein (U156); Carl Emmermann (U172); and Fritz Poske (U504). A fifth U-boat, U159, commanded by Helmut Witte, joined the group later. The most experienced of these commanders was Merten, who in three previous patrols in command of U68 had sunk 20 Allied ships totalling 125,000 tons.

On the night of 12th September Karl-Friedrich Merten, having reached a point just south of the Equator, opened the campaign by sinking a 5,000-ton steamer. As a more or less routine matter he took the master and the chief engineer prisoner, the object of the abduction being to create manning difficulties for replacement Allied ships. Later these two men were transferred to U459. Even more significant for the future, however, was the sinking by Werner Hartenstein on the same night of the passenger vessel *Laconia*, 19,695 tons. The 3,000 people on board included 1,800 Italian prisoners of war and their Polish guards and 80 women and children.

When the extent of the catastrophe was realised by Hartenstein he broadcast the location of the sinking by radio and undertook not to attack any vessel coming to the rescue of survivors. Other U-boats were ordered to the scene, taking aboard women and children and wounded, and assistance was given to make damaged lifeboats seaworthy and to tow some of them northwards. Meanwhile the Vichy cruiser *Gloire* was despatched from Dakar to help in the search for survivors. The Allies intercepted much of the radio traffic, but they suspected a trap: U-boats were in the habit of waiting in the area of a kill in order to attack ships coming to the rescue of survivors. Hartenstein's suggestion of a truce was not approved by U-boat Command, the Allies remained sceptical, and a sighting by an American Liberator of the rescuing U-boats three days after the sinking brought a series of aerial attacks. The U-boats, as it happened, escaped serious damage, but the work of rescue was disrupted, in some cases with tragic results.

The incident led to revised orders from U-boat Command: the rescue of survivors was in future to be limited to the capture of ships' captains and chief engineers and the interrogation of those who might have information of value. This specifically excluded any humane gestures towards women and children.

Knowing how distasteful this order would be to many U-boat commanders, a conscience-easing paragraph was added. 'Be severe,' it exhorted. 'Remember that in his bombing attacks on German cities the enemy has no regard for women and children.'

The offensive by the Polar Bear Group on the Cape Town traffic began in earnest shortly after the *City of Cairo* left Bombay.

A surprise attack on shipping in Table Bay failed, but in the space of four days fourteen ships in the Southern Ocean were sunk. Of these, six ships totalling 36,000 tons fell to Merten in a 48-hour period from 8th to 9th October, all in an arc off the Cape of Good Hope. The whole operation recalled for the German crews the 'happy times' of 1941, but the reaction of the South African Air Force was swifter than expected. The concentration of U-boats was driven away from this lucrative area, and the campaign declined into a succession of individual ambushes and raids.

Warning of the departure of Allied ships from Bombay was suspected of being given by a spy network fed by disaffected Indians and operated by radio from German merchant ships interned in the port of Marmagoa, the chief port of the neutral Portuguese colony of Goa, 260 miles south of Bombay. News of the sailing of the *City of Cairo* does not appear to have reached the Polar Bear Group; but Merten, having been forced to stay submerged off Cape Town in daylight by continuous air patrols, headed towards the Indian Ocean in search of further victims. All he found was a hospital ship, which he duly spared. An inhibiting factor was that the group as a whole, having been refuelled by U459 before the assault on the Cape Town traffic, could not hope for further supplies; they were running short of diesel and would soon have to head back to their bases. Thus the ponderous progress of the *City of Cairo*, combined with a five-day stopover in Durban, seemed likely to protect her, however fortuitously, from the depredations of the group.

Durban in October, to spinsters Evelyn Ashdown and Cecilia Norris, was very like their own Delhi in winter. Avenues of jacaranda were in full bloom, there were bougainvillaeas everywhere, and the gardens were a blaze of colour. What struck them most, however, was the appalling cleavage between white and coloured folk. 'Coming from India,' noted Evelyn Ashdown, 'it horrified us. We were thankful it had not been our lot to work in South Africa.'

Bert Waddell (having finished *The Sun is my Undoing*) teamed up with a lad named Allan Tempest, aged 17, owner of the bicycle

Dr Quantrill had seen being loaded at Bombay. Tempest was on his way home to take the Dartmouth entry examination in March of the following year. With young Tempest as chaperon, Waddell was joined by a girl named Betty Birchman, 27, going home on sick leave from the St Andrew's Homes in Kalimpong, where she was a matron of one of the hostels. An attractive, loquacious girl, fair and petite, she was full of animation and fun, and her friendship with Waddell might have gone farther but for the fact that he was already engaged. They too were horrified by the ubiquitous proclamations of FOR EUROPEANS ONLY and FOR NON-EUROPEANS, and at the way the Africans were treated. 'They say it is necessarily so,' noted Waddell, 'but coming from India it seems quite dreadful.'

Another of the padres on board, a Welsh Presbyterian named Davies, travelling home for health reasons with his wife and two little girls, was similarly outraged. One morning when the four of them were standing at a bus stop with a coloured man, the man was refused entry 'because we were boarding and we were white', noted Davies. 'We were visitors in his country.'

Two other passengers – Diana Jarman and Joan Redl – were practising their own brand of apartheid. Finding the docks a long way from the town, and enjoying their freedom, they put up at a Durban hotel.

The long sea voyage, and the sojourn in Durban, proved noticeably therapeutic for the many passengers under mental or physical stress, and none benefited more than the sick Ellerman Lines stewardess Ada Taggart, who wrote from Durban to her sister in Montrose: 'I have improved so much under Dr Quantrill's care and treatment and I am getting better every day. I feel sure I shall be fully restored to my usual good health by the time I reach home.'

Home, for Ada Taggart as for everyone else, still seemed far distant, but the magic phrase 'home for Christmas' was beginning to be heard. Security forbade any cabled forecasts of arrival dates, but cryptic references to this exciting prospect were made in letters home. Joan Redl, writing to her parents, expressed the hope that 'turkeys were plentiful'.

Among the 'distressed British seamen' joining the ship at Durban was 27-year-old Bill McGregor from Leith, being repatriated after sustaining severe burns in a boiler-room explosion. Tall and fair, with a pleasing personality, he was looking forward to spending Christmas with his 'wifey', as he called her, and their small child. Diana Jarman was attracted to him, and she arranged for him to sit at Quantrill's table. Strangest of the embarkations were those of three Russians, two men and a woman, whose only practical method of travel had been overland through Turkey to South Africa and onwards by sea. One of the men had been appointed to be Ambassador Ivan Maisky's chauffeur in London, the other, a Tass agency reporter on his way to Stockholm, was travelling with his wife. Conspicuous by their sombre attire, they maintained a cautious neutrality.

These additions to the passenger list were scarcely counterbalanced by the single disembarkation, that of the stowaway ginger tom, unceremoniously dumped ashore the night before sailing. Where he had hidden in daytime, and who had fed him at night, remained unsolved mysteries; but the animal, biding his time, crept back unnoticed up the gangway under cover of darkness.

News of the multiple sinkings off Cape Town had inevitably filtered through to the passengers, and while they were at Durban they were further alarmed by a sudden and complete black-out of the city and harbour. Another Ellerman Lines vessel, the *City of Johannesburg,* was sunk that night, 23rd October, off the African coast 200 miles to the south. Surely they would be given an escort now.

Captain Rogerson would have welcomed company, but he knew only too well that convoys in these waters were the exception rather than the rule, by far the majority of vessels sailing alone and unescorted. He had no reason to suppose that the situation had changed.

The run from Durban round to Cape Town, with a stricter black-out in force, and no music of any kind allowed after dark, was the tensest period so far. Keeping in sight of the coast all the way, Rogerson and his crew had every reason to make the best possible speed. They proved conclusively that their ship, properly bunkered, could cruise at its advertised rate without making smoke, provided the fires were cleaned, raked and re-stoked with care. The ship reached Cape Town unmolested well inside three and a half days, and the licence to carry passengers unescorted was safe.

With no fast escort vessels available, Naval Control Cape Town routed the *City of Cairo* for a lone crossing of the South Atlantic to Recife (then known as Pernambuco), in Brazil, avoiding the U-boat-infested Freetown route to the north. From Recife they would hug the coastlines of South and North America until they reached Halifax, Nova Scotia, after which they would enjoy the luxury of being convoyed and escorted across the North Atlantic to Britain. It was the first few days of the Cape Town—Recife section which held the main threat. The distance to Recife was 3,600 miles, but evasive routeing and a zig-zag course in daylight would extend this to over 4,000. Captain Rogerson was confident of reaching Recife in 15 days.

Three days at Cape Town gave passengers and crew a further opportunity for Christmas shopping, hairdressing for the ladies, and for sightseeing, though some of the shopping, with the hazards ahead in mind, devolved on the purchase of 'panic bags' – light rucksack-type hand luggage with shoulder straps – and useful items to fill them. These emergency bags would be all they could expect to take with them into lifeboats. One whose purchases included a special birthday gift was David Williams, a Welsh engineer who had completed his service in India and was on his way back to Swansea; it was a present for his wife Mary, on behalf of himself and his daughter Violet, the youngest of his three children. It was Violet, having joined her parents in India on leaving school five years earlier, who had persuaded them to come home: Violet's mother had a heart condition that was aggravated by the climate. Her birthday, 14th November, would fall during the crossing, and husband and daughter combined, in such secrecy as they could contrive, to buy her a wrist-watch.

A young man who found Cape Town less attractive than some

was E. Randolph Godlieb, a Sinhalese. An Oxford graduate, whose father was chief civil surgeon for Ceylon, he was turned away from Cape Town hotels because of his colour. Bob Skea, who was with him, stumped out in protest.

Walking up the lower slopes of Table Mountain on a sightseeing excursion, having learned that the cableway was closed owing to high winds, Evelyn Ashdown and Cecilia Norris, the two retiring Delhi missionaries, seemed unlikely transgressors against South African laws and regulations, however Draconian. Between them they picked a magnificent bunch of wild flowers, which much to their astonishment caused quite a stir in the tram on the way back. Everyone seemed to remark on them. It was not until they arrived at the house of their missionary hosts that they realized their mistake: the picking of flowers on Table Mountain, they were told, was strictly forbidden, and penalties for doing so were severe. Their hosts, for ethical reasons, found themselves unable to accept the flowers, so the two middle-aged ladies, accustomed from their lifelong work in India to taking a practical view, smuggled their ill-gotten gains back to the ship, greatly savouring their involuntary venture into law-breaking. Arranged in a vase on their dining table, the flowers were the envy of all.

Sailing delays were endemic in wartime, and the two women laughingly expressed the wish, after earlier partings had proved premature, that they would not meet again, a proposition from which their embarrassed hosts did not dissent.

Another law-breaker had meanwhile been apprehended. The uninvited feline guest, caught in the act of petty theft, had been incarcerated under a convenient crate on the dockside, to be released by a watchman after the ship sailed. But the crate, perhaps in response to the cat's entreaties, was lifted too soon, and as the vessel sailed a prodigious leap landed the stowaway back on the well deck. The nightly caterwauling that had caused a minor annoyance between Bombay and Cape Town was thus resumed. Some, however, thought the cat might bring them luck.

Sinkings in South African waters, although still occurring (as the passengers had been made painfully aware), were becoming less frequent, and indeed all four original members of the Polar

Bear Group expedition, although on the look-out for stragglers, were on their way back to France. The *Cairo* had been running to and from eastern ports since the outbreak of war and she had got through so far: this was the attitude of the crew. Sailings in any case could not be postponed indefinitely without conceding dominance of the sea routes to the U-boats, and that way lay certain defeat. The vessel would be routed to take maximum advantage of land-based air patrols in the early part of the voyage, when the danger from U-boats was greatest; and intelligence on U-boat movements might lead to further evasive routeing. Yet whatever the importance of the *Cairo's* cargo, and the real or imagined urgency of some individual travel, the responsibility for despatching the vessel on a lone ocean crossing, with a complement of 298 that included 101 fare-paying passengers, of whom 25 were women and 19 were children, was a daunting one. The misgivings of the *cognoscenti* were rendered even more acute by the suspicion, not generally voiced, that once South African waters were left behind there was no hope of aerial reconnaissance and very little of rescue.

All these factors had presumably been considered by Naval Control Cape Town and the risk judged acceptable. Be that as it may, at 06.00 on Sunday 1st November the *Cairo* sailed. Captain Rogerson was ordered to maintain a mean northerly course parallel with the African coast for 800 miles, zig-zagging during the day and keeping about 45 miles out. At latitude 23.30 south, some 70 miles short of Walvis Bay, he was to turn due west, straight out into the South Atlantic. Not until he was in mid-Atlantic would he turn north-west for Recife.

'We must be ready for anything now,' was the general opinion, and Evelyn Ashdown suggested to Chief Officer Britt that full dress rehearsals should now be conducted for abandoning ship. She felt they had been taking boat drills too casually, strolling to their boat stations just as they were and taking nothing they were likely to need, instead of going first to their cabins to collect the 'panic bags' they had been told to prepare. Britt disagreed. His policy was that if they were torpedoed without warning the passengers were to go straight to the boats. To accustom everyone

The *City of Cairo* in her peacetime livery, limned against the barren rocks of Aden. In wartime the vessel was painted grey and the two smaller lifeboats astern, port and starboard, were moved to the boat deck to make room for a 4.7″ gun.

The lounge/music-room, where Sidney Britt played the piano and Bob Gerner sang.

This luxury double-bedstead cabin, with elaborate fittings, had a bathroom attached.

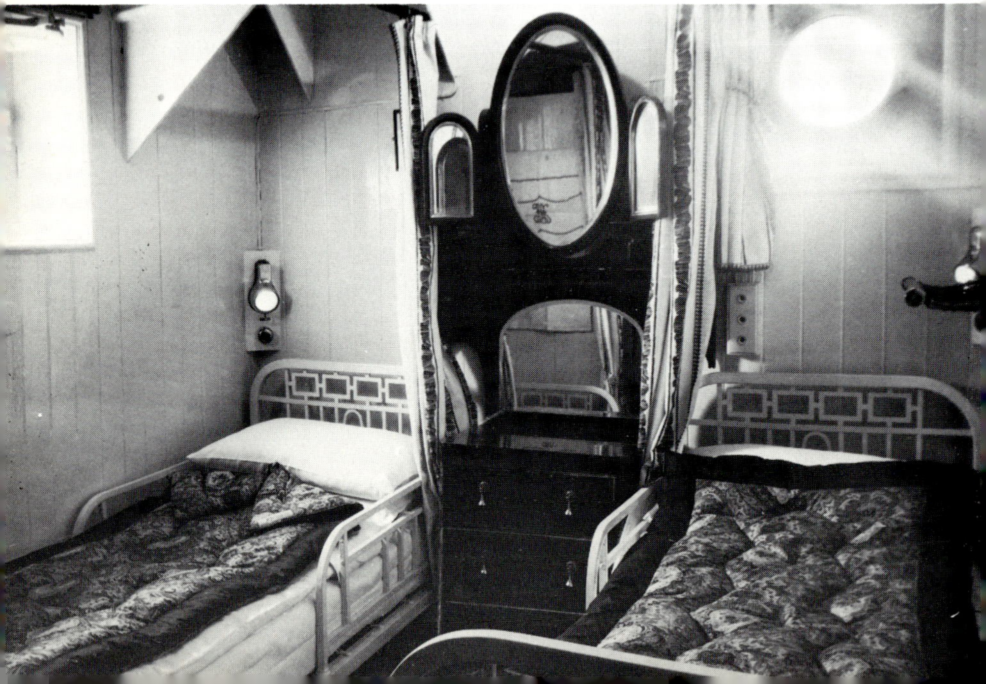

to going first to their cabins might lead to disaster. He had found volunteers to help mothers who had to go back for young children, and he had made similar arrangements for invalids and the aged. That, he believed, was enough. Too much organization would only confuse and frighten the passengers. Provided they took their lifejackets with them wherever they went he was satisfied.

'That's one more port behind us,' remarked Purser Francis McQuone to his assistant Jack Edmead as they left Cape Town. 'And one less for you, sir, before you "swallow the anchor",' responded Edmead. But McQuone was uneasy. 'I don't like it, Jack, it's too quiet. I've been having a word with Harry Peever to see if anything's coming through on the radio, and there's nothing. I don't believe the U-boats can have faded away just like that.' Noted for picturesque speech, he added: 'One of these nights we'll get shot up the arse like a garden thrush.'

Two days out from Cape Town, on Tuesday 3rd November, a submarine warning was indeed received, but it proved a false alarm. Next day the *Cairo* reached her first turning point south of Walvis Bay and altered course to the west.

Great excitement was caused towards noon next day by the sighting of two Italian hospital ships heading south. It was a perfect day, warm but not yet equatorial, and visibility was good. They were ordinary passenger ships with big red crosses painted on their hulls and on deck, and they were sailing in the direction of Cape Town. Soon afterwards Harry Peever, the *Cairo*'s chief radio officer, heard them transmit their position. While they were entitled to do this under International Law, the suspicion that such signals might carry some other interpretation to listening U-boats, such as the sighting, in the position indicated, of an Allied vessel, brought additional anxiety. The passengers, although not told of the message sent by the hospital ships, felt certain that the *Cairo*'s position and course would be given away. Captain Rogerson shared their cynicism, but beyond maintaining his zig-zag course and ordering a boat drill before sunset and a daily practice thereafter, there was little he could do.

When Evelyn Ashdown and Cecilia Norris, the two spinsters

from Delhi, turned up for boat drill early that evening in coats, hats and topees, carrying bags stuffed with all sorts of oddments, and with pockets bulging with passports and other personal effects, many of their companions laughed. But the principle of 'Praise the Lord and pass the ammunition' was one in which these two ladies, in the course of their missionary work, had learned to believe. They were quite unabashed, and next day they added a torch and a pair of flat shoes to their emergency gear. That night and the following night, several of the passengers reverted to an earlier habit of sleeping fully or partly clothed.

Bert Waddell was another who was mildly critical. He thought there ought to have been practices in actually lowering the boats, at least when in port.

Anxieties, however, receded in proportion to the distance the African coast was left behind. A sports committee was appointed and lists of competitors drawn up, and on Thursday 5th November, the day after passing the hospital ships, the passengers became absorbed in playing off the first heats of a deck games tournament. Others were planning a concert, to be held at the week-end, by which time, so they were told, they could expect to be virtually out of danger from submarines.

For Allan Tempest, the youngest of those travelling alone (his parents lived in India), the tournament made a welcome break from his cadet-entry studies. Satisfying his conscience by putting in two hours' work before breakfast, Tempest won at bucket quoits but lost at deck tennis. That night he went back to his studies.

The children's games, although less formal, were keenly contested, and since the children's lifejackets had to be either worn or kept handy, they sometimes got damaged. On the other hand, even the youngest children got used to them. Among those who had prepared their panic bags somewhat sketchily was Dulcie Kendall, but after Cape Town she took to packing warm clothing at night for herself and Colin and placing it at the foot of Colin's bunk. On 5th November Colin brought his lifebelt to her saying it was 'broken', and it proved to be badly torn. She took it to the young quartermaster allotted to her boat – Boat 6, the third boat on the port side – and he mended it and returned it to her that evening. It was to prove a timely repair.

One who missed the games that day was the teenage Violet Williams, in bed with a cold. Next day, Friday the 6th, she insisted on getting up and playing off her heats. Hampered by the cold, she lost them all, but she thoroughly enjoyed the day. The weather was becoming distinctly warm, and several of the ladies were planning to return to light frocks for dinner. 'If it weren't for the daily boat drill,' someone remarked, 'we might almost imagine we were on a pleasure trip.' The Belgian Pierre Jaspar agreed. Only the British, he thought, could have achieved the compromise that made it seem like a holiday cruise.

Chief Officer Britt, however, was undeceived, and before dark he made a thorough inspection of the life-saving gear. It was during this inspection, in the last of the lifeboats on the port side, No. 8, that the hiding place of the ginger tom was at last discovered. Most ships' cats became domesticated, attaching themselves to some section of the ship, and jealously guarding their territory as the engine-room cat, the bridge cat, or the galley cat. But the ginger tom, wild and unloved, was the cat who sailed by himself.

It was the animal's unfastidious habits that gave it away. Efforts to entice it out from behind the water breakers failed, and in the absence of a vet the ship's surgeon was consulted. Quantrill elected to smoke the cat out with a sulphur candle, normally used for fumigating cabins after infection, and soon after seven o'clock that evening he went up to the boat deck with Britt. Lighting the candle, he pushed it under the lifeboat's canvas protective cover, holding it there until a column of sulphurous smoke escaped and coiled upwards. But the cat stuck it out. With the light beginning to fail, and black-out regulations still in force, Quantrill was eventually obliged to postpone the operation until the morrow.

It did not occur to him, or to Britt, that from some sixth animal sense the cat had chosen the safest place to be. Nor did it occur to them that the column of sulphurous smoke that escaped from the lifeboat might be spotted through Zeiss binoculars on the horizon.

*

Korvettenkapitän Karl-Friedrich Merten, of U68, was running on the surface on a north-north-westerly course at economical speed, on his way home but taking his time, extending his patrol as long as was practicable. Since his spectacular series of sinkings off Cape Town four weeks earlier he had not had so much as a glimpse of a target, unless one could count the hospital ship he had sighted and ignored in the Indian Ocean; but dusk was one of the most opportune times for a sighting, enabling an attack to be made after dark on the surface, whereas in daylight, in view of the armament introduced on all merchant vessels, it was prudent to submerge.

In the evening at sundown, and in the morning at sunrise, Merten was always on the bridge of U68, accompanied by his first lieutenant, using both short- and long-range periscopes, scanning the very fine line between surface and sky. Thus in the late evening of 6th November, with the eastern horizon already darkening and a paler, refulgent light colouring the cloud formations to the west, Merten and his crew were fully alert to the significance of the hour.

Suddenly they noticed, far to the west, almost beyond the limit of their extended visibility, and lasting scarcely more than a second, what looked like a thin, vertical smoke-puff, solitary and ephemeral. Probably it was no more than a wisp of rain-cloud, or perhaps the spouting of a whale. It was altogether peculiar, not at all like the smoke-trail of a ship. Within seconds the phenomenon was repeated, at the same point of the compass, so brief and evanescent as to be almost subliminal. It might still be nothing more tangible than vaporization, yet in that dry, windless atmosphere it held its image just long enough to imprint itself on the retina.

There were no further exhalations, whether they were vapour or smoke, and Merten was not optimistic. Almost certainly it had been an illusion. But he gave orders for a change of course. Slowly, very slowly, the minutest of smudges on the horizon, inseparable at first from the wave-crests, began to acquire definition.

On the *City of Cairo*, with the African coast 1250 miles to the east and the South American coast 2,000 miles to the west, the passengers felt they were entering safe waters. Six days out from Cape Town and eight or nine days from Recife, they were approaching mid-Atlantic. It had been the warmest day so far; but above all it was another day nearer home. The exertions of the games tournament had left them comfortably tired and pleasantly hungry, and they went to their cabins for a bath before dinner in complacent mood. The general air of well-being was enhanced by the belief that the worst dangers were past.

Gladys Usher, of the Council for World Mission, liked to eat early, and she patronized the first sitting at 18.30, undismayed by the mothers with small children who occupied the dining saloon. Children – Indian children particularly – were her life. After the meal she took her coat, handbag and lifejacket up to the promenade deck to catch the last of the natural light. The fading glow of a magnificent tropical sunset was reflected in the calm, translucent waters, and the evening star was shining in the west. Her thoughts drifted back to Bengal, where she had worked for twenty-two years, and where she looked forward to returning. Sitting here, watching the colours change, and listening to the lap of disturbed water and the throbbing of engines, she felt an odd detachment. She was living a dream-like existence, cut off from India and all her friends and pursuits; even the war, on this enchanting evening, seemed impossibly remote.

For five weeks Gladys Usher had been living in a vacuum; but tomorrow, with the help of the young Welsh girl Violet Williams, and the limited use of the dining saloon for an hour each morning that Purser McQuone had approved, she would be starting a school for the children on board, and she was stimulated by the thought. When the sun finally went down she went into the lounge and sat at a writing-table, put her handbag under the seat, and discussed with Violet the basis of a curriculum.

Leaning over the forward rail of the promenade deck, also admiring the sunset, were Bert Waddell and his new friend Betty Birchman. 'We can't be so very far from the island of St Helena,' he remarked. 'It's somewhere to the north of us – about two days' sailing I should think.'

Evelyn Ashdown, too, sat spellbound watching the sunset, and she tried to identify the myriad colours, a teeming canvas of rose, vermilion, cobalt and gold. She had heard it said that sunrises at sea were even more uplifting. 'I'm going to get up early tomorrow morning', she promised herself, 'to see one.' Then it was time to join her colleague Cecilia Norris at dinner.

Kate Richardson and the Chapmans were dining as usual at the chief engineer's table. 'What a glorious sunset it's been!' exclaimed Sybil Chapman. The chief engineer was less enthusiastic. 'Don't overpraise it! It could be dangerous. We're too good a target.'

Another crew member, a cheerful, solid Tees-sider, was less apprehensive: this was the fourth officer, Bill Stubbs. It was one of his tasks to deliver daily to the wireless cabin a projected list of the ship's co-ordinates for every hour of the day, so that an approximate position could always be transmitted instantly in emergency. He himself had never even bothered to organize a panic bag. He had been at sea all the war – mostly in the *Cairo* – without being torpedoed, and he was firmly convinced that it couldn't happen to him. This evening, off duty, he was leaning on the rail on the starboard side of the promenade deck aft, gazing at the luminous sky on the eastern horizon.

With the children out of the way, the dining saloon, for the second sitting, was restored to its pristine glories. To the sheen of linen, the sparkle of cutlery and the gleam of glass the Bengali stewards added a tincture of Oriental colour with their blue sashes on white uniforms and white headgear as they glided between the tables, to the accompaniment of the percussion of steel on crockery and a lively, continuous chatter.

Donald and Marjorie Miller were dining at Chief Officer Britt's table, and when they came up from their cabin on 'C' deck the ship was already blacked out. Not a chink of light escaped through doors or portholes, yet the saloon was brilliantly lit. Miller had lost his heat at deck quoits, but his wife had won hers at deck tennis. Trust her!

At Dr Quantrill's table were Tommy Green, the British-India Line chief officer, Bill McGregor, recovering from burns, Diana

Jarman and Joan Redl. The Belgian couple, Pierre and Janine Jaspar, who normally sat with them, were in the bar. Their absence could be traced to a playful remark of Diana's at lunchtime. 'You are too fat, M'sieur Jaspar,' she had said teasingly, when he complained of exhaustion from his exertions that morning at deck tennis, 'and you're becoming more so every day. If you don't do something about it. . . .' They all laughed, but the shaft went home, and that afternoon Jaspar, at the captain's invitation, joined with the crew in a strenuous round of medicine ball on the bridge. The session had given him such a thirst that a single whisky and soda proved insufficient, and he had prevailed upon his wife Janine to join him in another, and then a third. They would be late – perhaps too late – for dinner.

Diana had spent the day, between heats of deck quoits and deck tennis, in the swimming pool, and after a five-course meal, followed by coffee, nuts, cigars for the men, and port and liqueurs (the latter at sixpence a glass), she felt replete and was hoping for a relaxed evening. 'We're going to play chess, aren't we, Douglas?' she asked Quantrill.

'Yes, Diana – that would be lovely.'

'I'll go and set up the board in the smoke-room.'

As Quantrill admired her trim retreating figure, he could scarcely credit the tragic circumstances that surrounded her. Her zest for life was unimpaired, embracing physical pursuits without excluding the cerebral. The secret of the simple philosophy engraved inside her wedding ring ('One crowded hour') was not one she shared with many, but Quantrill was privy to it. She was certainly living up to her motto.

Many of the diners were reluctant to exchange the convivial atmosphere of the saloon for the more repressive comfort and inferior illumination of the public rooms, and they lingered over their meal. Bob Skea and the Gordons were among the few who pushed back their chairs and moved to the lounge. Others found their way to the bar. At the chief engineer's table, Sybil Chapman excused herself and went along to Ada Taggart's cabin to get her ready for bed.

When Lady Almond finished her dinner she went to her cabin,

which she was sharing with her youngest child, Susan, to collect cards and score sheets for a rubber of bridge. The three boys were in a cabin further along the corridor. Susan, a young lady of forthright character, felt she had been perpetually travelling throughout her childhood, back and forth to India by boat and across the sub-continent by train, so she was perfectly accustomed to an itinerant life. She had packed her own panic bag with warm clothes, but otherwise the voyage, and her mother's comings and goings, seemed no more than routine. She certainly didn't properly understand the danger. When her mother crept into the cabin, anxious not to wake her, she was dozing.

Of the Simms children, Mary, the eldest at twelve and by far the most mature, was sitting on the top bunk of the two-berth cabin she shared with her ten-year-old brother David. A knock on the door heralded the arrival of a cabin steward with a special treat, a tray of ice cream, and her eyes, saucer-like at the best of times, opened even wider. 'Come in! Yum, yum – how lovely!' Sharp and alert, she had long since gone beyond the stage of exasperation at the slow wits and inconsistency of adults, learning tolerance but finding animals more logical. When the ice cream was finished she climbed back to her bunk and resumed her reading of Kipling's *The Jungle Book.* She knew perfectly well that the ship might be torpedoed, but it was silly to worry about that until it happened.

Since sighting the wisp of sulphurous smoke at 19.21, Karl-Friedrich Merten, in U68, had been closing the range. Soon he was focusing on what he judged to be a cargo/passenger ship, her masts, funnel and superstructure slowly taking shape. She seemed fairly high in the water, not, he thought, heavily loaded, and she was steaming without lights. She was probably a troopship, and he detected anti-aircraft armament and a sizeable gun, probably 4-inch, astern. The vessel had indeed operated as a troopship in the past, so Merten's conclusions were not unsound.

Merten estimated that the liner, of about 8,000 tons, was steaming at roughly 10 knots on a west-nor'-westerly course of 290 degrees. He could hear the vessel's engine revolutions on his listening apparatus, and he worked out her probable speed from these. It took him over an hour to manoeuvre into an attacking position, but at 20.26, having called his crew to battle stations some time earlier, he fired a single bow tube at her from a range of 500 metres.

Merten's underestimate of the *City of Cairo*'s speed did not save the vessel. 29 seconds later, abreast of the after-mast, the torpedo struck.

CHAPTER 3

'We've Got it This Time!'

From the bowl of mixed nuts in front of him on the dining table, Donald Miller, mindful of his destination, selected a brazil. He fitted the wrinkled husk into a pair of nutcrackers and squeezed. The result exceeded his expectations. Simultaneously, as the nut disintegrated, the steady, pulsating rhythm of nautical progress was shattered by a muffled explosion astern. The babble of conversation was stilled, and the ship shuddered to its rivets before lurching drunkenly, sending glasses and crockery sliding off tables and shelves and pitching those on their feet to the floor. In the next instant the lights failed and the entire ship was plunged into darkness.

'That's us! We've got it this time!'

'We're in for it now!'

Then came the clear, incisive voice of Chief Officer Britt, at whose table the Millers were sitting. 'Get to the boats!'

'Are you there, dear?' Miller anxiously enquired of his wife.

'Yes.'

'Let's keep together.'

They felt their way round the table, joined hands and began to grope towards the doorway and up the stairs towards the promenade deck. Their boat was No. 8 – the last boat astern on the port side. There was no time, it seemed, to go down to their cabin for coats or panic bags. Britt's instructions were clear.

The last thing Evelyn Ashdown saw, as the lights failed, was the vase of flowers, remnant of that illicit harvest on Table Mountain, sliding into her lap. Instinctively she tried to retrieve it, but it crashed from her lap to the floor. The ship was recovering its balance, and she started to join the exodus, then remembered she had left her lifejacket on the back of her chair. Jostled by the tide streaming against her, and momentarily disorientated, she felt physically sick. But she found her table, fumbled for her lifejacket, and pulled it on.

How long did they have? Had she got time to go to her cabin? Wearing as she was a flimsy evening gown and court shoes, she was sorely tempted. Knowing that most of the children were in bed and would have to be fetched, she left the saloon and made for her cabin. She might also be able to help with the children.

The staircase was crowded, with most of the people on their way up. There was no panic, and although voices were raised in nervous excitement there was no shouting. A young woman named Flossie Gavin pleaded to be allowed through to collect her ten-year-old daughter, and the crowd divided.

Pierre and Janine Jaspar, fearing for Michel, were among those pushing against the dense mass of humanity coming up. When they got to their cabin on 'C' deck, two decks down, they found Michel calmly sitting up in bed. 'I think', said the six-year-old in a detached tone, 'we've been torpedoed.'

Margaret and Crawford Gordon held hands and went quietly down from the lounge to their cabin on the saloon deck to collect their warm clothing and panic bags. They were half-way down when an authoritative voice shouted: 'Don't go down to your cabins! Go straight up on deck!' But having got so far, and knowing that mothers had to go down for their children, they disobeyed the order. Donning some warmer and more suitable clothing, they slung their panic bags round their necks under their lifejackets and returned to the promenade deck.

Fourth Officer Bill Stubbs, leaning on the rail on the starboard side aft, suddenly found himself flying through the air. Hurled from the promenade deck to the saloon or tank deck, he was pinioned by a wall of water as the stalagmite thrown up by the torpedo cascaded on top of him. When he eventually scrambled to his feet he found that the accommodation ladder on the starboard side had been blown away. He was standing directly above No. 4 Hold, where the torpedo hit. Above him, hanging on its davits from the boat deck, he could see Boat 7, the last boat aft on the starboard side, with its rudder missing, blown off by the blast.

Staggering across to the port side, where the ladder was undamaged, he climbed up to the boat deck and went forward to his cabin. He had bought a lot of presents to take home, but the ship's steam whistle was shrilling and all he could find in the darkness was his 'monsoon' coat. He ought to have prepared a panic bag; what he had been sure would never happen had happened. Losing no time in self-reproaches, he hurried back to the lifeboat he was assigned to take charge of, Boat 5.

Others who suffered the maximum convulsion and shock were those in the smoke-room. Among them were Betty Birchman and Bert Waddell. Nothing in their previous experience compared with that ominous sound and the knowledge of what it portended. The whole smoke-room seemed to turn a somersault on top of them and they were hurled from their seats. The initial cataclysm was followed by a tinkling avalanche of glassware and the tell-tale sibilance of escaping steam. For a moment they lost their bearings as the lights dipped, flickered and went out, but they had their lifejackets to hand and they hurried through the black-out curtains and out on to the narrow after-part of the promenade deck. Here the air was vaporous with steam and spray and thick with flying coal-dust. The boats had not yet been lowered, and Waddell, wearing a light hopsack suit, was considering a dash to his cabin when another padre, the Welshman Davies, who had been in his cabin preparing Sunday's sermon, thrust his daughter Ann into Waddell's arms and went off to collect his wife and second child. Betty Birchman, however, was able to get to her cabin and collect some warm clothing.

Allan Tempest was sitting in the lounge when he heard a dull thump – a distinctive, non-resonant sound that to him was unique. He was wearing a green blazer, white sports shirt and light grey shorts, and he had warmer clothing in his cabin, also some cine-film he valued; but his passport, military papers, exam certificates and cheques were in his pocket. In the stories he had read of torpedoing, anyone who went back to their cabin got trapped and was not seen again, and he was determined not to make that mistake. In any case, losing the books he was studying wouldn't be half as bad as losing the brand-new bicycle that had been loaded for him at Bombay. He went straight out on the promenade deck to his boat station, No. 5, and at once smelt the stench of explosive. Then the emergency lighting, eerie but effective, came on, providing ample light in the interior and for lowering the boats. Meanwhile the ship seemed to right herself. Perhaps his bicycle – and the books – might be safe after all.

The *Cairo*, still under way, had stabilized, but she was slowly settling by the stern, and Captain Rogerson, alerted by officer of the watch Knocker Whyte, rang the engine room telegraph to stop and ordered all water-tight doors to be shut. Finding telephone and alarm bells out of action he blew the steam whistle and gave orders verbally from the bridge.

'Prepare to abandon ship! Lower the boats!'

The next essential was to get a distress message out, giving their position, and word was passed to second wireless officer Tom 'Sparkie' Humphries, the man on watch in the radio cabin. Checking the ship's position from the list Stubbs had given him, the spare, diminutive Humphries tapped out an S.O.S., giving all relevant information and adding that amongst the hundred passengers on board were 44 women and children. After transmitting this message twice on the distress frequency he was delighted to receive an acknowledgement, so loud and clear that he could hardly believe it came from Walvis Bay, though the call-sign confirmed it. Walvis Bay would repeat the message at once to Naval Control Cape Town, and if the *Cairo* sank the Navy would know where to look for survivors.

Lancastrian George Nutter, of the Roman nose and straw-coloured hair, was in the alleyway leading to his cabin when the lights went out and he heard the steam whistle. In the darkness he stumbled on a woman who had fainted in the corridor, and his calm Mancunian tones helped to revive her. She told him her boat station and he carried her up. People were still hurrying down to their cabins to collect their belongings and he had to fight his way through. Having volunteered for duties as a boat warden he was left with no time to return to his cabin, and he went straight up to the port side of the boat deck to take charge, with the help of two Indian seamen, of lowering Boat 6.

Dulcie Kendall and Freda Bullen were lingering over their coffee in the saloon when they were almost thrown out of their chairs. In the ensuing darkness they grabbed their lifejackets and made their way to their cabins, which were at the opposite end of the ship. Dulcie missed her way in the dark and had to feel her way back along the corridor wall. The torpedo had exploded immediately below her cabin and the disorder was such that she was frightened to look at Colin's bunk. But he was sitting up in bed rubbing his eyes. By the time she had gathered a few essentials into her panic bag, a tall, grey-haired, well-groomed retired Army colonel named Arnold Silcock, a man with such a veneer of discretion that he was popularly supposed to be attached to M.I.5 (he admitted to being a King's Messenger, but that was dismissed as a 'front'), appeared in the doorway as pre-arranged, and, although carrying an armful of coats, jackets and jerseys, he took charge of Colin. Dulcie felt quite unperturbed now. The ship did not seem to be sinking, she was in good hands, and it didn't occur to her that there might be another torpedo.

Silcock *had* served in Intelligence, he was a Fellow of the Royal Institute of British Architects, and his wide-ranging interests included Chinese porcelain, on which he was an authority, and comic verse. But only his military training was of use to him – and to Dulcie Kendall – now.

Freda Bullen, whose cabin was on 'C' deck, had even farther to go to reach the twins. A shy person, she had not liked to trouble anyone else, but one of the distressed British seamen had offered to help and had kept his promise. The twins, lying naked in their bunks, were asleep. Freda selected a few items of clothing and they grabbed one twin each. Pulling the miniature kapok lifejackets over bare flesh and gathering up two tiny pairs of pyjamas, they hurried up to their boat station, No. 1 Boat, the farthest forward on the starboard (torpedo) side.

At Douglas Quantrill's table, Tommy Green took Joan Redl up to her cabin on the promenade deck, then went on up to the boat deck to help with the launching. 'See you at Boat 1,' he called as he left. Meanwhile Diana Jarman, after a quick dash to her cabin, made her way independently to Boat 3. Joan Redl's cabin too was in darkness and she had to struggle to get little Qunk into his lifejacket, but even in her haste she paused to make doubly sure it was fastened as tightly as the child could comfortably bear. Then she grabbed her emergency bag, collected her coat and lifejacket, and continued to her boat station.

Meanwhile Quantrill was running down the main corridor to his cabin, and as the ship recovered its equilibrium he bumped into Violet Williams as she came out of her cabin and sent her flying. But she seemed all right, so he continued to his cabin and rescued his medicine bag. Running on to the end of the alleyway, he came out on the well deck by No. 4 Hold. The hatches had been blown off by the explosion and he found himself looking down at the rectangular boxes he had seen being loaded at Bombay. He had forgotten to ask what was in them, but several had burst open, and they glistened in the half-light like the secret hoard of some eighteenth-century pirate. They were crammed with silver rupees.

Sybil Chapman was stranded in Ada Taggart's cabin. 'Now,' said the stewardess unselfishly, 'run for your lifeboat – and take your lifejacket.' She thrust the jacket into Sybil's hands.

'No, you can't be left. You can't even walk.'

'Don't worry about me, I'm provided for. The doctor has instructions from the Company to look after me.' At this Sybil Chapman left to join her husband at Boat 1.

Quantrill was already making for Ada Taggart's cabin. On the way he was delayed by a badly shocked Kate Richardson, who had been taken down to her cabin by her son-in-law after an early dinner. Someone was looking after her but they wanted Quantrill's specialist advice. He examined her briefly and suggested getting her into the first boat available. When he got to Ada Taggart's cabin she had gone. Sidney Britt had provided for her.

Running up the companion way to the promenade deck, he looked into the smoke-room, which was empty, then went down to the engineers' quarters, where he feared someone might have been injured. But his friend Bob Gerner (the baritone) told him:

'Everyone's all right here.' He ran back up to the smoke-room, intending to get a bottle of spirits from the bar, but some conscientious barman, over-zealous in protecting the company's property, had locked it.

Gladys Usher, her plans for starting a school stillborn, put on her coat and lifebelt, thought about going down to her cabin on 'C' deck, decided against it, and set off for her boat station, Boat 5. She could hear people running about on the boat deck above, but as yet there was no one to be seen at her station. Then she remembered she had left her handbag under the seat in the lounge, containing her passport, reading glasses, and valuables. Deciding to go back for it, she was intercepted by Freda Bullen, on her way to Boat 1, who asked her to hold one twin while she dressed the other. Then the Gordons arrived, and Margaret Gordon, who was also on her way to Boat 1, took the child from her, so once more Gladys Usher started off for the lounge. By this time Flossie Gavin arrived with her daughter Sheila; in her anxiety to collect Sheila from the cabin she had left her own lifejacket in the dining saloon. 'I'll get it for you,' offered Gladys Usher; but a stylish young woman with chestnut, shoulder-length hair named Cynthia Saunders, who was sharing a cabin with her, wouldn't let the older woman go. Cynthia, the wife of a tea-planter who had joined the Indian Army, had already been down to collect her own and her cabin companion's things; now she set off for the saloon. At last Gladys Usher was free to get her handbag from the lounge; but at that moment Boat 5 was lowered to the promenade deck and a quartermaster shouted: 'All women and children to the boats!' So she gave up the attempt, and when Cynthia Saunders came back empty-handed from the lounge the two women followed Flossie and Sheila Gavin into the boat.

The shock of the explosion jerked Lady Almond to one side and spewed the two packs of cards she was collecting across the cabin. Accustomed as she was to the tradition of the stiff upper lip, she betrayed no discernible surprise – such interruptions were only to be expected in wartime – and certainly no fear. Susan was frightened as much by the sudden darkness as by the crash of the torpedo, and for a moment she whimpered. Reassured by her mother, however, she quickly recovered her natural composure, and between them they began to collect torches, blankets and warm clothes into a bag. After helping her daughter put a coat on over her nightdress and cramming a lifejacket on top of that, Lady Almond donned her own lifejacket and balanced a fur coat over her arm, and together they made for the promenade deck, resolving to dress themselves while they were waiting at their boat station. Meanwhile the three Almond boys, who had been preparing for bed, had organized themselves efficiently, and the family was reunited at No. 2 Boat Station, the farthest forward on the port side.

For Susan, still not properly awake, the sequence had a dream-like quality, enhanced by the dim emergency lighting and a queer stifling of sound now the engines had stopped. She didn't feel particularly frightened because nothing seemed real. Yet she was vaguely aware that it *was* real.

At their boat station they were joined by Pierre and Janine Jaspar and Michel. There was no boat warden in sight. Looking up they were dumbfounded by what they saw. Directly above them, where their lifeboat should have been swinging on its davits, was an empty space. Beyond it there was nothing but deep-blue, star-studded sky. No. 2 Boat had already gone.

In their haste the launching crew had lost control of the winch and instead of halting the boat at the promenade deck they had allowed it to crash to the water. There was still too much way on the ship for a successful launching, and to compound their error they had omitted to put the plug in; it was normally removed when the boat was on its davits to allow rain water to drain. The boat immediately flooded to the gunwales, and, although still attached by a single painter to the ship and supported by its flotation gear, it tipped up and became uncontrollable for boarding.

Dragging their scanty belongings with them, the horrified Almonds hurried aft to try to find places in the next boat, No. 4. This was one of the two smaller boats. 'No more room here!' called a voice. 'We're full up and just going down!'

At any moment, out of the darkness, a second torpedo might strike. But if Lady Almond was panicking inside, she remained outwardly cool. It never did to let people see one was put out; this was ingrained in her. Once one got flustered, all command of a situation was lost. It was not that she shut her eyes to distasteful facts. It was simply that she would never let anything outface her. She would find places in the boats for her family and herself provided she retained her poise.

'There's a boat going from the other side!'

The shout came from quartermaster Angus MacDonald, a blue-eyed, ginger-haired Scot, small, wiry and tough, and a man of few words, who had been in charge of lowering Boat 4. Hearing his quartermaster friend Bob Ironside, another Scot, calling that he was having trouble lowering Boat 3 on the opposite (starboard) side, he left the launching of Boat 4 to others and hurried across the deck to Boat 3. Climbing into the boat, he cleared a rope that was fouling the lowering gear; once this was accomplished he signalled to the Almonds to get in. Two who were already safely established in this boat, which was crowded, were sick stewardess Ada Taggart and Diana Jarman.

Sitting in the boat while it was suspended on its davits felt precarious enough, but it was nothing to the fear induced as the boat was lowered. First one rope and then the other jerked down too far, throwing the occupants towards opposite ends alternately and nearly tipping them out. As the teetering, spasmodic descent continued they held on like limpets, while quartermaster Angus MacDonald, somehow keeping his balance in the middle of the boat, struggled to steady the descent by prodding an oar against the hull. Incredibly they reached the water without being somersaulted out, and then a rope ladder was lowered and the men started down.

Ship's writer Jack Edmead went forward and reported to Captain Rogerson. 'The boats are being lowered, sir. Is there anything more I can do?'

'Yes – release as many rafts as you can. But leave them trailing on the rail until she goes farther down. Then we'll cut them adrift.'

Accompanied by Bob Gerner, Edmead proceeded to pull the slip-hooks that attached the rafts to the rigging. On the way he saw Purser McQuone walking calmly across to Boat 3, dressed in a light-brown tweed suit and carrying a satchel stuffed with the ship's papers, for all the world as though he were just going ashore to the agents. 'See you in the morning, sir,' called Edmead. But when he next saw his friend McQuone he would not be looking quite so immaculate. Edmead then went to Boat 1.

The two older Simms children, Mary and David, were still reading when the lights went out, and they guessed they had been torpedoed. Mary scrambled down from her bunk, but her mind was a blank. Where was her lifejacket? She must have left it in Mummy's cabin. Forgetting for the moment about David, she felt her way along the corridor and tried to open her mother's door. It was locked. Eileen Simms had had dinner with the children and gone to bed early.

'Mummy! Have you got my lifebelt?'

Eileen Simms had the two younger children to cope with, and in any case she hadn't got Mary's lifejacket. She sent Mary back to her cabin to look for it. After a short search Mary found it and ran up to the deck. She knew her boat station was No. 8, the last one on the port side, and the emergency lighting made it easy to find. The boat had already been lowered to the promenade deck. David too started off without his lifejacket, dashed back for it, grabbed his coat from the cupboard handle, tore a blanket off the bed, and joined his sister.

Eileen Simms and the two younger girls arrived soon after. Two Scots quartermasters, both Glaswegians in their forties, were in charge at Boat 8 and they were standing no nonsense from passengers or crew. 'Now, Mrs Simms, are your four children all here? Yes? Then over you go.'

The names of the other women assigned to this boat were then called: they were the inseparables Evelyn Ashdown and Cecilia Norris; and Marjorie Miller. 'I don't want to go before you,' said Dr Miller to her husband. But for once he was the dominant partner. 'You must, dear. I'll follow directly.'

The operation of launching the boats was complicated by the fact that when suspended from their davits they would support not more than a third of their capacity. Women and children, and the aged and infirm, were embarked at promenade deck level, and then the boats were lowered to the water and the men shinned down rope ladders attached to the falls. But the task of the boat wardens in checking and restricting the numbers embarking had been complicated by the flooding of Boat 2. Boat 4, too, once Angus MacDonald's back was turned, had been launched prematurely, placing an intolerable pressure on the remaining boats.

Fourth Officer Bill Stubbs, in charge of launching Boat 5, had the help of one quartermaster and one Lascar, instead of the six crew members who should have been there. 'You take the forward end and I'll take the aft end,' he told the quartermaster, and they lowered away. When the boat reached promenade deck level Stubbs looked over the side and was appalled to see the numbers crowding in. Some idiot was shouting, 'Lower away forward . . . lower away aft. . . . We're getting pitched out.' Stubbs feared the load would bring them all to disaster. Fortunately, this was a newly installed boat, with new launching equipment, and it stood the strain.

Over-anxious to get away before the arrival of a possible second torpedo, Europeans and Asians alike were shouting prematurely that their boats were full. Allan Tempest was allocated to Stubbs's boat, but he had barely set foot on the ladder when there came a cry from forty feet below of 'Boat full!' Tempest, though only seventeen years old, had seemed so mature that no one had bothered to make themselves responsible for him, and now he was all too conscious that he was on his own. Hitherto in his life there had always been someone to make decisions for him. Now there was no one. 'Bugger you,' he thought, 'this is my boat. If I don't get away in this one, I shan't get away at all.' So down the ladder he went, chancing that the boat might push off before he could reach it. There proved to be plenty of room.

This was Quantrill's boat, and by the time he got to the promenade rail he looked down to see masts, sails, oars and boathooks occupying all the room down the middle, and heads everywhere else. 'Sorry,' called someone, as he peered over the rail, 'no more room.' Quantrill turned back to look for a raft, but at that moment the chief engineer arrived. He had been torpedoed before and was not so easily fooled. 'There's plenty of room in there,' he told Quantrill. 'Come on.'

Last to leave the boat deck above Boat 5 was Bill Stubbs; after unhooking the falls he slid down the lifelines running from the davit heads. Men were already manning the oars and trying to pull away, but the boat was repeatedly sucked back against the side of the ship. Fears of another torpedo drove the rowers on, and an oar was broken as they tried to push the boat off. Stubbs saw at once that the rowers were attempting the impossible: painters were still tethering the boat to the ship. Alerted by Stubbs, Quantrill produced his surgical scissors and cut the lines. 'You can pull for your lives now,' said Stubbs.

George Nutter, helping to launch Boat 6, marvelled at the speed with which the boat filled up. He was supposed to embark nineteen Asians, but he could see at a glance there were many more. Had he known of the problems with the two boats forward of him, Boats 2 and 4, he would have understood it.

The majority of the Asians, being saloon, galley and cabin staff, were of little help, and the spare Lascar crews, owing no allegiance to the *City of Cairo*, put self-preservation first. But two Asian seamen helped Nutter lower the boat, and discipline, helped by Nutter's firm but friendly manner, was maintained. When the boat had filled up after reaching the water, Nutter slid down the falls. In the process he badly chafed the palms of his hands.

Nutter's boat was one of the first away. He found he had thirty-three Asians instead of his allotted nineteen, ten European men, the three Russians, the Sinhalese, seven European women, and one child. (Dulcie Kendall was in this boat with Colin.) One of the men was the young aircraft tradesman in search of adventure, Victor Chambers, whose home town was Southampton and whose knowledge of small boats and affinity with the sea were a welcome reinforcement for Nutter.

One man who baulked at getting into this boat because of its over-loaded state was Francis Marr, 49-year-old geologist with the Burma Oil Company. Having seen his wife Peggy safely aboard, he stood back. Violet Williams was in this boat – with her parents – and she was a witness to Francis Marr's unselfishness. She hoped he would get away on a raft.

With such a full load – fifty-five people in a boat rated to hold forty-eight – George Nutter, finding himself virtually in charge, wasted no time in shoving off and recruiting oarsmen to pull away from the ship.

Bob Skea, another of the volunteer boat wardens, dashed up to the boat deck to help launch Boat 7. This boat, the farthest aft on the starboard side, was the one that had been damaged by the torpedo. What other weakening it might have sustained was not immediately apparent, but it had clearly lost its rudder. Since this was the only powered lifeboat on board, its serviceability was doubly important.

The man in charge of this boat was the ship's second officer and senior navigator, the poker-playing Les Boundy. Forty-five-years-old, rough hewn, moon-faced and jovial, he cut a comical figure to the whimsical Bob Skea when he first appeared. He had been in bed when the torpedo struck, and he had pulled his uniform over his striped pyjamas, crammed his cap rakishly on his tousled head, and hurried to Boat 7. Helped by the tindal (a sort of Lascar bosun's mate), he and Skea lowered the boat to the promenade deck, where the passengers began piling in, together with four of the DEMS gunners and a large number of Asians.

'I've got my sextant in the cabin,' said Skea. 'I'll dash down and get it.' Reliable navigation in the lifeboats, in the middle of the South Atlantic, would be impossible without a sextant, and he wanted to have his own.

'No, you stand by the boat,' replied Boundy. 'I'll get my sextant from the bridge, it's nearer, and I'll get a chronometer as well.'

'In that case,' said Skea, 'I shall claim a half-share in your sextant.'

'All right,' said Boundy. 'But see they don't launch the boat before I get back.' As he left he bumped into the Dutchman Ferdinand Dieckhaus, one of the wardens for this boat, who had just rescued a sleeping Ferdy – having wrapped him in blankets – from the cabin. 'Go up to my cabin,' Boundy instructed, 'and get my panic bag. My navigation books are inside it.' Dumping Ferdy in the lifeboat, Dieckhaus obeyed.

Boundy soon returned with the sextant, as did Dieckhaus with the nautical tables; but without being aware of it Boundy had dropped the chronometer. The process of launching had been started when there came a shout from the deck.

'Stop!'

The Belgian family, like the Almonds, had crossed to the starboard side when they found Boat 2 had gone, but, unlike the Almonds, they had missed their way and finished up at Boat 7. Here too they found themselves rejected.

'Sorry – there's no more room!'

'There must be – for one woman and one child at least!'

This time it was the officer in charge who shouted 'Stop!' Whether Boundy had recognized the voice of his poker-playing friend, or whether he had baulked at refusing to accommodate a woman and child, he was too poker-faced to reveal. The Jaspar trio were taken on board and the launching was resumed.

The lifeboat aft on the opposite (port) side, Boat 8, also got away about this time. 'Have we put the plug in?' someone shouted, and nobody seemed to know, but a *mêlée* of equipment and bodies made checking impossible. The boat leaked but not dramatically, so they concluded the plug must be in. They expected some initial seepage through the seams.

Once clear of the ship the rowers rested on their oars. Mary Simms noticed that as soon as they stopped, everyone produced cigarettes and began smoking. David Simms looked back and saw the dark form of the ship looming against the sky.

Donald Miller's thoughts were conflicting: on the one hand was the sight of the stricken ship, with some of the boats not yet clear, emphasizing their own unenviable plight; on the other was the backcloth provided by nature. The stars were shining in unbelievable brilliance and profusion, casting gleams of phosphorescence wherever the water was ruffled. Was there ever, he asked himself, such a marvellous night since creation? He found himself repeating:

When I consider Thy heavens, the work of Thy fingers,
The moon and the stars, which Thou hast ordained,
What is man, that Thou art mindful of him?

Would God, he wondered, be mindful of them now?

Boat No. 1, farthest forward on the starboard side, was Knocker Whyte's boat, and he had fitted it out superbly. All the boats carried water breakers, rations, general and emergency equipment, first-aid boxes, and so on, but Whyte had prepared his boat to a higher standard than most. He had already packed a spare sextant in it; and this was also the boat that carried the emergency radio, which might be vital to the survival of them all. Helping Whyte on the boat deck was volunteer boat warden Tommy Green.

The boat was lowered in orderly fashion to the rails on the promenade deck, but then there was a rush for it by some of the spare Lascars who had failed to find places in the boats on the opposite side. With no public address system, and no walkie-talkie radios, there was no system of monitoring progress or of distributing loads evenly under central control. Britt toured the promenade deck after the loss of Boat 2, pacifying the hysterical and shouting orders to 'Hold on! Wait till the way's off the ship!' But as one by one the boats filled up, the remaining passengers and crew could see themselves being left behind.

Already embarked in Boat 1 were Margaret Gordon, wearing a long check overcoat with trousers underneath and grasping her precious panic bag; Freda Bullen and the twins, still naked apart from the tiny kapok lifejackets the ship's carpenter had made for them; and Joan Redl and Qunk. Boarding with some misgivings were James and Sybil Chapman; could they safely assume that Kate Richardson was in one of the other boats? Suppose no one had fetched her? She might be in her cabin still. 'Oh, my poor mother!' moaned Sybil Chapman. 'We're not sinking,' replied her husband, looking over the side. 'There might be time to get her.' At this Crawford Gordon volunteered to go and look for her. 'I know where her cabin is,' he said as he left.

As the scramble to get into Boat 1 continued, many voices were raised in protest. Some of the Indians, momentarily shocked, had held back. Now they pressed forward. 'Hold it!' shouted one of the quartermasters. 'Women and children first! Any more women?' Several of the more senior European men, however, those in their fifties and sixties, had already climbed in, and the sight of them provoked the Asian crew. Women and children first was one thing, Europeans first was another. As more and more Indians crowded over the rail, the sudden excessive weight resulted in Tommy Green's hand and arm being jammed in the block on the davits.

Green's efforts to extract his arm only tautened the ligature, and with the launching of the boat indefinitely delayed, and forty or fifty people, seeing other boats leaving, and, fearing another torpedo, clamouring for action, a major catastrophe seemed imminent. To Tommy Green, trapped even more irrevocably than those in the boat, there seemed only one remedy.

'Cut off my arm!'

Knocker Whyte, horrified, thought he could see a way out, and after drawing back from the chasm where the starboard accommodation ladder had once been he crossed to the port side and descended to the promenade deck from there. If they could lighten the boat, the pressure on Green's arm would be eased and he might be able to extricate it. 'Tommy Green's arm is caught in the winch!' he shouted at the occupants of the boat. 'You'll have to get out!' And when no one responded: 'We're all stuck here until you lot move!' This brought a reluctant exodus, hastened by Whyte and others as they manhandled the uncomprehending Asians on to the deck.

Hurrying back to the boat deck, Whyte was accompanied by former military bandsman Jim Chapman, who had offered to help. Before leaving his wife Chapman threw her his coat, into which he had earlier sewn the deeds of his mother-in-law's house in Cornwall and their wills and passports. With the assistance of Chapman and others Whyte was able to take enough of the weight for Green's arm to be released. It was badly furrowed and contused, but the horror of amputation had been averted.

Although in great pain, Green helped Whyte and Chapman

lower the boat to the water, in jerks and starts that again terrified the occupants. Then Europeans and Asians alike swarmed down the ladder.

Leaving Green to take temporary charge, Whyte went forward to see what else remained to be done, and what help Captain Rogerson might need. There were still a number of people, including passengers, on board, and as officer of the watch he saw it as his duty to remain.

In Boat 1, Margaret Gordon was nursing one of the twins and Freda Bullen was trying to dress the other. Qunk, too, nursed for the moment by Stewardess Annie Crouch, still had nothing on but his lifejacket. Dressing the children, in these cramped and crowded conditions, was further complicated by the necessity to keep their lifejackets firmly over their bodies in case they were all tipped into the sea.

Starting down the ladder was Crawford Gordon, having returned from finding Kate Richardson's cabin empty. She had been in Stubbs's boat, Boat 5, all the time. Gordon's gesture was no less courageous for that. Now, with one of the boat crew hanging on to the hull with a boat-hook, someone shouted 'Boat full!' and cast off from the bow. 'But they're not all in yet!' shouted Margaret Gordon, pointing to her husband. Meanwhile the boat drifted aft, out of Gordon's reach.

In the adjacent boat, Boat 3, quartermaster Angus MacDonald was still standing up, fending the boat off and trying to push it clear. Between the two boats, within the range of neither, someone was hanging on to a rope near the water. 'Hold on, there!' Green shouted to Gordon. 'There's a chap trying to get in down here. We'll pick him up and come back for you.' Margaret Gordon, too, shouted to her husband to hang on.

All eight lifeboats were now in the water, although one was flooded and unmanageable. All the boats on the port side, and two of those on the starboard side, were clear of the hull. But Boats 1 and 3 were still being sucked inwards by the undertow. It was from the starboard side that the torpedo had come. And with the U-boat still somewhere out there in the darkness, this was the side still exposed to U-boat attack.

*

To Karl-Friedrich Merten the effect of his torpedo on the target seemed inconclusive. The *City of Cairo*, as he now took her to be from her radio call-sign, had listed at first, then recovered. He had seen the emergency lights glimmering on the decks and watched the boats being lowered, but it was quite possible that a skeleton crew was being retained, ready to organize a re-boarding if that should prove practicable.

Soon after Merten's torpedo hit, his wireless operator had come up to the bridge to say that the steamer was using her radio to report, on the international distress frequency, that she was under submarine attack. Had the presence of U-boats in the South Atlantic not been demonstrated already, Merten would have issued standing instructions to his radio operator to jam any transmissions from stricken vessels, so as not to disclose his whereabouts or attract a sub-hunt. But as it was he preferred to deal with the message by answering it immediately, using the call-sign of the coastal radio station at Walvis Bay. This fore-stalled repetition of the message, which otherwise would have been picked up sooner or later by some Allied vessel or ground station. Hunter and hunted were far enough from land for Merten to gamble that a brief exchange of signals would pass unnoticed. At the same time he was rewarded with confirmation which every U-boat commander was conceited enough to want to hear: the name (from which he could trace the tonnage) of the vessel he had torpedoed.

If successful, this Machiavellian deceit, encouraging false hopes, as it did, on the *Cairo*, would keep the Allies in ignorance of the progress of U68 on its homeward journey. It would also delay news of the sinking and perhaps prevent its receipt altogether; but that unfortunate fact had to be accepted. Merten was a humane man, but humanity came a poor second when the safety of U68 and its crew was at stake.

Thus it was to the U-boat that 'Sparkie' Humphries, unaware of the subterfuge – although he had been surprised at the signal strength – gave full details. From these Merten learnt that the *Cairo* was carrying women and children. His reaction to this, knowing nothing of the priority accorded the vessel's cargo or passengers, was that the despatch of an unescorted ship with a cruising speed of 10 to 12 knots, carrying women and children across the South Atlantic in wartime, bearing in mind the recent exploits of the Polar Bear Group, was the height of irresponsibility, if nothing worse. He could not let it deflect him from his duty.

Merten was an opportunist whose professional task, in a war to the death, was to sink enemy ships, whatever the cost in human suffering. He was merciful enough to give the lifeboats twenty minutes to get clear. Then, from the safe range of 800 metres, he fired a second torpedo at the now stationary ship.

CHAPTER 4

'Nice Night for a Bathe'

The heart-stopping roar of a running torpedo was heard in all four lifeboats on the starboard side, and for a fraction of a second all action was frozen, as though someone had stopped the film. When the torpedo, as timed by Merten, had run for 42 seconds, a blinding flash was followed by a guttural explosion and a crumpling sound as of a vast demolition. The impact, forward of the funnel between engine-room and stokehold, released a column of water three times the height of the ship and obliterated the night sky with a volcanic eruption of flames and smoke.

Boats 5 and 7, although rocked by the displacement of thousands of tons of ocean and showered with debris and spray, were far enough away to escape serious damage or injury. But Boats 1 and 3, still cringing under the hull, lay right in the path of the torpedo.

Boat 3, which Angus MacDonald was trying to shove clear with a boat-hook, was blown to splinters and its dazed occupants hurled to the depths. The tangle of limbs and bodies in this small but over-loaded boat was abruptly unravelled by the scatter effect of the explosion, which rocketed the occupants head-first in a score of individual and, as it seemed, irreversible descents.

This, thought May Almond, as the water pressure thundered in her ear-drums, is the end. Yet the kaleidoscopic replay of her past life that she expected to see did not come. She remembered a long-forgotten instruction by a swimming teacher to turn her hands upwards to surface after a dive, and despairingly she tried it. Soon, to her intense surprise, she found herself above water, half-blinded by straggling ringlets of hair. So much for her Cape Town perm.

'Mummy!'

It was her eldest boy, Basil, and he was grinning. 'Nice warm night for a bathe!' She called the names of her other children, but only Francis answered. A moment ago David and Susan had been sitting beside her in the boat. Now they were nowhere to be seen.

Susan had gone a long way down, and she too wondered if she would ever come up again. She could hardly swim, yet even now she didn't feel frightened. The experience was so preposterous as to be dreamlike. When at length she surfaced she couldn't see anyone near, but she didn't panic, and her lifejacket kept her afloat. Then Basil grabbed her and towed her towards her mother. The family was complete but for David.

May Almond faced an appalling dilemma. Should she concentrate her energies on getting the three children as far from the ship as possible before it sank and dragged them down with it, as it threatened to do, or should she risk all their lives in a desperate search for David? She made her decision, as always, with perfect confidence that what she was doing was right. They must stand or fall together. Soon afterwards David, who had thought it was the others who were lost, bobbed up beside her.

The adjacent lifeboat, the much larger Boat 1, although escaping the core of the blast, was lifted up like a cork and turned over, pitching nearly everyone inside it into the sea. Someone fell on top of Margaret Gordon and knocked little Michael Bullen out of her arms, and when at length she came spluttering to the surface the child was gone.

After a frantic but fruitless search she struck out away from the ship. Meanwhile Freda Bullen, similarly flung out, felt herself sinking, and she wondered, without any great curiosity, how soon she would drown. She could imagine no other *dénouement*. But she too came to the surface eventually. She was still clutching Peter.

Joan Redl was precipitated into the water so violently that she was knocked out, either by the blast or the impact. As consciousness flickered and returned she knew she was drowning. She had always heard that drowning was not unpleasant, but now she knew it was a horrible death, and she longed for it to be over. Somersaulting down, she thought not of herself or her child (unaware he had slipped from her grasp), but of her husband. How, she wondered, would he like being a widower? Then she remembered that he too was in mortal danger, many thousands of miles away. For a time she lost all orientation: then she sensed she was no longer going down but coming up.

One deep breath on the surface and her next thought was of Qunk. Where was he? She had clung to him to keep him safe throughout the voyage so far. Somewhere in that tumbling descent to the depths she had lost him.

She uttered a hysterical prayer – and in the next moment heard a child screaming twenty yards or more distant. To her the cries were utterly unlike those of any other child. It could only be Qunk. She hadn't realized that humans, like animals, had such an unerring ear for their young.

A poor swimmer, she mustered her strength to strike out and reach him, and her lifejacket gave her confidence. 'Go on!' she exhorted herself. 'Swim for him! You've got to get him before he can drown!' Behind her the ship was foundering, and it seemed to be dragging her back, but at last she reached little Qunk. How glad she was that she had tightened those straps!

Even now she could scarcely manage him, and for a time she dragged him around by one leg. Then a middle-aged man named Marshall Crichton, a bank manager from Bombay going home on retirement, offered to take him and she gladly accepted. Very soon, in the confusion and darkness, she lost track of them both.

In Boat 3, Sybil Chapman had been sitting next to quartermaster Bob Ironside when they were thrown into the water. Both were hurt in the explosion. Sybil was a non-swimmer but her lifejacket brought her to the surface. 'Jim! Jim!' she called. 'Help me!' But there was no sign of her husband. She remembered he had told her to lie on her back and float in an emergency, and she tried it and it worked. How long could she last? One side of her face had been paralysed by the explosion, she had lost her husband's coat, with all their valuables sewn into the lining, and as for her 78-year-old mother, she must surely be dead.

Gradually she got used to the darkness, and she could see

planks of wood floating about, sections of the splintered lifeboat, and hear people shouting. 'Jim! Jim!' she called again, but he still did not answer. He too must have drowned. Then someone spoke to her out of the darkness.

'I know that voice – that's Mrs Chapman.'

'Who is it?'

'It's Mr Little.'

What a mercy to find someone she knew! Bob Little was a railway official from Central India, 61 years old, on his way into retirement. 'I know you can't swim,' called Little, 'but I've got an oar here from the boat. Could you put one arm over this oar? I'll try to tow you to one of the boats.'

The boat Bob Little aimed for happened to be Boat 1, which, although overturned and swamped, had righted itself and was lying waterlogged some distance away. Some of those originally in this boat had managed to retain their positions, others were trying to regain them. Disputing their right was a tattered group of castaways from Boat 3, Bob Little, Sybil Chapman, the Almond family and Diana Jarman among them.

Margaret Gordon, still looking for the missing twin, hoped he might still be in Boat 1. She reached it, and strong hands pulled her in, but there was no sign of Michael. Marshall Crichton, however, had reached this boat and climbed aboard with young Qunk. Europeans and Asians, passengers and crew, were sitting in water up to their knees, and others were making things worse by clinging to the gunwales, which were sinking to water level. No one was bailing or taking the initiative, and there was no one in charge.

People kept swimming up and dragging themselves aboard, until the boat became almost completely submerged and in danger of rolling over. Yet there were more women and children still clamouring to get in. 'You can't come in here!' shouted the terrified occupants. 'Don't try it! Can't you see we're sinking?' Several more women and children still managed to climb over the gunwale.

Among those in the boat were stewardess Annie Crouch, who had hurt her leg and was in some pain, Freda Bullen and Peter –

Captain W.A. "Bill" Rogerson, master of the *Cairo*.

Kapitan zur See Karl-Friedrich Merten, commander of U68.

First Officer Sidney Britt, MBE.

Fourth Officer Bill Stubbs and Douglas Quantrill the Ship's Surgeon.

Robert "Tiny" Watts.

Quartermaster Angus MacDonald.

Third Officer James "Knocker" Whyte.

there was still no sign of Michael – Marshall Crichton and Qunk, Margaret Gordon, and the three smaller Almond children, Francis, David and Susan, the latter helped aboard and comforted by Crichton and the Australian. Lady Almond and Basil were hanging on to the grablines, as were Joan Redl and Diana Jarman. The two friends were thus reunited in the water. Diana sounded as cheerful as ever. 'I'm dying to spend a penny!' she confided. 'Considering where we are,' said Joan, 'it shouldn't be difficult.'

Margaret Gordon was trying to bail the boat out, and two who were helping were Francis and David Almond. But it was an impossible task. No sooner had they reduced the level than the swell slopped over and swamped the boat afresh.

'I found this child – anyone know whose it is?'

The new arrival was 32-year-old Mona Rooksby, who had embarked at Cape Town with her husband Billie: he had been recalled to England by his firm. Thrown out of Boat 1, Mona Rooksby had found the second Bullen twin floating perfectly happily in his lifejacket, quite alone, gurgling away to himself as though he were enjoying a bath. He was handed into the boat, to be restored to a grateful Freda Bullen. She knew someone else had been nursing Michael but she had not realized he was lost.

Quartermaster Angus MacDonald, half-blinded by the flash when he was thrown out of Boat 3, found himself floating amongst all kinds of flotsam in a darkness that seemed far more intense than before. Slowly, as his night vision recovered, he picked out the biggest piece of wreckage in sight and swam to it. It proved to be not wreckage but the waterlogged Boat 1. Once he was recognized he was welcomed, and he dragged himself aboard to try to examine the boat and assess the damage and what had to be done.

The boat had held together, but it had clearly been holed. Everything inside it was hopelessly entangled, such emergency gear as he could find was under water, and he feared that much of the boat's equipment had been lost when it capsized. This, he knew, was Whyte's boat, into which the emergency radio and a spare sextant had been packed. But he could not check the boat in its present state, completely submerged as it was except for the bow and the stern. Somehow he would have to persuade most of those in the boat to get out, for perhaps half an hour or more, trusting to their lifejackets and hanging on to pieces of wreckage if necessary. Then he could bail the boat out, plug the holes, and make it seaworthy.

'Look,' appealed MacDonald, 'you'll be quite safe in your lifejackets. The boat itself is unsinkable, but if you get out and hang on to something – not the grablines, that will only pull the boat down – a few of us can bale the boat out and get it shipshape. Then you can all get back into a dry boat.'

Most of the Indians in the boat were in a state of shock. MacDonald could see they would be difficult to budge. The European men were in no better shape; some were elderly, and one had been violently sick. MacDonald was left with the women, and they immediately set the example, swimming to a water-tank that was floating nearby. MacDonald was an unemotional man, a confirmed bachelor and loner, but he felt proud of them. Now he could get to work on the Indians.

Marshall Crichton, having entrusted Qunk to stewardess Annie Crouch, got back into the water, and Margaret Gordon was about to follow when she saw, reflecting the starlight, a tiny ashen face slopping about between the thwarts amongst the boat's loose gear. Bending down, she realized it was the body of a child, lifeless as far as she could see. It was Qunk. The injured stewardess had let his wet, greasy body slip from her grasp. As Margaret Gordon seized him he opened his eyes. Mercifully he had floated face up.

'I'll get out,' she said to MacDonald, 'but who's going to look after this baby?'

'Stay where you are – one more doesn't make any difference.'

Amongst those still on board the *City of Cairo* when the second torpedo struck had been Captain Rogerson and a dozen others, a mixture of passengers and crew. Crew members included Sidney Britt, Knocker Whyte, First Radio Officer Harry Peever, who had taken over in the wireless cabin, and Sparkie Humphries, who had sent the original S.O.S. Passengers included Crawford Gordon, Francis Marr, and Bill McGregor, the young engineer who had been burned in a boiler-room fire. Apart from Harry Peever, the crew members had been on duty at the time of the torpedoing. The remainder had all been involved, in one way or another, in helping to get their fellow passengers off the ship.

Rogerson knew from Gordon that two boats aft had been damaged and probably sunk by the second torpedo, and with nearly 300 people to care for he was determined to make use of Boat 2 if he could. This boat, prematurely launched, still lay flooded and unoccupied, precariously attached to the ship by painter, but within reach forward on the port side. Now that the ship was stationary the boat was recoverable. With the ship sinking rapidly, Captain Rogerson ordered all those remaining on board to climb down the ladder and get into this boat. It was so full of water, however, that they were unable to pull it away from the ship.

The *City of Cairo*, now a blazing mass amidships, began to slip backwards in a smooth, slow-motion glide. And as the stern disappeared, the suction dragged Boat 2 back over the forward well deck. Lifting her bows to an alarming height in a final expression of defiance, the stricken vessel tipped Boat 2 over and dragged it down with her. The last thing the occupants saw, as the bows towered above them, was the mast vanishing beside them.

Anticipating what was about to happen, Knocker Whyte and others jumped for it, swimming away as fast as they could. But some were caught in the suction as the 8,000-ton liner was swallowed up by the ocean in a single gigantic gulp. Captain Rogerson was dragged down to a considerable depth, and as a result of the buffeting he received he swallowed a great deal of water. He was retching violently when he finally surfaced. Britt and Humphries of the crew, and McGregor of the passengers, trapped for a time by the swirling vortex below, were somehow regurgitated. But nothing was seen of the others.

As the vessel went down a succession of waves corrugated the surface, each with the force of a tidal bore, rocking the lifeboats, tilting them crazily, and nearly capsizing Boat 1 a second time. Susan Almond, terrified, tried to get back into the water to join her mother and brothers, who were still clinging to the water-tank. Margaret Gordon pulled her back and pacified her, but in doing so she lost her grip on the slippery Qunk. Francis Almond calmly grasped the child by the legs and retrieved him.

Violet Williams, having watched the bows of the ship shoot up to the vertical in its death-throes, found she was smothered in coal dust. People all round her were half-choked by it. Stubbs had entertained hopes – until now – of reboarding. The crew mourned the loss of a home, the passengers the loss of their possessions. Valued belongings, collected by some over half a lifetime, had gone to the bottom.

Allan Tempest, worried that because his books had perished he would never pass his cadet-entrance examination, forgot for the moment about his bicycle. Quantrill could not help thinking of all those silver rupees.

Closest to the grave of the vessel was Boat 5, and urged by Bill Stubbs the men rowed back towards the bubbling whirlpool, which was slowly becoming quiescent. They saw an old Indian, whom they recognized as the cook, sitting in a stunned state on a raft, so they rowed over and took him aboard. Next they sighted Rogerson himself, also on a raft and also concussed, and they hauled him in. Then, hearing more cries for help, they rowed on and found someone in an even less enviable state. It was the purser, Francis McQuone. Thrown out of Boat 3 when it disintegrated, he was almost done for. No one had entered the lifeboats better prepared, as Edmead had noted, but the blast of the explosion had torn his brief-case from his fingers and removed every item of his clothing except his underwear. In view of his bulk he was not hauled in without difficulty.

'Look! There's the sub!'

'For God's sake put those cigarettes out!'

'Don't say another word or they'll hear us!'

All these exclamations were hissed in a whisper as the dark outline of a submarine, dripping with water as though it had just risen from the depths, was glimpsed from the boats, transfixing the survivors with a new terror. Silhouetted against the night sky was the conning tower. Was the submarine German or Italian? Would it make any difference? Nothing intimidated them more than the oppressive shadow thrown, forward of the conning tower, by the submarine's long-range gun.

Still hoping they might not be seen, the survivors in the boats, ostrich-like, remained silent and still. But those in the water, the red lights on their lifejackets flashing with phosphorescence, went on shouting for help. Mary Simms, safely ensconced in Boat 8, thought they were mad to attract the submarine like that. Surely they could wait for just a few more minutes?

The expectation in the boats was that they would be rammed or machine-gunned, probably both. Horrific stories, not all of them propaganda, had been told. They were utterly at the mercy, or so they believed, of a fanatical and ruthless enemy.

Violet Williams, having persuaded her parents to sail, wondered just what she had done. Dulcie Kendall had heard of women and children being taken aboard U-boats, and she was unsure what she should do if the opportunity came. Fingering her St Christopher's medal, she decided she would take her chance in the lifeboat. Douglas Quantrill got ready to dive into the water the moment the guns opened up. There were no heroes, he reflected, at moments like this. He thought he might be able to stay submerged for at least a minute.

'Stand by to come alongside!'

George Nutter's boat, Boat 6, was the nearest to the submarine, and indeed the only one properly within earshot. The occupants could see four or five figures in the conning tower; one of them, presumably the commander, was addressing them through a megaphone. Bronzed and athletic, he was wearing white drill and a peaked cap. His English was perfect, with only a trace of an accent.

The throb of the submarine's diesels faded as the two boats closed. 'Keep still and stop rowing,' ordered Merten. The black silhouette of a 4-inch gun stifled argument.

Godlieb, the Sinhalese, noticing the gun, shouted: 'Take care! There are women and children!'

Merten knew this already, from the signals he had intercepted.

At the same time he was appalled at the number of people still in the water. Some of the lifeboats looked half-empty, with no one seeming to care.

'What ship are you?'

Surely it couldn't possibly help the enemy to reveal the name of a sunken ship? Yet so ingrained was the habit of avoiding careless talk – even at Cape Town they had been bombarded with warnings – that the only answer was a muttered 'Go to hell!'

Merten, determined to get confimation of the intercepted signal, tried again, and this time there was a peremptory edge to his voice. *'I said, what ship are you?'*

It came grudgingly, in little more than a mumble. 'The *City of Cairo*.'

'What name?'

This time it came in a chorus. 'The *City of Cairo*.'

'Good. The *Cairo*. Where is the captain?'

Already, in Boat 5, both captain and chief engineer, knowing the habits of U-boat commanders, had removed their uniform jackets and stuffed them under the thwarts. Boundy, in Boat 7, removed his cap. There was no one in uniform in Boat 6, but someone had the presence of mind to answer.

'He's gone down with the ship.'

This was at least partly true, and Merten accepted it. As it happened he had no plans to take the captain or anyone else prisoner. He wanted to tell the captain that some of the boats looked half-empty and to urge him to hasten the rescue of those in the water.

For the shipwrecked survivors it was difficult to tell, as swell and currents caused headings to crab this way and that, whether the submarine's guns were trained on them or not. Most believed that they were. For Nutter, seeing figures in the conning tower and a gun facing him, and detecting a sound like a ratchet, which he interpreted as the swivelling of a gun, the assumption was automatic. Face to face with the enemy, he appreciated that he and the helpless occupants of the lifeboats were, for the men on the U-boat, the enemy too. Even Nutter could not be certain that no one in his or some other boat carried a gun. A warning burst from the U-boat's guns – which comprised one 10.5 cm (approximately 4-inch), one 3.7 cm and one 2 cm – would be no more than they must expect.

Merten, in fact, had not ordered his guns to be trained on the boats. He had never experienced resistance from any of the lifeboats he had approached in the past, and he did not anticipate it now. Such weapons as rifles and pistols were under lock and key and had not been distributed. Yet there were many survivors who saw – or thought they saw – two men in the conning tower and two on deck manning the 4-inch gun.

'Where are you from?'

Nutter decided to assume the role of informant. It could do little harm to give their last port of call.

'Cape Town.'

'Where are you bound for?'

The ship's course must have given this away. 'Pernambuco. Destination U.K.'

'What was your cargo?'

'General cargo. Pig-iron, timber and wool.' Nutter knew nothing of the boxes of silver.

'Have you any prisoners of war?' Merten had not forgotten the *Laconia* incident,[1] and he repeated the question in German.

'No.'

'Have you anyone who would prefer to be taken prisoner?'

Nutter avoided putting this to the test. 'No.'

'Do you know where you are?'

The officers of the ship would know their position exactly, but none of them was in Boat 6, and there was no harm in getting confirmation from the U-boat. 'No.'

'Your nearest land is the island of St Helena. It's four hundred and eighty miles to the north-north-east, course zero-zero-five degrees. You are a thousand miles from Walvis Bay and three thousand from South America.'

These were very approximate figures. In fact they were 1250 miles from Walvis Bay and 2250 from Brazil. But everyone tried

[1] See page 26

to memorize the details. Someone even said: 'Thank you very much, sir.'

'Take care for those in the water.'

Merten's manner throughout had been considerate, once answers were forthcoming, but the impression he had formed of a complete breakdown of discipline in the lifeboats, with women and children left struggling in the water while boats drifted about half-empty, failed to take account of the chaos he himself had created. The sinking of a ship was a familiar occurrence to Merten. To most of those in the *Cairo* it was unique. The firing of the second torpedo, and the destruction of one boat and the capsizing of another, had been an additional catastrophe, not yet fully absorbed. With the sudden and unexpected appearance of the U-boat, and the terror it engendered, everyone had stopped rowing, and the task of rounding up those in the water had been halted. Nutter's boat was the only one in direct contact with the U-boat, but people in all the other boats were aware of its presence, and many heard snatches of the conversation. For Violet Williams, as for many others, the five minutes occupied in talking to the U-boat commander were the tensest of her life.

It was now two hours since Merten had first sighted the *City of Cairo*, and 54 minutes since he fired his first torpedo. Distress signals had been sent and might well have been heard. He had been in the area long enough. But for Merten the destruction of any ship, triumph though it might be in the context of the maritime war, was an unpleasant if necessary evil, hell for everyone concerned. He was already rating the sinking of the *Cairo* as one of the cruellest and most merciless acts of his submarine life. Now he coupled his farewell to his victims with an apology.

'Goodnight. Sorry for sinking you.'

At 21.20 he turned on a westerly course, coming back on a northerly course for home when he was out of sight of the lifeboats. It was a sensible precaution, yet there was nothing his victims could do in retaliation. And revenge, as it happened, was not in their minds; the last thing they had expected was the courtesy they got. When the U-boat made off, many were left with a feeling of elation.

Not so Bert Waddell. Two hours earlier he had been talking glibly to Betty Birchman about St Helena being quite close, as though it were only just over the horizon. 480 miles in a lifeboat sounded totally unattainable. Others had different reasons for scepticism. 'Go to St Helena?' said one. 'That's out of the question. It's French territory, which means it's controlled by the Germans. Don't you remember Napoleon?'

'I'm sorry, sir,' said Pierre Jaspar. 'You are mistaken. St Helena belongs to the English.' Trust a foreigner to know more about the British Empire than the British. It was some time before his view prevailed.

Ferdinand Dieckhaus was struck by the U-boat commander's ambivalence. After sinking them without warning he had apologized and given them a course to steer to reach the nearest land. He seemed perfectly sincere. Yet he could have eliminated them all there and then. Soon they would be resuming their journey to England, their objective to fight back and kill Germans. The Germans, he reflected, had something to learn from the Japanese about total war.

Following his ducking and the salt water he had swallowed, Captain Rogerson was suffering a severe attack of diarrhoea, and in his weakened state he gave his orders from Boat 5 to the other boats through Bill Stubbs. 'All lifeboats and rafts, keep searching for survivors,' called Stubbs. 'Tie up together where you can and stream sea anchors.' By riding to these they would hold their relative positions. 'The captain will call a muster at dawn.'

Six boats had got safely away, though several were damaged. Boats 5 (Rogerson/Stubbs), 6 (Nutter), and 7 (Boundy) were virtually full. Boat 1 was being rehabilitated under Angus MacDonald, and Boat 4 was adrift with a handful of Asians. This left most of the rescue work, for the moment, to Boat 8. This was another boat with no officers; but no community of which Marjorie Miller was a member lacked leadership, and the two Scots quatermasters who had supervised the loading of this boat, Campbell and McKelvie, gave tremendous support. Seeing the bobbing lights of lifejackets in the distance, and hearing shouts, they rowed in amongst the wreckage, while those in the bows pushed aside the accumulated flotsam, including crates, heavy furniture, suitcases and fittings, with their hands. Eventually they came up with the waterlogged Boat 1.

Mary Simms, in Boat 8, had her head in Dr Miller's lap and her feet across Evelyn Ashdown, but she couldn't sleep. Suddenly she heard voices, and looking over the side she saw several funny-looking objects bobbing about in the water. Then she realized they were people. In the darkness the boat nearly rammed some of them, much to the disgust of another young lady, who was not accustomed to being ignored. 'You nearly ran me over,' complained Susan Almond as they hauled her aboard, 'and I was shouting as loud as I could!'

Three Indian seamen threw themselves across from Boat 1, and then Lady Almond and Basil were hauled in, though because of their waterlogged clothes it took a lot of pulling and pushing to get them aboard. Inevitably they dripped all over those who were snugly asleep in the well of the boat, forcing David Simms to come out from under the seat. Mary Simms didn't see these two, but she knew they were safely aboard. 'I recognized Lady Almond', she told David, 'by her la-de-di voice.'

Francis and David Almond had remained in Boat 1, but Basil and Susan were reunited with their school-friends. Lady Almond, too, was glad to have the company of a distinguished Indian Civil Servant going home on retirement, Old Tonbridgian Sir John Dain, until recently Governor of Bihar.

Joan Redl was picked up by Boat 8, but the boats drifted apart and lost contact before Qunk could be passed to her, so once again she was separated from her offspring. Under Dr Miller's direction the newcomers, who were shivering with cold and shock, took off their clothes to be dried. Mary Simms gave up her blanket to the lady she knew as 'Mrs Qunk', and another coarse grey blanket was provided for Lady Almond. Donald Miller noted the bizarre contrast of the drab Army blanket that enveloped her and the luminous pearls that peeped through.

The traumas of the night stimulated in some an urgent need for relief, one of the first to be affected being May Almond. None of the boats carried a portable toilet, and there would have been scarcely room to use it if they had. What could she do? The boat's equipment included two galvanised buckets, but in the crowded darkness it was impossible to locate them. The example of going over the side had already been set, and Dr Miller confirmed that there was at present no alternative. For a woman of Lady Almond's reticence in such matters it was a solution she shrank from, yet she showed herself perfectly capable of bowing to the inevitable. The sea was still calm, but the danger of falling overboard was real, and she looked round for help. With Marjorie Miller holding one hand and Sir John Dain the other, she managed her affairs, as always, without looking in the least bit put out.

Bob Little had meanwhile towed Sybil Chapman to Boat 6. 'There's no room here,' said a voice. 'We're too full already.' There were 56 people on board. 'We can't take another soul in here,' said Nutter. 'You'll have to strike out and find another boat.'

Turning away in desperation, Little saw a raft in the distance. 'Try to hang on a little longer,' he asked Sybil, and made for the raft. Suddenly the beam of a torch shone in their faces. 'Good God!' they heard someone say. 'It's Mrs Chapman!' They knew that voice – it was Knocker Whyte. Whyte had swum to the raft when the ship went down. He jumped into the water and helped the two of them clamber on.

There were seven people on the raft, and soon they spotted the empty lifeboat – Boat 4. This was the boat MacDonald had been preparing to launch when he crossed over to starboard to help Bob Ironside with the ill-fated Boat 3. Like the disintegrated Boat 3, it was a much smaller boat with a low freeboard; these were the boats which had been moved from the stern to make room for the gun.

Boat 4 presented a curious spectacle: the sole occupants were four bemused Lascars. How this had happened no one knew, but Merten's impression of culpable indifference may have been gained from a sight of this boat.

Whyte transferred those on the raft to the lifeboat, then got the

Lascars to help him row to Boat 1, where people were still in the water. By the time they got there, MacDonald and others had reduced the flooding to manageable proportions. Fresh faces in Boat 1 included Jack Edmead, Bob Ironside (with his injured back) and Ada Taggart, picked up from another raft, also two of those who had gone down with the ship but fought their way to the surface, Sidney Britt and Bill McGregor. As the senior officer present, Britt assumed command.

'How many are you?' Britt asked Whyte.

'Twelve men and a woman.'

'Who is the woman?'

'Mrs Chapman.'

'Thank God. Mr Chapman is in this boat.'

To Sybil Chapman this seemed like a miracle. She was allowed to join her husband in Boat 1. Most of the women and children in this boat, however, were transferred to the drier and half-empty Boat 4. They included Margaret Gordon, Billie and Mona Rooksby, Freda Bullen and the twins, Diana Jarman, Francis and David Almond, and Qunk. Margaret Gordon looked for her husband in this boat in vain, but Whyte was able to tell her he had seen him since the incident on the rope ladder when Gordon was left stranded. 'He was with us when we left the ship,' Whyte consoled her. 'He must be in one of the other boats.'

Another woman fraught with anxiety was Peggy Marr: torchlight messages flashed from boat to boat brought no firm news of her husband, the man who had chosen not to add to the overload in Boat 6. Joan Redl, however, wearing nothing but a fur coat – her clothes were being dried in Boat 8 – was reunited with a cold and apparently lifeless Qunk in Boat 4. The child was still naked apart from the lifejacket, and his distraught mother, baring her stomach, wrapped him round her waist like a body-belt in a desperate effort to transfer some of her own warmth to him. Meanwhile Margaret Gordon produced a small bottle of brandy from her panic bag and they tried to get a few drops down the child's throat. Frantically Joan massaged his stone-cold little body, but it was a long time before he showed any signs of reviving.

Best news of the night came from Sparkie Humphries, who had gone down with the ship but had since been picked up by Boat 5. Still unaware of the deceit practised on him, he confirmed that his S.O.S. had been acknowledged.

All the boats were leaking badly, not so much from damage as from dryness of the timbers. The joints would tighten, it was expected, with prolonged immersion, but the pumps could not cope with the inrush of water, and the boats were so packed it was difficult to use buckets and bailers. All six boats were now full to the point of discomfort, and torchlight signals for help to relieve overloading were flashed in vain. With one or two exceptions everyone had eaten before the sinking, so few felt hungry or thirsty, and only those who had been in the water noticed how the night got colder and colder as it wore on. There was even some community singing. Meanwhile the hunt for survivors went on.

The last thing Mary Simms saw before falling asleep was a shooting star. When she woke up it was still dark, her toes were frozen, and she sat up to see what was happening. The two Scots quartermasters were still scouring the sea for survivors, and she could hear the squeak of the rowlocks and the splash of the oars. A senior chief engineer in his middle sixties named Lewis Scaife was sitting next to her, and he asked if he could lean against her back. It meant she had to sit up, but she knew he had a weak heart and was on his way home to retire. Someone had told her he had been torpedoed six times, so Mary smiled at him and said, 'All right.' But he grew heavier and heavier until she thought her back would break. Eventually he slumped into the place she had vacated and took up even more room; but she did not wake him.

Many of the passengers helped with the rowing, and typical of their experience was that of Bert Waddell in Boat 7. He spent most of the night up to his knees in water, struggling with an oar he could scarcely lift, with a stark naked black stoker as his fellow oarsman.

At length it became clear that there was no one else in the water, at any rate alive, and since no bodies were seen it was hoped that all those who got off the ship had been saved. The boats were scattered over a wide area, but torchlight contact was maintained.

Eventually the rowers shipped their oars, and although few slept, no one talked. As people sat alone with their thoughts, a vast silence descended. The night remained spectacularly beautiful, but it seemed never-ending. All their hopes were vested in the morrow, and Gladys Usher, in an unspoken petition, encapsulated all their prayers. Quoting from the shipwreck of St Paul, she 'wished for the day'.

CHAPTER 5

Sharks and Cats

For Evelyn Ashdown, when dawn came, the display of colours was every bit as uplifting as she'd been told, though her vantage point was not quite what she had planned. In all the boats, however, daylight brought renewed hope. Thanks to the sea anchors all six boats lay within a radius of half a mile, but the occupants, as the boats assembled, viewed each other with dismay. They were a pale, bedraggled lot, their wan faces streaked with grime from the coal dust that had permeated everything after the torpedoing. But the day was fine, the sea was as smooth as a lake, and the companionship of other boats raised their morale.

'Bacon and eggs for breakfast?'

'Coffee and toast?'

'Don't forget we're playing deck tennis at ten!'

The banter from one boat to another, with its element of forced gaiety, was quickly imitated by the children. Basil Almond, eldest of the Almond children, called out to Sheila Gavin: 'Sheila! You won't be able to go to school now!' David Simms adopted a tone of mock affront. 'I don't think much of this boat. There's no deck to play on.' Someone asked lugubriously if anyone thought they would still be home for Christmas.

There remained for some a gnawing anxiety about their loved ones. Jim and Sybil Chapman started calling for news of Kate Richardson, while Margaret Gordon and Peggy Marr scanned boat after boat for their husbands. Kate Richardson was discovered in the captain's boat, but the names of Crawford Gordon and Francis Marr were called in vain. Captain Rogerson confirmed that both men had been with him when he boarded the waterlogged Boat 2, but there was no sign of them now. By mid-morning it was tacitly accepted, by all but the two women concerned, that they had gone down with the ship. For many hours, however, Margaret Gordon and Peggy Marr refused to believe it.

The absence of these two men, and of three others lost with them, among them Harry Peever, suggested in each case an element of personal sacrifice.[1] All five had stayed on the ship to help in various ways. Together with a Lascar fireman, killed in the first explosion, they were the only people lost in the sinking.

The men appointed to take charge of the various boats were (or were soon to be):

Boat 1 – Chief Officer Sidney Britt
Boat 4 – Third Officer Jimmy 'Knocker' Whyte
Boat 5 – Captain Rogerson, with Bill Stubbs
Boat 6 – George Nutter
Boat 7 – Second Officer Les Boundy
Boat 8 – Tommy Green

(George Nutter, already effectively in charge of Boat 6, was later to be confirmed as leader, and Tommy Green was transferred to take command of Boat 8 on the following day.)

Captain Rogerson held a conference with his officers that morning to review the situation and make a workable plan. Confirmation from Humphries that his S.O.S. had been acknowledged encouraged optimism, but to set against this was the loss of the emergency radio, which had been tipped out of Boat 1 when it flooded. Whyte's sextant had gone too. What hope was there of rescue? The distances from land – 1250 miles from the African coast and 1500 miles from Cape Town – made rescue operations virtually impossible due to lack of resources, although this was not generally realized, and their routeing had deliberately avoided the known shipping lanes. There seemed a good chance that some

[1] The other two, both passengers, were 56-year-old Rev. Lachlan McLean, from Perthshire, one of the four chaplains aboard, and a British-India Line master named Wilfred Tingle, a Tees-sider, aged 44.

long-range flying-boat, probably a Catalina, might be sent to search for them, and the S.O.S. had given their position; but finding them would be another matter. 'Keep a good look-out for a plane,' Captain Rogerson told them; but privately he made the assumption that salvation lay in their own hands. Somehow they would have to reach land.

Any attempt to make a landfall on the African coast would be frustrated by the prevailing winds – the south-east trades – while South America, although to leeward, was outside any practical estimate of their endurance and range. Even the nearest point on the Brazilian coastline was some 2250 miles distant, which at 50 miles a day (averaging 2 knots) would take 45 days – and that assumed accurate navigation. Even with the strictest rationing their water would not last more than half that time. They were thus left with a Hobson's choice. 'We shall aim for St Helena,' announced Rogerson; and whether or not agreement was unanimous, there was no argument.

St Helena was indeed a British possession. A tiny island in mid-ocean, nearly 500 miles distant, it was 10 miles long by 6½ miles across, a remote outpost in a vast wilderness of water. Rogerson would have regarded finding it as an unlikely chance but for Boundy's sextant. 'Every boat has a compass,' Rogerson reminded them, 'but only Mr Boundy in Boat 7 has a sextant, so it's vital we keep together. Mr Boundy will take sights daily at noon and any changes of course will be passed to all boats.

'We'll sail independently by day, rendezvousing before dark and laying to at night so as to keep together. If currents don't take us out of our course I expect to reach St Helena in a fortnight. But we'll ration ourselves for twenty one days, in case we have to search for St Helena.

'We'll rig and hoist sails in case we get some wind, but there's none at the moment so we'll just have to row. Once we get into the south-east trades we'll be all right. If we can make some progress today we should hit the trade winds tomorrow.'

Much of this, to the occupants of the lifeboats, sounded academic. Their S.O.S. had been acknowledged, it was unthinkable that it could be ignored, and already they were alert for signs of a ship or a plane. Many thought it would be wiser to stay where they were: surely that was the golden rule. Few appreciated that the forces necessary for a search operation were simply not available, and that their only hope of rescue was a chance sighting by a passing ship. Although they did not know it, it would not be until the *Cairo* was reported overdue at Recife in one week's time that anyone would be alerted to their plight, and even then no one would know where to look. Yet for the castaways the prospect of spending up to 21 days in a leaky and over-crowded lifeboat, with no room to sit comfortably, let alone lie down, was too painful to contemplate.

The knowledge that they were being organized as a group was reassuring, but 480 miles sounded impossible, and to bolster morale they clung to the belief – unaware that it was an illusion – that, knowing their whereabouts, the authorities would find some way to reach them. It was just as well that Merten's fake acknowledgement remained undiscovered.

An essential, for use in conjunction with Boundy's sextant, was a reliable time-piece. Whyte had picked up the chronometer dropped by Boundy and it had eventually found its way into the captain's boat, but it had suffered too many soakings *en route* to be serviceable. Captain Rogerson had a Rolex 'Oyster', and this too had suffered immersion, but it seemed unaffected. Boundy's and Rogerson's boats were thus inter-dependent and would keep together at all costs. Even then, much depended on the accuracy of Rogerson's watch, by which Boundy's watch was regularly set. 'If it gains or loses more than a few seconds a day,' Rogerson told Quantrill, 'we shan't find St Helena.' Quantrill kept this confidence to himself.

The rest of the morning was spent checking names for the muster, examining equipment, salvaging food and water from rafts – with little success – and re-distributing loads. Incredibly, no one was missing from the capsized boats, so only six out of 298 had been lost. No bodies were found. Each boat was equipped to a specified scale, which in addition to oars, masts, sails and rigging included such items as a magnetic compass of the liquid type, mounted on gimbals in a small hooded binnacle (with a tiny oil lamp for illumination); a sea anchor; galvanized buckets; a rotary bilge-pump and hand-bailers; an oil lantern; two hatchets, a torch and a jack-knife. There were also signals, parachute and hand flares, and a first-aid box.

All boats carried a plentiful supply of concentrated food, consisting of ship's biscuits, tins of pemmican (a paste-like meat extract with a high protein content), malted milk tablets, and chocolate. But in every boat the water situation, assuming a voyage of 21 days, was critical. The five larger boats were each fitted with six 6-gallon tanks or kegs, 36 gallons per boat, or 288 pints. For their rated capacity of 48 persons, this exactly fulfilled the laid-down minimum of six pints per person. Each of these larger boats, however, was overloaded, reducing the individual share, while Boat 1 had lost one of its tanks.

What was the water ration to be? A pint a day, or 20 fluid ounces, was reckoned to be sufficient to sustain life in the tropics, but at that rate the water would not last a week. Even a ration of six ounces a day, less than a third of that recommended, would find them running out of water after two and a half weeks, and Rogerson was budgeting for three. His problem was to strike a compromise that would keep them alive and at the same time give them a chance to reach land. He settled for four ounces per person per day, two in the morning and two in the evening; in some boats this was increased to six. But four ounces allowed some flexibility in the issue of rations according to need and still gave a margin of two or three days beyond the budget of three weeks.

Water was extracted from the kegs by lowering a white enamelled dipper attached to a lanyard through a bung-hole in the top of the casing. A dipper, conveniently enough, held two ounces.

The overloading of the boats meant that they sailed lower in the water than normally, exposing a greater area of their parched timbers to the sea. They were clinker-type boats, and the water that slopped around inside them, defying all attempts at pumping and bailing, greatly aggravated the general discomfort. All the boats suffered in this way, but Boat 1 was the worst. Jack Edmead tore up a lifejacket and used the kapok and some white lead he found in a locker to plug the holes and caulk the seams, but two-hour pumping watches were necessary throughout the day. All the children were transferred from this boat because of its excessive porousness, but the 54 adults who remained felt themselves lucky to have Chief Officer Sidney Britt in charge, with the efficient but less communicative Angus MacDonald in the fore part of the boat to attend to the sails and running gear. 'There are no passengers in a lifeboat,' Britt reminded them. 'We're all in this together, and we won't get to St Helena unless we all pull together.' One man who responded at once was aeronautical engineer Robert 'Tiny' Watts, a powerfully built Londoner, one of Vic Chambers' colleagues on the abortive glider project. 'I don't know much about seamanship,' he told MacDonald, 'but if you want anything done at any time, just explain the job to me and I'll do it.'

Every single body above the 48 prescribed for these boats had a disproportionate effect on the comfort of the whole, and this was worsened in Britt's boat by two invalids for whom room had to be made to lie down. These were quartermaster Bob Ironside, who had injured his back when Boat 3 disintegrated, and sick stewardess Ada Taggart, whose recovery had been sadly reversed when she too was thrown out of Boat 3. Spaces were cleared for Ada Taggart in the bows and for Bob Ironside aft. There was a surgeon in this boat, Dr Ronald Tasker, who in circumstances like these would normally have been an asset. He had served in the Royal Navy in World War I, and besides enjoying a distinguished medical career he had been in his day an outstanding athlete, playing football as an amateur for Bristol City. He was still only 50 years old. But as an employee of the Burma Oil Company he had suffered the inevitable privations of the retreat, and, although he seemed to have recovered his old form on the *Cairo*, his recuperation, like Ada Taggart's, had gone for nothing when he was thrown out of Boat 3. He had since suffered a mental and physical disorientation that left him listless and vague.

*

Every boat had its problems. In Boat 4, Whyte had a serious imbalance in his complement: he had twelve Indians, six women, five children, and only one European male besides himself, Mona Rooksby's husband Billie. With people spread all over the boat's gear Whyte found it impossible even to begin the task of getting things shipshape for the days ahead, and the low freeboard of this 21-foot boat magnified the sense of exposure and posed problems of safety, especially for the children. As Rogerson had Dr Quantrill in his boat, he agreed to take the three infants and their mothers, Freda Bullen and Joan Redl; to make room for them he transferred two of his more troublesome Asians to Boat 8, away from their cronies, and he called for able-bodied volunteers to change boats to help Whyte. First to do so was Sparkie Humphries, an old shipmate of Whyte's, an act of comradeship which was to be ill-rewarded. The same was true of the other volunteers, William 'Solly' Solomon, the senior of the returning glider men, and the *Cairo's* third engineer, Bill Pirrie. To get away from the influx of screaming children in the captain's boat Allan Tempest also volunteered, but others beat him to it. He viewed his rejection with mixed feelings; there might well be advantages in being in the captain's boat.

Francis and David Almond stayed in Whyte's boat – and earned praise from Margaret Gordon for their eagerness to help. Margaret herself, although dazed and pre-occupied with her thoughts, was determined not to be a drag on the others, and the two boys gave her a chance to forget her sorrow in the exercise of her motherly instincts. Francis, upset by his first taste of pemmican, which he found too rich, had a languid spell, and David, red-headed and freckled, showed a touching concern for his ailing elder brother. It was Francis, though, who contributed most to their well-being: the tool box, well-equipped otherwise, lacked a jack-knife, and Francis proudly produced his scout-knife and lent it to Whyte. It was used by Whyte for innumerable tasks and became his most prized possession.

All that day nuggets of coal kept turning up in the strangest places; Margaret Gordon even found lumps in the pockets of her tweed coat. She was one of the best off for warm clothing, and she was able to help several others. Her panic bag became a kind of Pandora's box in reverse, though hope, as in the mythical box, lay at the bottom.

Captain Rogerson had still not recovered fully, and the routine in Boat 5 was left to Bill Stubbs. The immediate problem was Kate Richardson: the terrible experience of the previous night had unhinged her mind. 'Has anyone picked up Mrs Chapman?' asked Stubbs, and Britt, from Boat 1, answered: 'I have both Mr and Mrs Chapman here.' 'Mrs Chapman's got to come to my boat,' ordered Rogerson. 'We've picked up her mother and she's off her head.' But Sybil Chapman, with one side of her face still paralysed, was too shocked to be moved, and her seasick husband was in no better shape.

The only quartermaster in Boat 6 was a 19-year-old from the Isle of Barra named Patrick McNeil, and not surprisingly his maturity did not extend to the unenviable task of controlling such a polyglot crew. He was glad to hand over to those with more experience, among them George Nutter and Vic Chambers, helped by a little Jewish lad from the East End of London called George Racher who knew nothing about boats but proved a willing helper.

Les Boundy cut a bizarre figure at the tiller of Boat 7, still wearing a striped pyjama jacket and a peaked officer's cap, and this boat, with its sextant and motor, was the envy of all. But there was fuel for a maximum of ten to twelve hours' running, some of which would have to be saved for finding a landing place, perhaps against wind and current, on the craggy and precipitous coast of St Helena. If the engine was started at other times it could only be used, in all conscience, for towing the other boats, greatly reducing potential speed. The engine installation, too, was a mixed blessing: it encroached on the space available, reducing the rated capacity of the boat to 45, though this had not been allowed for in the distribution of loads. Most crippling, however, was the loss, during the torpedoing, of the rudder. Bob Skea was in this boat, and his skill with a steering oar made him indispensable. He knew well enough, though, that the method put a brake on a boat as much as it steered it.

In Boat 8 (soon to become Tommy Green's), an ominous crack in the mast gave cause for concern. It might be no more than a surface cleft, but whether it would stand the strain of long days of sailing seemed doubtful. Worse still, the compass in this boat had been smashed, presumably during the torpedoing; if they became separated from the other boats, say through being dismasted, they would stand no chance. But this was to reckon without the resourceful Dr Miller. 'I've got a compass in my pocket,' she announced. 'I'm a Guide, you see.' It was no toy compass but a precision instrument which she had used when trekking with the leper girls at the Purulia Leper Home and Hospital. Captain Rogerson checked it against the compass in Boat 5 and found it accurate.

Mary Simms, who was seasick that morning, recovered quickly, and she was ravenous by the time the rations were distributed. Marjorie Miller, fearing for the children's digestions, slowed them down by declaring a race – to see who could finish last. Meanwhile her husband was pointing to a neat arrowhead formation of small black-and-white fish that were following the boat, their stripes sharply defined in the translucent water. 'Aye,' said Campbell. 'They're pilot fish. They lead the sharks to their prey.' Sure enough another creature was cruising in their wake, a huge, menacing, milk-and-slate-coloured shark. They could have had no grimmer warning of their fate if things went wrong. Those who had been in the water the previous night shuddered the most. Fortunately the explosions that had precipitated their exit from the *Cairo* must have temporarily stunned or scattered the sharks.

They were back now, though, clearly with breakfast in mind, and they glided backwards and forwards under the boats as though looking for some way of capsizing them. Just when it seemed there must be a collision they skimmed underneath, but they kept up their sinister escort all day.

Francis Almond, watching apprehensively from the boat with only six inches of free-board, began to wish he still had his jack-knife. Fishing, which had seemed to offer possibilities for the complementing of rations, was thus early discouraged.

'Is the doctor all right?' The question came from Diana Jarman, one of those picked up by Whyte's boat. Hearing that he was busy attending to Kate Richardson, she asked next for Bill McGregor. McGregor was in Britt's boat, Boat 1, and Britt and Whyte were agreeable to giving them the opportunity to get together. Diana felt Bill was the right sort of person to be in a lifeboat with, and she was also attracted to Britt. But as the two boats closed, with Diana aft in one boat and McGregor forward in the other, a misunderstanding on McGregor's part resulted in both parties jumping across simultaneously; having had experience of sailing small boats, McGregor thought he was wanted in Whyte's boat and that he was to join Diana there. Before they could correct an error that was to prove of considerable dramatic consequence the two boats drifted apart, leaving Diana in Boat 1 with Britt and McGregor in Boat 4 with Whyte. Captain Rogerson was now impatient to get the little convoy moving, and the opportunity did not recur.

It soon became clear to Diana that she was needed in Boat 1, just as Bill McGregor was an acquisition in Boat 4. There were many people in Britt's boat requiring bandaging and first aid, and with stewardess Annie Crouch's help she was able to attend to them all. 'Stop calling me Mrs Jarman,' she told them. 'Call me Diana.'

Although sails were hoisted to catch whatever breeze might develop, scarcely a ripple disturbed the surface and the only feasible method of propulsion was manual, which Captain Rogerson was determined they should attempt. Preposterous as the idea appeared of rowing these cumbersome craft any distance, it could scarcely be more futile than drifting aimlessly in mid-ocean. Like a flotilla of fishing smacks at Brixham regatta, the six lifeboats with their scarlet sails presented a picturesque sight as the strongest of the crewmen exercised their muscles, oars dipping in unison, sails casting purple reflections on the royal blue of the sea.

There was a limit, though, to the stamina even of the fittest. There was scarcely room to bend to the task, and against the need for progress had to be set the importance of preserving their strength. A fix taken by Boundy at noon placed them more than 500 miles from their goal rather than less. Those unaccustomed to sea-going oars found them unbelievably heavy. Different combinations were tried in different boats, but four oars each side proved impracticable for want of elbow room, and most of the boats were reduced to two oars a side and then one, two men to an oar. Many of the European men were either too old or too feeble for the sustained effort of rowing, and few of the Asians had handled an oar in their lives. Most of them in any case lacked the necessary brute strength and tended to lean on their oars. Few of those who did make the effort had any idea of keeping together, or of backwatering when told. Whyte could manage an oar by himself, but the Indians in his boat, two to an oar, were quickly exhausted.

Of the 26 Indians in Boat 8 only two were genuine seamen. Lady Almond and Basil took a turn on the oars but they found they were too weak to be of much use. Some tried manfully to keep going, refusing to give in until their hands were blistered and raw.

Susan Almond and Mary Simms found the afternoon heat unbearable and they were allowed to go forward and find what shelter they could under the sail. Then in the late afternoon it grew chilly and they moved aft again. Only the children were suffered to move around at all freely. Susan, in a fit of irritability, went into a sulk despite all Sir John Dain's efforts to amuse her with nonsense rhymes, and although she knew she was behaving like a spoilt brat she couldn't unbend. Mary Simms knew that Basil Almond had a lurid 'thriller' in his pocket which she was dying to read, and she could not forgive him, or anyone else, for allowing this precious commodity to be passed round for an unmentionable purpose.

Margaret Gordon was not alone in regarding the effort expended on rowing as folly, a sapping of physical reserves that might be desperately needed. So little rhythm was achieved that she doubted whether any real progress was made. But for Captain Rogerson, anything that got them nearer the south-east trades was worthwhile.

Rowing was stopped at five o'clock on orders from Rogerson and the boats got together for the night. For the rowers the respite was welcome, and all derived comfort from re-assembling as a group, led by men who were trained for just such an emergency. Again there was a mood of false gaiety, and raucous jokes were shouted from boat to boat. As usual the sky was shot with colour, and the singing of 'Red Sails in the Sunset' seemed so appropriate that it evoked general enthusiasm.

A full issue of rations was now made, for the first time in most boats, but eager faces soon contorted as the contents were sampled. The biscuits were hard and dry, and the pemmican, spread on top, was strong and salty. The combination proved difficult to chew and almost impossible to swallow without water. Yet it seemed sensible to defer the issue of water until after the meal. The chocolate was good, pleasant to the taste and not too sweet, and the malted milk tablets were sucked as a savoury after the meal. Then the white enamel cylinders were dipped into tanks and passed round in turn, while the children cheered. Some objected to drinking out of the same utensil as their neighbours, but as yet they had no alternative. Empty pemmican tins were saved to be used as receptacles later. Everyone sipped their two precious ounces – less than a small medicine glass – slowly, retaining the liquid in the mouth for as long as possible. By the time the issue was completed darkness was falling.

Bob Skea noticed that the rations were marked 'Good till November 1942.' This appealed to his wry sense of humour. 'We've been torpedoed', he said, 'just in time.'

The arrangement in some boats was that the Europeans occupied the bow and the stern while the Asians huddled together amidships. What they suffered in being even more constricted than the Europeans they gained in protection at night, when the temperature fell dramatically and they snuggled under the boat cover. In other boats they occupied the bow. There were six blankets per boat, a totally inadequate number which was divided equally between the races. Many of the women were wearing thin cotton evening dresses, and one of them, an elderly widow named Minnie Clark (she was 66) who had gone to India in 1938 to be with her schoolteacher son (since recruited into the Indian

Army), was given the yellow lifeboat flag in Boat 6 as a shawl. A few people, among them Evelyn Ashdown, Dulcie Kendall and Arnold Silcock, as well as Margaret Gordon, were able to distribute warm clothing, but for many there was no escape from the cold. Sleep too was virtually impossible, and any form of rest was disturbed by the movements of others and the need for continuous pumping or bailing and occasional rowing. Lifejackets provided a cushion to sit on and to soften the many sharp edges, but except in the less heavily loaded Boat 4 there was no room to stretch out along gunwales or thwarts. Even in Boat 4 these surfaces were so narrow and hard that they scarcely provided a vestige of comfort. Lifejackets laid in the bottom of boats as mattresses soon became soaked as the water seeped through.

During the night Susan Almond felt something scratching her feet. She called but no one believed her; they thought she was having a nightmare. When it happened a second time, however, her screams carried conviction. A banshee wail from behind the water casks confirmed the survival of the incorrigible ginger tom. Hunger and thirst, for a creature who had missed the issue of rations, had overcome timidity and fear.

Superstition alone had preserved this unfortunate animal this far, and superstition – and the cat's own distrustful nature – saved it now. No mariner, ancient or modern, was going to slay this particular albatross, however much of a nuisance it might be. The cat kept itself hidden, but water and food were put down for it, and when morning came both were gone. The cat's habit of scratching at Susan's feet alienated her completely. 'I hate this cat!' she said crossly. But the animal instinctively attached itself to her.

Contact between the boats was maintained through the night by means of torches, each boat flashing in Morse the initial letter of the name of the officer in charge. When their second full day at sea eventually dawned, two boats had dropped far behind, which meant a long wait for the others while they caught up. Cramped and chilled, they were more conscious than ever, now the initial shock had been absorbed, of the discomfort and precariousness of their plight. Surely today they would see some signs of a search?

They cheered up as rations were issued and consumed and as routine tasks were performed, such as washing in salt water, which they found refreshing, and spreading clothes and blankets out to dry. This latter activity had to be practised carefully, as unguarded clothes, even shoes, had a habit of disappearing.

The men were stiff and sore from their efforts of the previous day, and when at length they took up the oars it was with a symptomatic lack of inclination and vigour. Fortunately it was not long, as Rogerson had foreseen, before a light breeze gave promise of the trade wind they sought. As the rowers rested gratefully on their oars, sails were hoisted, which immediately billowed out in the breeze.

The boats were basically little more than survival craft, beamy, keel-less and barge-like, and in an increasingly choppy sea it was not easy to maintain a correct heading. Wind and tide kept sweeping them west, and their actual progress towards St Helena was slight. Sometimes the mainsail would swing right round, when oars had to be slotted into rowlocks again and it was a tough job to pull the boat back on course. Boat-handling skills varied from boat to boat and from watch to watch, one man in the captain's boat emerging as particularly adept. This was a shipboard friend of the chestnut-haired Cynthia Saunders named George Waters, an all-round sportsman and a specialist in regatta racing; in his thirties, and of athletic build, he was one of the most vital people in the whole flotilla. He was also one of those exasperating men who seem good at everything. His knowledge of sailing small boats far exceeded that of Rogerson or anyone else in the captain's boat and at critical times Rogerson left it to Waters.

Right from the start some boats sailed faster than others, and this was not always a matter of seamanship. Britt's boat seemed to be the speediest and it continually forged ahead. Nutter and Chambers, taking spells at the tiller in Boat 6, found they did better when they dispensed with a jib.

Just before eleven o'clock on that Sunday morning a gravelly Scots voice called across the stern of Boat 8 to Donald Miller: 'It'll soon be time for a spell of praise!' The speaker was Daniel McNeill, born in Perthshire 60 years earlier of humble stock and apprenticed as a boy to an ironmonger. Seeking to better himself, he had applied for a job with a famous Scottish company in Burma, of which, after many years of service, he became a director. Life in the tropics had aged him, but he had made enough to retire in 1939. With all his investments in Burma, however, he went back there when war threatened to salvage what he could, which was little enough. He had survived the great trek across the Shan mountains into Assam, but to virtual impoverishment was added the anxiety that his younger son had been reported missing in the Libyan Desert. Yet it was Daniel McNeill who revived their spirits that morning with his call to lift up their hearts.

Miller had been hoping that the initiative for a corporate act of worship would come from others, and he welcomed McNeill's request. (Ministers and missionaries in the other boats, too, mostly waited for a layman to give a lead.) 'You're right,' answered Miller warmly. 'It's certainly time. Suppose you choose the first hymn?'

McNeill's years as an empire-builder had not coarsened his gentle, kindly disposition, and he gave some thought to his choice. It must be something uplifting, nothing sentimental or morbid. After Miller had offered a prayer, McNeill led them in the hymn he had chosen.

'Let us with a gladsome mind
'Praise the Lord, for He is kind:
'For His mercies aye endure,
'Ever faithful, ever sure. . . .

Mercies there certainly were, but there were afflictions too, and many more, perhaps, to come. Yet despite their plight they were singing that God's mercies would endure. How could they be said to do so, wondered Miller, when six lives had been lost in the sinking and many more were threatened? He justified his faith by making a distinction between what God did and what men did. Again, whatever might befall their mortal bodies, they could not pass beyond the range of God's mercy. But he did not attempt to preach to others. They must work things out for themselves. Certainly the words of the hymn were sung with fervour, though with more hope, Miller imagined, than conviction.

The Six Lifeboats – Table of Occupants

BOAT 1 (54)
Chief Officer Sidney E. D. Britt

Annie Crouch
Marshall Crichton
Jack C. Edmead
James (Joe) Green
Robert J. Ironside
Diana Jarman
Robert Little
Angus W. D. MacDonald
Thomas McCall
John (Jack) Oakley
Frank Stobbart
Ada Taggart
Dr Ronald H. Tasker
Basil Watkins-Ball
Robert Watts
Serang Budroodin Baba

Also in this boat, not mentioned in the text by name, were Sydney H. Barnes, Albert R. C. Dobson, Harry Lane, George E. Napier, David D. Noble, John Nuttall, John Tagg, and 30 other Asians.

BOAT 4 (17)
Third Officer James Allister Whyte

Margaret Gordon
Thomas A. V. Humphries
William McGregor
Fred Powell
William T. Pirrie
W. C. Solomon
10 Asians

BOAT 5 (54)
Captain W. A. Rogerson

Freda Bullen, with Michael and Peter
James and Sybil Chapman
Chief Engineer R. A. Faulds
Florence Gavin and Sheila
John MacFarland
Lawrence and Catherine McGaffney, with Catherine and Patricia
Francis B. McQuone
Dr Douglas Quantrill
Joan Redl and David (Qunk)
Kate Richardson
Cynthia Saunders
Herbert Shenton
Fourth Officer William Stubbs
Allan B. Tempest
Gladys Usher
George Waters

Also in this boat, not mentioned by name, were Leonard Codling, D. Dick, Charlie McKechnie, M. McLean, George Norton, Thomas Parkinson, Cadet W. B. Ritchie, Charlie N. Williams, one Gunner, and 20 Asians.

BOAT 6 (55)
George Nutter

F. George Blagrave-Dean
H. D. Broomby

Victor Chambers
Minnie Clark
Ruby Cooke
E. Randolph Godlieb
Vassili and Galina Kariakin
Dulcie Kendall and Colin
Gregore Krakovski
Patrick McNeil
Peggy Marr
George Alfred Racher
David and Mary Williams and Violet Williams

Also in this boat, not mentioned by name, were John Cullinane, Alexander Day, Edward V. Elliott, Elsie M., Petrie, and 33 Asians.

BOAT 7 (57)
Second Officer Leslie Boundy

Elizabeth Birchman
David and Jenny Davies, with Ann and Janet
Robert and Elizabeth Dickey
William and Avis Dieckhaus and Ferdinand (Ferdy)
Robert H. Gerner
Pierre and Janine Jaspar and Michel
Leslie Mountain
William and Mona Rooksby
Robert Skea
Arnold Silcock
James Turner
Robert Waddell

Also in this boat, not mentioned by name, were M. Campbell, Roland Dodds, Andy Green, 5 Gunners and 27 Asians.

BOAT 8 (55)
Tommy Gerard Green

Lady Almond, with Basil, Francis, David and Susan
Evelyn Ashdown
Michael Campbell
Sir John Dain
Robert McKelvie
Daniel McNeill
Donald Miller and Dr Margaret Miller
Cecilia Norris
Lewis Scaife
Eileen Simms, with Mary, David, Lisa and Esther

Also in this boat, not mentioned by name, were George E. Faun, Third Radio Officer James Friel, Robert Keith, Alexander Marshal, James A. Scott, 4 Gunners and 26 Asians.

The four gunners in this boat were John H. Jones, Bryce Kerr, James Murphy (all R.A.) and Kenneth MacKinnon, RN. The other six gunners on the *Cairo*, precise distribution in the lifeboats not known, were Corporal-Gunner W. A. Edwards, RN, Albert Cockill, RA, and Seaman Gunners John Martin, John V. Morris, Hugh M. Porterfield, and David Skinner.

They had the blessing of the trade wind all that day, but their speed of necessity remained that of the slowest boat, and Boat 8, with its cracked mast, dropped a long way behind. It was when they rendezvoused that evening that Rogerson sent Tommy Green to this boat to take charge. The two quartermasters Campbell and McKelvie were proving their worth, but they shied at the responsibility of command, and Tommy Green, despite the hand he had damaged in launching Boat 1, was a welcome volunteer.

George Nutter, too, felt his boat was under-officered, as indeed it was; already the high proportion of Asians in this boat – 33, more than in any other boat, against only 13 European men – was presenting a challenge to his tenuous authority. He protested that Boundy in Boat 7 had the support of a master mariner in Bob Skea: would it not be fairer to transfer Skea to Boat 6? 'There's two navigators in Boundy's boat,' argued Nutter, 'and none here. What happens if we get separated?' But Boundy would have none of it. 'I can't steer without a rudder,' he told Rogerson. 'I need Bob for that. In any case, a navigator's no use without a sextant. Nutter will just have to keep up with us.' Selfish as this might seem, Boundy was acting for the general good. Everything depended on making a landfall on St Helena, and that lay largely with him.

Fearing that their little fleet might become fragmented during the hours of darkness, Rogerson ordered the boats to down sails at sunset and to tie up with ropes stem to stern. Thus secured as a group, the boats rode to sea anchors all night.

CHAPTER 6

Britt goes it Alone; and the Night of the Sea Anchors

'How far have we sailed today?'

By Monday 9th November, their third full day in the boats, the survivors of the *City of Cairo* were still scanning a vast and empty panorama of sea and sky, framed only by a few broken clouds on the horizon; they were tiring of straining eyes and ears in vain. The hope that their S.O.S. would bring rescue, or at the very least a long-range Catalina, receded, and they began to accept that they faced a long and arduous voyage. Thus they took a more lively interest in their progress. Most of them set themselves to last it out, tending to withdraw into themselves but settling into a routine. This was much the same in all boats; yet each boat developed its own peculiarities. One boat always seemed to have a line of washing out; this was the boat in which Marjorie Miller, one of whose mottoes was 'cleanliness is next to godliness', imposed the regime. She did not neglect inner cleanliness either, setting aside two periods a day for attempts at 'keeping regular'. Several groups had rigged themselves out with canvas hats for protection from the sun, cut from spare boat covers. Whyte's smaller boat, with the strong profile of Margaret Gordon silhouetted astern, was also conspicuous, as was Boundy's with its lack of a rudder and the steering oar manipulated by Bob Skea.

Rousing themselves at dawn, the castaways rolled up the boat covers, emptied their bladders, which yielded a surprising amount, washed in sea water, attended to the sick and injured, and issued the rations. No one could move more than an inch or so and everything had to be passed by hand, a process which took nearly two hours. The children adapted quickly, and unlike the adults they seemed able to eat more as time passed. They soon got used to the idea of swallowing their ration of water in sips instead of gulping it down.

This third day brought a welcome breeze, up went the sails, and to everyone's delight they bowled along at about 3 knots. They soon discovered, though, that with the wind forward of the beam the north-north-east heading they were trying to maintain to counter the westerly drift could barely be held. In Vic Chambers' estimation they were virtually sailing close-hauled, if such a tactic could be applied to a heavily laden lifeboat with not much more than twelve inches of freeboard. Helmsmen quickly discovered that the slightest lapse in concentration resulted in their boat turning and heading off in the opposite direction, after which oars had to be set to pull the boat round. It proved impossible to get back on course by rudder alone. This, thought Chambers, didn't matter much while the rowers were fresh, but it might cause concern as they grew weaker.

Trouble between the races developed early on in all boats. Many of the Indians, particularly those who were not strictly seamen, appeared sullen and apathetic; either that or their natural stoicism was mistaken for apathy. They were not accustomed to playing any part in the actual sailing of a ship and they were unwilling or unable to do their share of rowing and bailing. Disdain amongst the Europeans was matched by resentment amongst the Asians at the way the Europeans took charge of the rations; they suspected that they might not be getting their share. It was true that, in some boats, those who exerted themselves most were given the only suitable reward, an extra ration of water. It was also true that, in the composition of the rations themselves, little thought had been given to religious taboos: few of the Indians would eat the pemmican. Many of them, in their ignorance of the situation they found themselves in, were unable to grasp the need for strict rationing at all. There were numerous exceptions, and some of the Indian seamen were outstanding, but the apparent indifference of the majority saddened those who, like Lady Almond, were firm admirers of the Indian race. She was glad when Donald Miller, who spoke Bengali, joined them in the well of the boat and took an interest in their welfare, finding out where they came from, where their families were, and so on.

Ignorance was not confined to the Asians; some of the Europeans, brought up to believe in the superiority of the white man, treated the Asians abominably. In the four boats where one of the ship's officers, recognised by all, was in command, divisive elements on both sides were eventually reconciled or kept under control. Rumblings of discontent on the one hand, and excesses of arrogance on the other, were less easily subdued in the two boats where a passenger had been appointed to command. Lacking the outward and visible sign of authority conferred by a uniform, they were not automatically respected or obeyed. Segregation was practised in all boats, as much for the Asians' convenience as for the Europeans', but the Asians in Boat 8 did not always take kindly to the authority their new leader, Tommy Green, delegated to a woman – Dr Miller – while some of George Nutter's 33 Asians refused to do any work and threatened to overturn the boat unless they were given more water. Security of the water stocks became a problem in all boats, and Nutter's was not the only one in which a continuous guard had to be mounted.

When Nutter appealed to Captain Rogerson for help in managing the Asians he got a short answer: 'Be firm with them.' That, with the ring-leaders accompanying their threats with a meaningful fingering of their *dahs*,[1] was easier said than done. Eventually the European passengers in Boat 6, in an attempt to give Nutter the authority he needed, held a poll and by a unanimous show of hands voted him leader.

A suggestion by Ferdinand Dieckhaus in Boat 7 that they improvise a 'jury' or substitute rudder out of various items of equipment in the boat, thus easing the task at the helm, gained little support because it meant sacrificing a valued protection for those on the weather side of the boat. A canvas side-screen,

[1] A small dagger or thin-bladed knife.

fastened to two eye-bolts which protruded from the gunwale, one forward and one astern, prevented or greatly reduced the drenching of those on the weather side and the danger of swamping; this side-screen had already been employed to good effect in most boats. Dieckhaus's suggestion included removing these eye-bolts, leaving nothing with which to anchor the side-screen.

The plan involved, first, removing the stern thwart, to which the magnetic compass was bolted, detaching the compass, and using the thwart as a rudder. Its dimensions – roughly six feet in length, one foot wide and one inch thick – approximated to those of the original rudder. The problem was to find the necessary fittings which would secure the jury rudder to the stern post and allow it to pivot as though on a hinge. This was where the eye-bolts came in. There were four in all, two on each side of the boat. By measuring the distance apart of the eye-bolts or gudgeons fitted to the stern post, which were still in position, the four purloined eye-bolts could be screwed into the long edge of the plank at the appropriate point, so that they fitted above and below the gudgeons on the stern post. All that remained was to improvise pintles – the bolts that would thread through the gudgeons and hold the rudder in place. These bolts, and the nuts to secure them, would be available once the compass was unscrewed from the thwart.

It was an ingenious plan, cannibalizing a number of suitable items that were readily available, and the only drawback was the loss of protection. But so long as Bob Skea could cope with the steering oar, this protection was preferred. In arguing that they could always bail the boat out, that it was unsinkable anyway, and that all their lives would be forfeit if they couldn't steer a straight course, Dieckhaus made himself unpopular.

Dieckhaus was a forceful character, which was why he had cut a niche for himself in Burma. But the sinking of the *Cairo* had done nothing to repair his shattered nervous system, and like Crawford Gordon before him his illness had left him with something of a persecution complex. His size, for instance – he was a hefty fellow – although not entitling him to extra water, doubtless increased his need. 'I'm a big man,' he said. 'I usually have two glasses of water in my office every morning.' But he got no sympathy from Bob Skea. 'You're not in your office now.'

The Dutchman's sense of persecution may not have been entirely psychological. He felt he was the victim of racial prejudice. This was something he had suspected ever since boarding the *City of Cairo*, and he traced it, rightly or wrongly, to the fact that he had married a Eurasian. She had an English passport and many ancestors from the British Isles, but this mattered little; in the eyes of some (or so he imagined), he had let the side down. At Durban, and again at Cape Town, he and Avis had been excluded from clubs and hotels. Even in the lifeboat he had sensed a veiled disapproval. Quite probably, because of his dark skin, they concluded he was a Eurasian himself.

The group who were running the boat, he felt, kept too much to themselves. As a boat warden, and a man of wide practical experience, he should have had a say in things, but they never consulted him, and he thought he knew why. To compound his resentment, he could not escape the suspicion that some were drinking more than their share.

In this, if in nothing else, he was mistaken. But he had made himself useful at the time of the sinking, going up to Boundy's cabin to collect the navigation books after already having had to go down to his own cabin to fetch Ferdy, and he had proved he was a man to be trusted. With his imaginitive and workmanlike suggestion brusquely rejected, he seethed with bitterness and frustration.

Games hours, instituted by the adults to amuse the children, proved generally popular, diverting adult minds as well. 'I went to the grocer's and bought,' or 'I went on holiday and took,' drew scandalized gasps of deprivation when lists of goodies totally unavailable in lifeboats were enumerated. Susan Almond, however, despite all the efforts of Sir John Dain, continued to sulk. He was such a kindly old fellow, and a man of distinction, as she vaguely knew, yet she was being quite horrid to him. He eventually shamed her by going on reciting his nonsense rhymes despite her pretended indifference. Yet she would not give in. She had a feeling that if she did she would be forfeiting her independence, which, with three older brothers alternately spoiling and bullying her, she was accustomed to defending with childlike tenacity. Why should she be obliged to sit here in the boiling sun, with nothing to eat or drink and no room to move? What right had they to put her to such inconvenience?

During the day the breeze stiffened, and Lady Almond, likening the rise and fall of the waves to a scenic railway, thought the buoyancy of the boats miraculous. Every boat closed with Boundy's that afternoon to get the right course before nightfall, and Boundy reported at noon that they were 106 miles nearer St Helena than when they were torpedoed. This still left nearly 400 miles to go.

That night all boats made fast again and lay to a sea anchor. This took the form of a canvas cone or drogue, open at both ends but with one end much larger than the other, streamed over the bows and secured to the boat by a cable. The object was to keep each boat's head to wind and sea. But the lack of progress at night worried Rogerson, and his cares were increased next day when the wind dropped to the lightest of breezes. There were complaints, too, from other boats. The night had been rough and windy, and several boats had had difficulty in keeping properly trimmed. It was impossible to stop the Indians, when the water splashed over the gunwales, from shifting the bulk of their weight from the weather to the leeward side, causing an imbalance. They had no more room to move than the Europeans, but the change of trim was palpable. Whyte's smaller boat, with its lower freeboard, was especially vulnerable, and although this boat sailed faster than most in calm conditions, it soon fell behind when the swell was pronounced. Half-swamped during the night, Whyte insisted next morning that his boat must be lightened.

Rogerson agreed, and among the eight people transferred were the Rooksbys, Billie and Mona, who went to Boundy's boat, and the two younger Almond boys, Francis and David, who joined the rest of the family in Boat 8. This was a change devoutly wished for by Lady Almond, though she had not dared suggest it herself, feeling that fate must take its course. Francis generously left his scout knife with Whyte, which Margaret Gordon promised eventually to return. The Almonds, accustomed to family separations, took the reunion without histrionics, but others found it almost unbearably moving. One of these was Donald Miller, and he quickly busied himself with other things to hide his emotion.

Margaret Gordon was originally to have gone with Mona Rooksby, but when she realized that Mona was to be separated from her husband she flatly refused to go. 'He can go in my place,' she insisted. 'It would be too awful for you to be in separate boats.'

The addition of these two bodies to Boundy's boat was a minor disaster, turning mutual harassment into physical torment. Neither of the Rooksbys was of a retiring or self-effacing nature but it was not their fault that they made themselves so painfully felt.

A young apprentice with a head injury was also transferred, in his case to Boat 5, to be treated by Quantrill. But Rogerson declined to take any more women. It was agreed that Margaret Gordon should go to Boat 1 when the transfer could be managed. Whyte's complement had already been reduced to 16. 'We can give Britt a half-cask of water now if he wants it,' said Whyte.

Another change was forced that day by the illness of Kate Richardson, who besides showing signs of insanity was becoming increasingly feeble and refusing to take any food. 'Why can't I go back to my cabin?' she wailed. 'It's much more comfortable there.' Boat 5 was promptly manoeuvred alongside Boat 1. 'This is an order,' said Rogerson. 'Mrs Chapman has got to come to my boat and take care of her mother.' Sybil Chapman agreed on condition that her husband went with her, and the two of them put on their lifejackets, held hands, and jumped together, landing in a heap in the bottom of the captain's boat. They spread the old lady across their combined laps and did their best to comfort her, but she seemed not to know them.

Rogerson was faced with another decision later that day, Tuesday 10th November, after Boundy's noon position had shown an advance on St Helena in the previous 24 hours of only ten miles, bringing a supplication from Britt. All the boats were still spongy and leaking continually, but Britt's was still the worst. Yet it was also the fastest. The speed of the flotilla remained that of the slowest boat, and Boats 4 and 8, Knocker Whyte's and Tommy Green's, were repeatedly falling behind, necessitating a general slowing down to let them catch up. Those in the faster boats fretted at the delay, and the hold-up was especially irksome for Britt. In addition to his characteristic independence of mind, he had sound practical reasons for the suggestion he was about to make. 'Captain Rogerson,' he said, 'I've got the fastest boat, I've lost some of my rations, and I don't want to hang about. I think the best thing I can do for everyone's sake is to go on ahead. I can be at St Helena in four or five days. Then I can send help for you.'

Rogerson saw this as the beginning of the fragmentation he sought to avoid. Anything resembling a boat race was madness. The key to their survival was Boundy's sextant. Rogerson did not doubt Britt's ability or courage, but he did question the good sense of trying to find so small a target without any navigational aid other than a compass. As for sending help, Rogerson doubted whether any facilities existed in an isolated spot like St Helena for long-distance search and rescue. The more he thought about the idea the less he liked it.

'It's such a tiny island, Mr Britt. You'd never find it without a sextant. We must all stick together.'

'That's all very well, Captain Rogerson, but I'm short of rations, and I'm responsible for the lives of the people in my boat. As officer-in-charge I'm entitled to make my own decisions. I may have to press on.'

'I'm responsible for *everyone's* lives, Mr Britt. You're still one of my officers, and you'll do as I say. Whyte's boat has been lightened and he can spare you some water. There's no need for you to be any worse off than us.'

Britt knew his man and said no more for the moment. But he also knew his own mind. Many of the steamship companies, in the days of Britt's apprenticeship in the 1920s, had insisted that their deck officers get certificates of competency in sail as well as steam, and Britt was no exception. He had complete confidence in his ability to sail his boat to St Helena. He believed he had the right to decide, and unless they made better progress he intended to go.

Meanwhile Rogerson had taken Britt's point. The boats were making so much leeway that a distance covered of 50 or 60 miles a day was actually narrowing the gap with St Helena by no more than 10 or 15 miles. Rogerson decided that when the other boats lowered their sails that evening he would keep his own hoisted. Instead of putting out a sea anchor he would keep sailing all night, towing the others. If they progressed no more than 12 to 15 miles in the night hours it might prove a decisive contribution over a period.

In case a rope parted during the towing and a boat lost touch, hourly flashlight signals were still exchanged. But in the troughs of the waves it was easy to miss a signal, and the luminosity of the sea often made it difficult to distinguish between the flash of a torch and a patch of phosphorus. The night was squally, and Lady Almond, like many others, spent anxious hours on watch, cold and periodically drenched, peering into the darkness for the promised signals. Standing up in the stern to extend her visibility, she experienced the illusion of moving steeply downhill in a wide stretch of parkland, the clouds forming themselves into stately avenues on either side. Bob Skea in Boat 7 had a similar impression: gliding down the long following swells, he felt he was riding over the tops of the green fields of Scotland and not sailing on water at all. The fact that the boats were being tossed alternately up and down did not affect the general impression of gliding downhill. Some of the cloud formations at night had an awesome magnificence, matching the sunsets that dazzled them each evening with their beauty.

The old Scot McNeill, numb with cold and cramp, was attempting to urinate over the side of Boat 8 when a vicious roll caught him off balance. Before he could grab anything to steady himself he was thrown over the side. 'Man overboard!' shouted those around him, and people in other boats saw a figure drift past them with arms flaying not twenty yards distant. The commotion reached Captain Rogerson in the leading boat, but with six boats strung out in a line and tied together, it seemed futile to try to bring the convoy round for a search in darkness in such seas. Indeed Rogerson dismissed the idea as impossible, and his voice rose grimly above the elements.

'Keep on!'

It was a shattering moment for everyone. Individuals didn't matter any more. They were all expendable, for the good of the whole. Survival of the fittest, that was the lesson.

For the children it was especially traumatic, their first acquaintance with death. Susan Almond had seen McNeill get up from his seat, and she caught a glimpse of his despairing clutch at the gunwale as he fell overboard. She knew there were sharks following the boat. In her imagination she saw him wrestling in vain with the sharks. That seemed to her far worse than dying. To her he was old Mr McNeill, for whom dying must seem almost natural. It was the manner of it that made her shudder.

David Simms' reaction, too, was an imaginitive one. He had been sitting next to Mr McNeill the day before. 'What would I have thought,' he wondered, 'if I'd known I was sitting beside a man who was soon to be dead?'

The squalls that had been responsible for McNeill's loss of balance caused difficulties of control in most boats, and disappointing progress was made. For Bob Skea, in Boat 7, steering with an oar was becoming increasingly difficult. Running to the north-east with the wind on the starboard quarter, he had to watch the seas carefully. If a wave lifted the stern, the boat was liable to broach to, and the drill was, first, oar on; then, when the wave moved past the bow, he feathered the oar. He also had to be careful not to let the boat get beam on to a wave, or be caught with a wave dead astern. Some of the waves were steep enough to have toppled them over. It was especially tricky at night, when it was difficult to gauge the waves as they came. Only Boundy and Skea could handle the boat in these conditions, so for them it was virtually four hours on and four hours off. No one admitted it, but the Dieckhaus plan was gaining adherents.

The boat with the most immediate problems remained Britt's. Like the others it was overloaded, and during the night, although riding the waves well enough, it suffered badly in the troughs, when the tow-rope nearly pulled the stem out of the water. 'We can't last out like this,' Britt told Rogerson next morning as the wind rose still further. 'If we tie up another night we'll sink. At this rate I doubt if my party will survive until we reach the island. We shall become a liability here, and in this weather we're going to get split up anyway. I'm requesting permission to go on ahead.'

Rogerson felt the challenge to his leadership, and to his plans for keeping together. He knew Britt could be headstrong, but he also knew there was sense in what he said. There was even some attraction in the idea that warning could be given to St Helena that five more boats were on the way. Yet Rogerson remained reluctant. If Britt had had a sextant, chronometer and navigation books it would have been different. Now he warned him again of the hazards. But he did not want another open clash with his chief officer, and to hold him against his will might be counter-productive.

Rogerson had been a sick man ever since the sinking, largely because of the quantity of water he had swallowed. To the shock and even humiliation of losing his ship had been added the bout of diarrhoea, in marked contrast to the chronic constipation that had afflicted most of the others. These factors may or may not have weakened his will to resist. Now, confronted as he was by a man who seemed utterly sure of himself and of what he proposed, he finally consented. 'Very well, Mr Britt, if you really think you can make it. It's your decision.'

'Then we'll go.'

A storm seemed to be brewing, and with it the hope of rain, but the sky was overcast, and Boundy had been unable to get a noon sight. Thus their last position confirmed by sextant was more than 24 hours old. Yet for Britt, further delay was intolerable. Their approximate position was known, and that was enough. 'You'd better see if anyone wants to change boats,' suggested Rogerson. Any large-scale reluctance to share Britt's gamble would have aborted it at the outset. But of his complement of 54, not a man – or a woman, and there were three of them, Annie Crouch, Ada Taggart, and Diana Jarman – hesitated. They were the lucky ones, they would be first to the island. Soon they were proving their boat's greater handiness by drawing ahead.

'Good-bye! Good-bye and good luck! See you at St Helena!'

'Don't forget to send someone to look for us!'

The chorus of farewells lifted everyone's spirits. Something was being done at last to speed their rescue.

Envy of those fortunate enough to be in Britt's boat was general. Watching them more wistfully than most were the Chapmans. Had it not been for the old lady they would have been with them.

Margaret Gordon, too, had her regrets. The seas had been too rough that day for her planned move to Boat 1 – the second time her transfer had been frustrated – and she was left as the only woman in Boat 4. Another in this boat who felt cheated was Diane Jarman's friend, Bill McGregor. But for a foolish error he would have been in Boat 1 with Diana.

Among the few who would not have changed boats at any price was Bob Skea. St Helena was little more than a dot in the ocean, and his canny Scots caution did not underestimate the difficulties of finding it. Taking his turn with Boundy at the helm of Boat 7, and checking Boundy's sextant readings, he was well aware of the leeway these lifeboats made. To make good a course of 005 degrees they were having to steer north-east, even east-north-east. He was glad to be in the boat with the sextant.

More precarious was the progress of Boat 8, where Tommy Green and the two Scottish quartermasters were eyeing the mast apprehensively at every fresh gust. Eventually, with a crack like a rifle-shot, the fissure widened. The sails were quickly lowered, and, fortunately, the boat was not actually dismasted, but it rolled helplessly on the swell. Campbell and McKelvie, working at speed, fashioned a splint from a broken oar, and there were cheers of relief when the splint was successfully lashed to the mast. The repair, however, became a perpetual focus of anxiety. 'My mast has cracked,' Green told Rogerson, who had been obliged to wait for him. 'We've repaired it, but I daren't use too much sail. If I fade out of the picture you'll know what's happened.' Here, for Rogerson, was a further threat of fragmentation. The transfer to a safer craft of the eight children in this boat – strictly seven, since the 16-year-old Basil Almond insisted on shouldering all the responsibilities of an adult – together with their mothers, could not be considered. There was no room for them anywhere else.

Shortly before dusk on that Wednesday evening, 11th November, Britt's boat, now a long way ahead, finally disappeared from view. It had gone without collecting the extra water from Whyte, again because of choppy seas. But Rogerson for one had not overlooked this, and when the five remaining boats gathered together to tie up that evening, he asked Whyte to hand over the half-keg of water. 'I don't see why, sir,' answered Whyte. 'I haven't got all that much for sixteen people. Britt was short of water and that was different. This keg belongs to the people in this boat and it's not for me to give it up.'

'I want that keg, Whyte. Hand it over.'

If Rogerson had revealed any uncertainty with Britt, he showed none now. Whyte continued to object, but short of mutiny he had no alternative. 'I'm officially complaining about this, sir,' he said. 'I want that recorded.' In a gesture of defiance he doled out a two-ounce measure from the keg to everyone in his boat. 'Look, they're drinking it!' came the screamed accusation from people in the other boats; but afterwards the keg was passed over to Rogerson.

'We'll record that, too,' said Rogerson. But he was not totally unsympathetic. It was natural for Whyte to fight for the people in his boat. The 32 ounces they had appropriated was less than two pints, and the half-keg held three gallons. Whyte was one of Rogerson's favourites – and a favourite, too, of his wife's. They were personal friends. He had had to be hard on him for the general good.

As night fell the sky blackened, and the wind blew chill. Few had any real protection against the cold, which proved doubly penetrating after the warmth of the day, and they huddled miserably together. The wind was whipping the wave-tops into white horses, which broke over the boats repeatedly, slamming into the bows and sides and drenching everyone in turn. The night was intensely dark, and whereas in daylight they could see the waves coming and anticipate them, the night assault was the more terrifying for being unseen. Gradually, however, a star-lit luminescence made the wave-tops dimly visible, and then they flinched at each oncoming blow. Allan Tempest, bailing furiously, had his back to the wind, but he winced just the same; he could hear the rollers roaring down on him out of the night.

Linked as they were, it became increasingly difficult to keep head to wind. Gunwales were awash, they were sitting in water, and all the boats, Whyte's especially, were in danger of being swamped. Anticipating this, Whyte ordered his boat-load to put on their lifejackets, a precaution that was soon followed in the other four boats. There was so much water in the boats that bailing became more and more frantic: they were bailing for their lives. Yet the overcrowding made fully effective bailing impossible.

Whereas the Europeans were mostly prepared to take their turn on the weather side, the Asians, most of them even more scantily clad, could only be persuaded to do so by threats, and their mumblings and grumblings grew. It remained essential to keep the boats head to wind and sea, yet without the correct balance it was impossible to keep them evenly trimmed. Boats kept swinging right round and running with the wind instead of into it. Oarsmen fought desperately to bring the boats back in a long and exhausting battle, posing an enormous strain on the few men competent to row.

The rain they had been praying for didn't come, but the seas, briefly floodlit by jagged shafts of lightning, became more and more fearsome. Most terrifying of all was the imminent danger of being dashed to pieces in a collision with the next boat, either the one behind or the one in front, necessitating even more feverish manoeuvring by over-worked oarsmen. The dangers were worst in Boat 4, where Knocker Whyte, the only one strong enough to pull the boat round, was almost irreplaceable at the helm, and in Boat 7, where Bob Skea at the steering oar remained indispensable.

As the wind stiffened it became impossible for Skea to keep the heavily loaded craft in line, even with someone dipping a 'backing-up' oar to his orders amidships. Twice Skea snapped an oar fighting to hold the boat against tempestuous seas. The imminent danger of foundering was especially exasperating for Dieckhaus, whose advice had been so hurtfully ignored. 'It's bloody no use!' he shouted. 'It's madness to go on with these oars!'

The knowledge that they had missed their chance of making the substitution he had recommended, and that it would be quite impossible to attempt it at present, drove Dieckhaus into a frenzy. At any moment the lifeboat would capsize, and although it wouldn't sink, no one would survive for long in these seas. 'Dive as deep as you can!' he shouted to his wife Avis. 'Get it over quickly! A lifejacket won't save you.' With this he forced his way to the side of the boat with the clear intention of throwing himself overboard.

Dieckhaus was such a heavyweight, even after five days in a lifeboat, that those who tried to stop him were almost overwhelmed. When at length he was hauled back into the boat, Arnold Silcock punched him on the jaw to quell his hysteria. Limp with exhaustion and utterly humiliated, he sank down in the after-well and sobbed with impotent rage.

Dieckhaus junior, who was sitting on his mother's knee, took fright at all this and began screaming. The child was a cheerful little lad who behaved better than most, and his appetite continued to amaze, but from this point on whenever his father went anywhere near the side of the boat he yelled in protest.

So the nightmare continued, bearing particularly hard on those who were invalids already. None was in worse shape than Kate Richardson. Stretched out on the duckboards in the bottom of Boat 5, with water continually sloshing over and around her, she was mercifully unaware of her surroundings. First she thought she was travelling in a bus, then she was back in Meerut or Darjeeling. Not even her daughter could do anything with her. Meanwhile Violet Williams had two parents to agonize over. Her father was getting weaker and her mother was delirious; all night long she stood against the mast, with only a thin dress and cardigan for protection, while Violet stood beside her to keep her from falling. What had she done to these two frail, middle-aged people in encouraging them to make this terrible journey? It would surely be the end of them. Even she herself became a prey to fanciful imaginings, and for a long time she thought they were being tossed about in a harbour, within tantalizing reach of land. Would the night ever end?

The dilemma facing each boat commander was the same: should they sever the link with adjacent boats or stay in the chain and risk being bumped or broached? It would be all too easy, in these storm conditions, for the tiny convoy to be irretrievably scattered, so the dangers of collision and capsizing were for a long time accepted. Vic Chambers, for one, was astonished that his boat didn't founder, and he came to the comforting conclusion, as others had done, that it really must be unsinkable.

Captain Rogerson's solution to the problem was to revert to a sea anchor. He, in the leading boat, would ride to a drogue, keeping his head to wind and sea and steadying the chain. But cone and cable, imperfectly stowed under innumerable feet, proved so tangled and knotted that it took fifteen minutes to unravel them and get them out. At once the cone developed a fault and had to be hauled in and re-set. Meanwhile the other boats in the line, despite frantic rowing and ruddering, were blown past the leader in a variety of directions, creating a scene of chaotic derangement. The drogue proved too small to have much effect on five heavily laden boats, communication became impossible, and one by one the boats dropped their tow ropes and detached themselves from the crocodile.

Riding the waves remained precarious in the extreme, and there was still much back-breaking work to be done by the rowers, even after individual boats got their sea anchors out. By this time it was after three o'clock on the morning of Thursday 12th November, but several hours of darkness remained, the storm showed no sign of abating, and contact by torchlight, despite continued flashing, was intermittent at best. Bailing and rowing remained essential, and there was no rest for anyone. They called it, when it was over, the Night of the Sea Anchors.

CHAPTER 7

And Then There Were Two

'All boats in sight at daybreak.'

This laconic entry by Fourth Officer Bill Stubbs in the log of the captain's boat was written with grim satisfaction. Britt's boat had gone on ahead and everyone wondered how it had fared during the night, but the remaining five boats, despite the night's vicissitudes, were still in visual contact. Another such night, though, would surely scatter them; they could not risk tying up again.

The entry revealed nothing of the terrors of the night, nor did it include more than a passing reference to the privations they were suffering. 'Pani, sahib, water, sahib,' chanted the Asians, and many of the Europeans found excuses to plead for special treatment, while the youngest of the children cried piteously. Fellow human beings, of whatever colour, got on the nerves of their neighbours, selfishness and ill-temper spread like a contagion, and standards of behaviour plummeted. Most debilitating of all – even worse than the acute thirst from which everyone suffered – were the extremes of temperature and the constriction of movement, the latter being the prime cause of the perpetual wrangling and vexation. Chivalry was at a premium, and the women behaved better than the men.

Ingenious methods of extracting water from the casks, by the surreptitious insertion of absorbent clothing or other material into bung-holes, were practised by Europeans and Asians alike, and guards had to be strengthened, two trusted passengers being posted to sit on the barrels. More serious was the boring of holes in the casks, which was traced to the Asians, causing the most acrimonious quarrels so far. To set against this, a European in

Nutter's boat drank the whole of the spirit ration, the after-effects removing all speculation as to the culprit.

Acts of generosity and self-sacrifice came mostly – but not exclusively – from the missionaries. Gladys Usher, in Boat 5, refused an extra ration of water, insisting that it go to the children. Betty Birchman was another who denied herself for the children in Boat 7. Mothers had to be watched to make sure they did not martyr themselves. Donald Miller in Boat 8 saw one of the Indians drink no more than a third of his two-ounce ration before passing it swiftly, before he could be stopped, to the youngest of the Simms children, the 3-year-old Esther, who was hunched up next to him in the bottom of the boat screaming for more.

The principles on which extra rations of water were granted varied from boat to boat. In some boats, women and children were favoured, but not in the captain's boat, where Rogerson decreed that those who were most active in running the boat must be accorded priority. 'If we miss St Helena and have to row for the shipping lanes,' he told Quantrill, 'we'll need fit men.' Quantrill did not demur. He recalled that in times of famine in primitive communities, emaciation was always most marked among women and children and the aged. Those on whom the tribe relied for survival were the last to starve. Nevertheless he administered the captain's policy with humanity. Those who fell ill or were in obvious distress were seldom denied something extra.

George Nutter's outlook was different. Lacking any mantle of authority, or any higher court of appeal, he took a rigid line. Everyone, from the oldest to the youngest, regardless of their protestations of illness or weakness, got the same. Then there could be no argument. Sickness and debility, he decided, were too easy to feign.

Tommy Green, in Boat 8, believed that by allotting the same rations to the children as to the adults he was giving them more in proportion, because of their size, and in this he was supported by the Millers. It seemed to Donald Miller that the older children managed their rations rather better than the adults. Tongues and throats had become so parched that biscuits and pemmican could not be masticated and even a malted milk tablet took hours to dissolve through lack of saliva. Only the chocolate was palatable. Yet the children continued to eat reasonably well. The infant prodigy in Boat 7 was the Dutch boy Ferdy, to whom most of the Indians passed their pemmican. His capacity for food was almost as unique as his facility for excreting it.

Physical deterioration, although general, continued to be more rapid amongst the Indians whose apathy declined into a torpor of resignation. What was to be would be. But there were many exceptions, among them the deck serang Baboo Allee, who pulled more strongly than anyone in the captain's boat when rowing was necessary. Suffering even more acutely than the Europeans from cold and exposure, and probably also from thirst, the Asians were the first to succumb to the temptation to drink sea water.

The Europeans, weaned on stories of shipwrecks and of castaways crazed with thirst, had a superstitious horror of drinking salt water; that way, they had been brought up to believe, lay madness. The Asians had had no such indoctrination. Quantrill kept an open mind, but the captain's orders were clear: everyone was to be discouraged from drinking salt water, and warned of its deadly effects. Many of the Asians, however, continued to supplement their water ration by drinking it.

Quantrill thought about it deeply. Medical opinion, he knew, was against it, but he could think of no compelling reason. Could it be that Europeans were so prejudiced against it that having succumbed they suffered agonies of fear and remorse which affected their reason?

As the days passed and lack of lubrication brought dry throats and cracked lips, Quantrill decided that it couldn't do much harm to wash his mouth out with salt water, and even to let a few drops trickle down his throat. He tried it and felt no ill effects, but he didn't find it thirst-quenching. He noticed that several other Europeans washed their mouths out similarly, but he couldn't be sure whether they swallowed the water or not. Officially he continued to discourage it.

Margaret Gordon had a toothbrush in her bag and for days she looked at it longingly but dared not use it; she didn't feel like lending it to the others, and anyway it meant dipping it in the sea.

Now she decided to try it. The sensual pleasure of freshening her mouth proved well worth the risk. Sea water, in any case, could be beneficial, and when Whyte developed a painful abscess in his mouth she persuaded him to rinse it frequently with sea water, and the swelling went down.

People in other boats experimented with washing their mouths out with salt water after eating and before drinking their water ration, and they found they got the best out of their meagre supply of fresh water in this way. Mary Simms noticed that everyone around her in Boat 8 rinsed their mouths out with salt water, which they sipped from empty pemmican tins. They said they spat it all out, but she watched Sir John Dain carefully and was sure he swallowed most of it.

It seemed to Quantrill that the Indians who indulged themselves most were suffering the worst, though so many of them lapsed into passivity it was difficult to tell. Some of them, he feared, had overdone it. That, he was sure, would be fatal.

Quantrill himself had no time to brood, being kept busy helping to relieve cramp and other circulatory troubles in others, providing dressings for blisters and sores, palliatives for seasickness, sunburn and sunstroke, and visiting or advising the other boats on similar ailments. Among the Europeans, the one who gave him the most concern was Kate Richardson. She continued to hallucinate for most of the day, and she could not be moved from the bottom of the boat, where water still lapped around her. At five o'clock on that Thursday afternoon, the sixth day after the sinking, she fell silent, and when Quantrill examined her he found she was dead.

It was a sad moment for the Chapmans, but a merciful one too; they had more or less given up hope. Distressed as she was by her loss, Sybil Chapman had a comforting feeling that her mother had had a genuine foreknowledge, that her journey through life had been accomplished, and that she had reached a destination that would not have been unwelcome to her. Although she had no maritime connections that anyone knew of, she had never wanted a conventional grave and had always wanted to be buried at sea.

Rogerson conscripted four men for a burial party, one of them the young Allan Tempest. In a boat that contained many experienced crew members, Tempest was dismayed to be singled out, but having been appointed he was not going to back out. He had never seen a dead person before. They had to lift the body up on to the thwart and then manhandle it on to the side of the boat, ready for Captain Rogerson to conduct some sort of burial service. As Tempest lifted the body, excrement stuck to his hands, but he and Jim Chapman draped a dressing-gown round the corpse and lowered it gently into the water. They still had the unpleasant task of going down into the bilges and cleaning up the mess.

That evening there was a second death in Boat 5, that of an Indian seaman. Quantrill was sure he was one of those who had been drinking sea water. He had been comatose for several hours but his companions, seeing the chance of an extra water ration, had not raised the alarm. Rogerson held another burial service and the body was put over the side. The reaction of the Indians was hard to fathom; their murmurings were strangely muted, and they showed little interest in their colleague either before or after his death.

Boundy's noon sight put them 329 miles from St Helena, and the breeze was too light to narrow the gap much that day. It was a day of stocktaking in all boats, with stricter rationing the only counter to their sluggish progress. In Boat 8, schoolteacher Evelyn Ashdown chose Basil Almond to help her work out how long their water would last at existing rates, and they confirmed that it would run out after another 18 days. With the clamour for extra water becoming strident, however, it was decided not to attempt a reduction. Things were difficult enough already.

Europeans and Asians alike were giving up hope, and the first deaths persuaded Rogerson that Britt, perhaps, had been right after all, and that the faster boats should go on ahead. Boundy's boat, under the retarding effect of the steering oar, was slower than Rogerson's, and Rogerson, prompted by helmsman George Waters, suggested to Boundy that he take over the sextant and strike out alone for the island. 'He'd be mad to say yes,' said Waters, 'but it's worth a try.'

Anticipating resistance, Rogerson made it an order from the start. 'I've decided to go on ahead, Mr Boundy,' he said, 'and I shall want your sextant. I'll come and get it now.'

This got a derisive laugh from Skea and a decisive negative from Boundy. 'I'm captain of my own boat, sir,' he said. 'I'm sorry, but you're not having my sextant.'

'That sextant', interposed Skea, 'is half mine. I agreed that with Mr Boundy. It's not leaving this boat.'

Rogerson had expected something like this and he did not pursue the matter. But his point was taken – and with it, indirectly, the Dutchman's. The calmer weather made an attempt to fashion a jury rudder opportune, and Dieckhaus more than redeemed himself in the eyes of his fellows by his flair and enthusiasm for the task in hand. With Bob Gerner he swam round to the stern of the boat on a rope to offer up the jury rudder while Skea dived under water to hammer home the bolts and fasten the nuts. They simply took a chance on any sharks that might be around.

It was not until the time came to get the three swimmers back on board that anyone realized how weak they had all become; only by a concerted effort did they succeed. Hauling Skea and Gerner in was awkward enough, but hoisting Dieckhaus was like landing a whale. With more than 300 miles still to go to reach land, it was an unwelcome revelation of their declining strength.

An earlier discovery in Boat 7 had come when the ship's carpenter went forward to release the eye-bolts for the jury rudder. He stepped on the body of an Indian, on which four others were sitting to conceal it. Their motive, as before in Boat 5, was to preserve their dead comrade's water ration for themselves. When they realised their ruse had been discovered they set up a discordant lamentation. The dead Indian was a Moslem, and his companions prolonged the funeral rites interminably before lifting him overboard. The delay, as it happened, was probably fortunate for the three swimmers, Dieckhaus, Gerner and Skea. When the body was released, the sharks returned.

Because the engine was astern, the magnetic compass had to be kept well clear of its influence, and someone had to call out the compass readings to the man at the tiller. What was needed was a voice of clarity and authority, and an obvious candidate was Mona Rooksby. Her natural 'presence' was ideal for the task. 'I'll use my high canteen voice,' she promised – something she had practised to good effect in the Services canteen in Bombay. Skea was greatly diverted by the cultured tones of command in which she announced 'North-east by east – you are a quarter of a point orf your course.'

The days were so hot that some cooled their heads by hanging them over the side and getting a neighbour to pour water over them. Skea borrowed a spare item of Mona Rooksby's underwear, soaked it in salt water, and wound it round his head like a turban. They washed daily, and although ordinary soap was latherless in sea water, someone passed round a cake of strongly impregnated toilet soap just for the luxury of the scent. All the men grew beards. Under the imperious rule of Marjorie Miller the women in Boat 8 cropped their hair, but this did not appeal to women of fashion like Christine Saunders in Boat 5 and Janine Jaspar in Boat 7, and the Belgian especially kept up appearances by making up punctiliously each day. She amused and eventually exasperated her companions, however, with a single over-worked English phrase: 'I am fed *op*.'

Squeamishness over bodily functions faded, although a measure of screening could still be obtained by the use of a blanket. Boundy, like Marjorie Miller, set aside two periods a day for personal hygiene. With one or two exceptions everyone was constipated, but they continued to pass water with a freedom that surprised them. For the women, periods of menstruation were normal.

Gladys Usher helped Quantrill with his medical work in Boat 5, and with Cynthia Saunders helped nurse the children; abandoning her shawl, she cut strips from it for head-coverings for others. In Boat 7 the sick were in the hands of a qualified nurse in Betty Birchman, who, despite suffering more than almost anyone from sun-blisters because of her fair skin, busied herself in prescribing and applying ointment and dressings for others, in massaging swollen limbs with whale-oil (provided in the boat's equipment for the relief of frostbite), and in administering sal volatile, brandy and extra water where it was needed. Margaret Gordon played a similar role in Boat 4, where one of the Indians had a horribly gashed finger, revealing the bone. She made him soak it in sea water while she explored the contents of the first-aid kit. There was no antiseptic other than a small bottle of iodine, but there were packets of lint and bandages, and she poured iodine into the wound when she was sure it was clean and bandaged it carefully. She did the same for a nasty scratch she had discovered on her own ankle.

Among the Europeans the most seriously ill were the old engineer Lewis Scaife, the man who had been torpedoed six times (three in the First World War and three in the Second), and Purser Francis McQuone. Scaife, who had been recalled to duty because of the war, suffered from angina and was a continual source of concern in Boat 8. McQuone had been stripped of his clothes when thrown out of Boat 3 and had spent far too long in the water for a man of his age and bulk, but he sat quietly in Boat 5, responding to treatment and never complaining. Stubbs lent McQuone his finely woven canvas 'monsoon' coat, the one he had rescued from his cabin, but when McQuone realized Stubbs had no other covering at night he insisted on returning it.

Quantrill had to move about to attend to the sick, but most people had no alternative but to sit where they were day and night. Only Boundy in Boat 7, where the crush was worst, insisted on some regular changing of places, and this only in the stern. Apart from the extreme discomfort, sitting in one position induced pins and needles and numbness, and although Quantrill, helped by Gladys Usher, was always ready with massage, circulation was not easily restored.

With no drugs to issue, Quantrill dished out sodamint tablets for almost all ills, and as time went on these were welcomed as a life-saving potion. Otherwise the only effective treatment was an extra ration of water, but this he used sparingly, not just for reasons of economy but because it caused more problems than it solved. So many people had become completely self-centred in the fight for survival.

Quantrill saw that the ordeal was bringing out the best in some and the worst in others, and he noted that the disproportion between the two groups was widening. For the first time he was realizing how perverse and covetous human nature could be. Failure to guard one's possessions was to invite the meanest of thefts. The explanation that something had 'gone overboard' acquired a cynical connotation. When people woke up from fitful sleep to find personal items missing, Rogerson collected all jewellery and attractive items in Boat 5 and stored them in a locker behind the helmsman's position in the after-peak. Unless the helmsman himself went to sleep they were safe.

In really difficult circumstances, decided Quantrill, heroism was not a very common characteristic. Some of the toughest men were losing heart, while the women kept cheerful. The children responded to the mood of their elders.

Sybil Chapman was so tired that she allowed her head to drop on to the shoulder of a man wedged against her and she awoke with a start as he pushed her away. When she protested he flared up. 'It's everyone for himself in this boat.' After all she had been through, this reminder of the frailty of human nature was especially painful. For the first time in her life this agreeable woman found herself making enemies rather than friends. In the daytime she got so tired of looking at disgruntled expressions and listening to grievances that she longed for darkness. But when night came there were continual disturbances and it was impossible to sleep, so that she became impatient for daylight.

There was still some camaraderie amongst the crew, even between one race and another. Some of the Indians had preserved their tobacco, and as cigarettes ran out they shared it. Captain Rogerson called to his personal servant Abdul Abdool: 'Have you got any tobacco left, Abdul?'

'Yes, Captain, a little.'

'Roll me a cigarette, will you?'

Abdul did so, lit it, and passed it down from the well of the boat to Rogerson in the stern. All who handled it on the way took a draw. The last to do so was Quantrill.

'Hurry up with that cigarette, Doc.'

'Just keeping it alight for you, Captain.'

All cigarettes were carefully stubbed, and Allan Tempest, as a non-smoker, was entrusted with the job of preserving the fag-ends. He stored them in the top pocket of his green blazer. When enough stubs had been collected, the tobacco was rolled into a cigarette, using the paper in which the malted milk tablets were wrapped. Seeing the pleasure and solace people derived from smoking, Tempest asked: 'Do you think I could have a drag?' To his surprise his request had to go to arbitration. 'You're a non-smoker,' said one accusingly. Another said: 'It'd be wasted on you.' As with everything else in the boat, the addition of one to the number meant less for everyone else.

The decision arrived at by the conference was that Tempest could have a drag provided he inhaled, and they watched to see that he drew the smoke down into his lungs. Within seconds of inhaling he almost passed out, and he felt giddy for several minutes. For the moment, as intended, they had cured him of smoking.

In most boats the hand-pumps had seized up through salt-water corrosion, and there were times when water poured in faster than it could be ejected. Bailing became so exhausting that short spells were all anyone could manage and a system of shifts was arranged. The changing of shifts caused disturbances in which people who felt they were being unnecessarily inconvenienced came to blows. The quarrels were not inter-racial: European struck European and Asian struck Asian.

In Boundy's boat, where one bucket had been lost overboard, work with the remaining bucket was shared between an Indian and a European; the Indian filled the bucket and the European lifted and emptied it over the side. To make room for this two-man operation, in a boat where space was more restricted than in any other, the remaining occupants had to split themselves into two sections, jamming themselves together on either side of the space created. If they spread themselves forward of the mast they upset the boat's trim, and if they spread themselves aft they obstructed the helmsman. The result was two dense compressions of humanity, so tightly wedged that it was almost impossible to change the shift when the time came. In theory the two men going off duty should have slotted into the space occupied by their replacements; but as soon as someone left his place in the pack the pressure from all sides immediately filled it. To get to and from the bailing station the shift-workers had to clamber over and through the intervening mass, bringing further blows and abuse. Most energetic of the bailers was a salt-of-the-earth Cockney named Jimmy Turner, who really did say things like 'Cor, stone the crows, guvnor.'

At night the shift system had to be abandoned, bailing being taken over by the ships' gunners (five of whom happened to be in Boundy's boat), in conjunction with an equal number of Indians. They took up position at dusk and stayed there till dawn. But even this did not bring peace, largely because of the intolerance of some of the gunners. Young lads of 18 or 19, they were cheerful and willing, but they knew no Hindustani and had no idea how to handle Indian seamen. Ignoring the censure of Bob Skea, they bullied them almost as a matter of course, called them 'wogs', and finally provoked them into going on strike. At this point Boundy stepped in. Although he had a strong personality he was not the 'officer-type', preferring to lead by persuasion and example, relying on his own good humour and optimism to keep order. But now he admonished the gunners and insisted that they call their colleagues 'Indian seamen' and treat them with respect. He then appointed the ship's barber, an Indian named Mohammed Isahak who spoke English, to be responsible for the good behaviour of his compatriots. 'Tommy Barber', as he was affectionately known by the crew of the *Cairo*, was also appointed to see that the food and water rations were properly distributed, removing a continual source of suspicion and resentment. Already Boundy had ensured that in cases of sickness it was the Indians who were the first to get extra rations.

Basically the Indians in this boat were no better and no worse than in other boats. They were a typical cross-section, so varied that they could be exasperating. Although they included a sprinkling of Hindus and Christians, they were mostly Mohammedans, and, as in other boats, they adopted a fatalistic attitude. If it was the will of Allah that they perish it was useless to resist. With the appointment of Tommy Barber, however, they responded a good deal better, and Bert Waddell thought them surprisingly co-operative in view of the abuse they had suffered. They adapted gradually to the benign execrations of the British soldier.

Waddell conceived a great compassion for them; they had been taught to rely on a hierarchy that had let them down. Certainly there were rascals among them, who caused endless trouble and gave a bad name to the group. But there were bad hats amongst the Europeans, and no one condemned them out of hand on that account. Physically they lacked the stamina of the young gunners, but that was to be expected.

Another boat that delayed the convoy that day was Whyte's: this boat had not been Whyte's originally, which might account for some of the equipment being sub-standard. The canvas of the sails had rotted in places, and Whyte had to stop to patch them. Very grudgingly, as it seemed to Margaret Gordon, Captain Rogerson waited for them, but they dropped a long way astern. The next time something goes wrong, she thought, they won't wait.

There was no alternative now but to sail at night, using torches to maintain contact. Rogerson did not pause this time for a general assembly at sundown, but all boats somehow kept him in sight. Whyte lost the others for a time but fortunately made a good enough speed to sight them before dark.

The nights seemed endless, and the torch batteries were weakening. 'What time is it?' asked Tempest, on watch in Boat 5. He thought the night must be half gone. 'Ten o'clock,' came the reply. It had only just started. 'You're flashing too often,' scolded Rogerson. 'Look out for that battery.' But Tempest stubbornly continued to flash. 'I haven't had a reply yet, sir,' he said. Their chances depended, he knew, on keeping in touch with Boat 7. He felt he was flashing for his life.

Oil for the compass lamps, too, was running out, making contact with the leading boat imperative for them all. But Nutter, in Boat 6, was getting no reply to his signals. For him it was the longest of all nights, yet for once he feared the dawn. When it came it brought a shock so stark that he could scarcely absorb it. It was the morning of Friday the 13th of November, and they were alone.

'All boats in sight at dawn except No. 6,' noted Stubbs dispassionately. *'Heavy swell and moderate breeze and sea. Proceeding steering north-east. Course and distance to go, N8E 302 miles.'*

Rogerson was thus presented with another agonizing decision. Where was Boat 6, and ought they to wait for it? After checking their food and water yet again, and noting the prostration of some of his complement, Rogerson felt he could no longer sacrifice the progress of the majority to round up the stragglers. At their present rate it might be another ten to twelve days before they could expect to sight St Helena, and Rogerson had serious doubts whether more than a handful from his boat would last that long. There was no certainty that Britt would reach St Helena to raise the alarm, or that anyone on the island would be able to help if he did. Boundy's noon sight, showing 302 miles still to go, settled it. From now on, if boats dropped out they would have to find their way independently. With Britt somewhere in the lead, the boat-race was on.

Progress towards their target that day, at an estimated 1½ knots, was slow but steady, and the four remaining boats were still together at nightfall. But Friday the 13th was not over yet. That evening the wind changed and Whyte, who had again got behind through the need for repairs, had to reef in his sail. His boat was peculiar in that the weight of the sails forward obliged the occupants to crowd together in the stern to keep her sailing; any weight in the bow raised the rudder out of the water. But they were continually finding that one or more of the Indians had crept forward to escape the crush. It was the Indians themselves who discovered that some of their number had been using these forbidden forays not to get a comfortable sleep but to steal water. They had half-emptied one of the tanks.

This was doubly serious in view of the half-tank given to Rogerson two days earlier, and in the commotion and upheaval that followed steering and navigation lapsed and it was some time before Whyte could calm tempers down and regain control. He resolved to get that half-tank back if he could; but when at length they got back on course, the lights of the other boats were no longer visible.

Once again they would have to catch up. But half an hour later, when they saw flashing lights, the direction seemed to Whyte to be altogether wrong. He answered with his initial, and then watched while a series of bewildering signals were transmitted that not even Sparkie Humphries could translate. They could only come from one of the *Cairo*'s boats, and as Humphries repeatedly picked out the letter 'G' they guessed it must be Tommy Green in Boat 8. Whyte and McGregor immediately manned the oars and began rowing towards the lights.

Earlier Green, too, had had to send someone forward to lower and adjust the sail. But as it was being hauled up again there was a sharp crack. 'The mast!' thought Green: but in fact the repair had held. What had snapped was the heavy wooden gaff or spar supporting the head of the four-sided sail. It came crashing down on the men resting below the mast.

Crawling forward in the darkness, Donald Miller found a fearful scene of entanglement and disarray. He grabbed an injured man from the *mêlée* of bodies and began pulling him clear, while others endeavoured to straighten out the sail; the man appeared to have escaped serious injury and was no more than stunned. A moment later an apparently lifeless body, suddenly released from the enveloping folds of the canvas, fell across Miller. Dragging himself clear, he recognised one of the gunners. The gaff had fallen squarely across his spine.

The gunner too recovered consciousness, but he was in severe pain, and Miller feared his back was broken. With the help of others he managed to clear a space for the gunner to lie down flat, and he spent the rest of the night protecting him from being bumped into or stepped on by those around him.

This was the only serious injury, but the accident halted Boat 8 completely, and although they signalled their distress by torch-light they were not seen until they were spotted by Whyte. There was nothing anyone could do before daylight, so the two boats tied up and waited for dawn.

Meanwhile Boundy was making such good speed that he almost left Rogerson behind as well. *'Only one boat in sight – at a distance,'* recorded Stubbs next morning, and it was not until four o'clock that afternoon, Saturday 14th November, that they came up with Boundy. By that time another member of the Indian crew, the old cook, the man they had picked up alone off a raft, had died from exhaustion and exposure. The fact that two more boats had dropped out was scarcely referred to; they had enough troubles of their own. Fragmentation was at last accepted as inevitable. 'No one seemed to mind,' noted young Tempest, 'and we pushed on.'

CHAPTER 8

Fragmentation

As the only woman in Boat 4, Margaret Gordon came under pressure next morning from the women in Boat 8 to change boats. It developed into a campaign. 'You shouldn't be over there with all those men,' said one, and if this smacked of sour grapes, Marjorie Miller's advice that 'It would really be much better for you if you came to this boat' sounded sensible. Margaret Gordon, as it happened, had been thinking on similar lines, though for different reasons. She knew that Knocker was still desperately short of fit men to help manage the boat. There were strong men to spare in Boat 8, and if she could get one of them to change places with her it must be good for Boat 4. Knocker didn't want to lose her, and he advised her not to go. 'You're much better off staying in this boat,' he told her. 'They're terribly crowded over there.' But Margaret had another reason: she wanted to talk to Tommy Green. He had been close to her husband at the time of the second torpedoing and might know more details of what happened to him. When it transpired that a volunteer to change places was forthcoming, she stepped over into Boat 8.

The man who took her place was a young engineer named Freddie Powell. Dapper but of good physique, Powell was very particular about his appearance, and even now his hair was neatly combed. The eldest of a close-knit family of seven boys and two girls from Romsey in Hampshire, Powell had improved himself at night school during an engineering apprenticeship and in 1937, at twenty, he had joined the British India Steam Navigation Company. He had been homeward bound in 1941 when he had been torpedoed, and to replace an earlier shipment of gifts for home that had never arrived he had bought a wedding present for his sister Elsie of a Japanese tea-set, together with many other luxuries unobtainable in wartime England. Among them he listed a kimono and pyjamas of Chinese silk, 'also a set of underwear, lovely silk, comprising knickers, petticoat, brassiere, and night-dress. Don't think me too bold writing all this but I had a brass neck buying it.' A girl in Romsey who had decided not to wait for him would be missing out – but not his younger sister. 'I've got the same for Molly too. All this I'm bringing myself so if it gets lost, well, so will poor Fred.' The luxury goods were already at the bottom with the *City of Cairo*, but 'poor Fred' had survived so far. He would be missed in Boat 8 for his friendliness and because he was one of the few who carried a comb. In volunteering to go into the smaller and more vulnerable boat he was taking a chance.

Before any further progress could be made, repairs were necessary in Boat 8. It seemed sensible for these two boats to stay together, and Whyte indicated that he was prepared to wait. He had a proper boat's compass, against Marjorie Miller's pocket compass, and he also had a sketch map, while for him the presence of another boat offered something more than mere companionship. Once they got going, however, it became apparent that the two boats were ill-matched for sailing in company. Green's, although much the bigger boat, was in continual danger of being dismasted and was therefore restricted in the area of sail it could safely put up. Whyte's boat, although its hull had been damaged, was a good deal handier in fair weather. They stayed together for the rest of that day, but progress was scant and both men had their misgivings.

Another with serious misgivings was Margaret Gordon. The gritty composure she had displayed in Boat 4 had been much admired from afar, and she was enthusiastically welcomed into Boat 8. For her part she was deeply impressed by the way Marjorie Miller looked after the welfare of everyone on board, from the issue of rations to general fitness and the treatment of illness and injury. Compared with the smaller boat the sides of this boat were much higher out of the water, giving more depth in the after well, and Dr Miller had had oars laid down the middle, leaving an enclosed space underneath but over the floor boards.

The smaller children slept down there, and in the daytime most of the adults took the chance to stretch out there, one by one, for an hour. Seeing how efficient the Millers were, Margaret remembered her own modest efforts in Boat 4 and began to feel she should not have deserted her charges. Some of the men there were in poor shape and there was much she could do for them. She had, as it seemed to her, selfishly abandoned her former companions to their fate.

Boat 8 too, was far more crowded, as Whyte had warned her. Sitting in the stern were five women besides herself: Lady Almond, Eileen Simms, Dr Miller, Evelyn Ashdown and Cecilia Norris. There were eight children (or seven children plus Basil Almond). And there were four men: Sir John Dain, Donald Miller, and Tommy Green, with one or other of the quartermasters at the helm. In addition room had to be found for the two sick men – Scaife and the injured gunner – to stretch out along the seats. Amidships were the Asians, 26 of them, and there were another twelve Europeans in the bow. Powell's departure had eased matters there, but that did not help in the stern.

Overcrowding in all sections meant that for all the work of the Millers and others there was a great deal of bickering and complaining, and with Esther, the youngest of the Simms children, whimpering almost incessantly, the atmosphere was sometimes explosive. It seemed to Margaret that there was nothing she could contribute to the general well-being, and she could not escape the conclusion that her very presence had made things worse.

Her new companions noticed her restlessness. Gone was her natural serenity; she felt she had let Knocker down. No amount of reassurance or persuasion would appease her, and next morning she asked Knocker if he would have her back.

There followed an unnatural pause. Some of Whyte's complement, it transpired, were undecided: word had gone round that it was bad luck to have a woman in a lifeboat. With the Asians indifferent, Whyte took a vote among the Europeans, and the candidate was returned with a bare majority. She took advice from Marjorie Miller on keeping the men fit, handed over some spare cold cream, liver pills and aspirins from her bag, which Dr Miller needed, and finally returned to what seemed her natural place in the stern of Boat 4. Twice before her transfer from this boat had been planned. It seemed now that she was fated to remain there.

Meanwhile Green and Whyte were reviewing their situation. They had made negligible progress in the past 24 hours, and the fault lay with Boat 8. 'We've no right to hold you up any longer,' said Green. 'Especially with that damaged hull. You ought to make the best speed you can.'

With health and morale in both boats deteriorating, it had become a question, as Captain Rogerson had already accepted, of every boat for itself. Thus it was that on that second Sunday since the sinking, Whyte, like Britt before him, went off on his own. Whyte's decision, too, was a gamble, and this time the good-byes and good wishes, and the exhortations to send help, held undertones of profound anxiety. What were their prospects? Both boats were now utterly alone in mid-ocean, nearly 300 miles from the nearest land, and that a remote and minuscule island. The decision to separate was a fateful one, a fact that was obvious to everyone, to none more so than Freddie Powell and Margaret Gordon, who had chosen to be in Whyte's boat. Margaret, however, was relieved to find that the men had got over their doubts and seemed glad to have her back.

As the smaller boat forged ahead, the final picture embossed on the minds of those left behind was of Freddie Powell ostentatiously combing his hair to make them laugh, and of Margaret Gordon, profile unmistakable, sitting next to Knocker Whyte in the stern and waving a cheerful farewell.

Tommy Green noticed after a time that Whyte appeared to be taking a course a few points west of the one they had been given when last in touch with the leading boats. That had been two days ago. The course circulated then had taken account of a substantial correction to the north-east to compensate for the excessive drift revealed by Boundy's noon readings. Whyte's boat had fallen behind during that Friday. Had he ever received that correction?

It was something the two men had never discussed. They had

made a compass check and that was all. Whyte was too far ahead now to be recalled. Was his solo effort doomed from the start? For Green, whose chances of reaching land were no better, and perhaps not so good, it was an uncomfortable thought.

In Boat 6, also sailing alone, George Nutter's North Country good sense and dependability did not imply any lack of imagination; he knew exactly what he was up against. Beyond St Helena, some 1500 miles to the north, lay the bulge of the West African coastline. Filling that gap lay an eternity of ocean; to miss the island meant sailing on to certain death. With no qualified navigator on board, no navigational equipment other than a magnetic compass, and with an unstable and at times unmanageable boat, he knew well enough that their chances of finding St Helena were poor, perhaps even negligible. But he knew, too, that that was the last thing he must reveal if he wanted to get there.

All they could do was set a north-north-easterly course on the compass and try to maintain it. But this, especially at night, tested their concentration to the full. Once, on their first night alone, a combination of wind and sea and a momentary inattention at the helm drove them drastically off course. Hitherto they had been able to row the boat round on to the correct compass heading, but now, in their weakened condition, they faltered. Unless they could make the turn they were lost, and every rower was recruited to help. They battled for an hour in a superhuman effort that finally achieved success, but by that time they were utterly exhausted. Every man who took part in the operation knew that in similar conditions it could not be repeated; if they were driven on to a reverse heading again they would never get back.

There were three men taking spells at the helm – George Nutter, the young aircraft tradesman Vic Chambers, and third engineer H. D. Broomby – and next day they gave anguished thought to the problem of maintaining course at night. It was not just a question of fatigue, though that was a factor. The paraffin-fuelled wick that illuminated the compass had functioned well and there was no shortage of fuel, but the wick had suffered repeated soakings as the boat got swamped, and now it finally flickered and went out. All attempts to dry it out and get it to burn proved futile, and the only means of illuminating the compass at night became by torchlight. This alternative source of energy, however, was declining like everything else, and the problems of night steering grew.

The night that followed was the severest test yet for the helmsman. Nutter had preserved one reliable torch for signalling, in case it was needed at night to alert a passing ship, and this he kept in reserve. As the other torches dwindled to nothing the helmsman was automatically deprived of compass aid. The course had to be 'sensed', by the feel of the wind, the sails, and the rudder; and the knowledge that a single mistake meant disaster so petrified Nutter and Broomby that in the early hours they handed over to Chambers. They no longer felt able to accept so heavy a responsibility. If Chambers seemed more confident than his colleagues it was because he welcomed a personal challenge. With the arrogance of youth, too, he was less prone to self-doubt. Yet he was equally aware of the consequences of error. Perhaps it was that as the youngest he found it harder to resist the combined pressure of his seniors. Certainly he did not blame them for passing the buck: if they genuinely thought he could cope and they could not, it was a wise decision. The only alternative was to give up sailing at night, and with nearly twelve hours' darkness that was a sacrifice not to be contemplated. So Chambers, not altogether without apprehension, agreed. As long as they continued to sail at night, the vital role of helmsman would be his.

In daytime the weather was cloudless, with no sign of any other living thing, neither bird nor fish. They didn't even see sharks. It seemed a long time since they had enjoyed the company of other boats, and they felt intensely lonely. The one compensation of being at the helm was that a more generous space had to be kept clear to allow for movement of the tiller, though at night Chambers found this of doubtful advantage. As he sat there sensing the wind, deliberately steering a degree or two off course to get the feel of where the stem should be pointing, and trying all the time to get indicators to guide him – the luff of the sail, the pressure of the rudder, sometimes a star – he had room to stretch out, and he was overwhelmed by tiredness. Only with a tremendous effort was he able to keep awake. Although gaining confidence in his ability to steer at night, he knew that to relax for only a few seconds could result in catastrophe. Trailing his free hand over the stern, he splashed his face with water at frequent intervals. Sometimes, despite the cold, he removed his shirt, dipped it in the sea, and drenched his head and torso in a cold-water douche. The shock to his sunburnt body brought full alertness, and the treatment became a nightly routine. Strangely enough when daylight came his fatigue vanished and with it all desire for sleep.

Saturday 14th November, the eighth day after the sinking, was for Violet Williams a painful reminder of her part in the family's misery; it was her mother's birthday. The wrist-watch she and her father had chosen so carefully was irretrievably lost, but she prayed for some sign, on this anniversary day, that would give them fresh heart. That afternoon she felt her prayer had been answered when a bird with a single-feathered tail flew past. Someone identified it as a bosun bird. Then as dusk fell came a sighting almost too good to be true: a speck on the horizon, too distant to be distinguished with certainty, but it must surely be – could only be – a ship. In a torment of incredulity they searched for the flares that would certainly be visible for miles so late in the day, while Nutter flashed *'SOS – Help'* on his torch. The flares were of a self-igniting type, and all that was needed was to pull an energizing strip off the flare and throw it overboard, contact with the water setting it off. Their expectations of a gleaming coruscation mounting the heavens were dowsed simultaneously with the watery fizzle that extinguished the flare. They had four flares in all – and one was a dud. A second flare, though not performing quite as dramatically as expected, sent dense clouds of smoke billowing into the air, sufficient, they felt sure, to be seen by the ship – if it *was* a ship. But would it be recognized as a distress signal? There was no answering sign, and in the gathering darkness they debated whether to expend any more of their precious flares. Nutter's decision to save them for a more definite sighting was supported, and by nightfall the speck on the horizon had gone.

Chambers' task at the helm was made much easier that night by

Nutter's ingenuity. Using batteries from the emergency lamps attached to the lifejackets, he took the red cover off one of the lamps and clipped the naked bulb to the binnacle. The batteries had a short life but there were plenty of spares.

When the water ration was issued next morning Nutter noticed a significant reduction in the weight of the cask. It had been half-drained in the night. The guard, it transpired, had fallen asleep. Inevitably the Indians were suspected, but they remained silent when questioned and continued to present a picture of passivity bordering on despair. It could well have been one or more of the Europeans, but Nutter decided that further interrogation was pointless, and he attempted no reprisals, issuing the rations as usual. The important thing was to prevent a recurrence. That night the East End Jew George Racher, although not officially on guard, armed himself with an axe and kept the casks obliquely in view. Just before dawn, suspicious movements near the cask were traced to a small group of Indians, one of whom was delirious with thirst. Little George Racher, whose hobby, pursued in the boat daily, was the tranquil one of crotchet, flourished the axe, but the Indians again threatened to mutiny and sink the boat if their sick men weren't given more water. Helped by David Williams, who spoke their language, Nutter managed to pacify them, but tempers remained volatile and there was no sleep for anyone that night.

Several of the Indians were drinking sea water, and although they seemed unaffected, these were the men who had advanced on the cask. The Europeans in this boat, cautioned by Nutter, were convinced that drinking sea water could only result in madness and premature death.

Nutter knew his boat was being set rapidly westwards, so each day he steered a course a little more to the east. The days remained insufferably hot, blistering the fair-skinned, and the nights were wretchedly cold, but they seemed to have left the rough seas of the first week behind, and the hoods and side-screens attached to the boat were usually sufficient to keep them dry. The boat itself needed a fair amount of running attention; the cleats worked loose, the sails started to rip, and the mast, as in

Boat 8, developed an ominous crevice and had to be lashed to a splint. Issuing and guarding the rations, and keeping the boat ship-shape, kept Nutter and his chief helpers busy.

One of these helpers was a middle-aged man named George Blagrave-Dean, a scientist with an oil company reputed to have spent his last weeks in Burma sabotaging oil and other installations to deny them to the Japanese. Hair brushed sleekly to his scalp, round expressive eyes, a narrow upper lip camouflaged by a moustache, and frequent jocular references, in a hoarse whisper, to the 'noggins' and 'chota pegs' he was missing, earned him the nickname of 'Ruggles', after a cartoon character of the time. His natural ebullience acted as a tonic, and he had a way of telling *risqué* stories in mixed company without giving offence that made him a popular figure. When someone asked him what had happened to his voice he explained: 'A man has seven vocal chords, but I've only got one.'

'What happened to the other six?'

'They rotted away with the booze in Burma.'

Nutter had helpers amongst the Indians too, who did all they could to protect him. They knew his value and sat beside him at the tiller and massaged his limbs to keep him going. Inwardly Nutter felt pessimistic, but he exuded confidence for the sake of the others, many of whom had no understanding at all of the problems. Some thought it was only a matter of time before they reached the island. Nutter was disconcerted by their faith, but he dare not enlighten them. For many of these people he had become a saviour, and he deprecated their adulation; so far as he was concerned he was saving his own life. That he happened to have others in his care, and that in saving himself he might save them, was coincidental. If acts of self-sacrifice were called for he didn't know how he would behave.

A self-sufficient bachelor, Nutter found to his surprise that he wished he was married. At 34 it was a gap in his life that he was suddenly and acutely aware of. He could die in this lifeboat, and there would be no one to care.

It was not the sort of thing that he or anyone else talked about. Indeed they talked very little. Few moved about to chat to others.

Each had his or her place in the boat and it became their territory, not to be violated. Property might not be sacrosanct, but ownership was fiercely defended. Every empty pemmican tin belonged to someone. These tins were something to drink from, something in which to conserve their ration for an hour or so instead of gulping it straight down, and something to trap water in if it rained.

The women in this boat – there were eight of them – had more privacy than the women in other boats because they were congregated in the bows. Hardly anyone in the boat, however, male or female, had a bowel movement, though as evidence of their slow desiccation they passed far more water than they drank. Peggy Marr, who had lost her husband in the sinking, and Mary Williams were extremely unwell, while Galina Kariakin, the Russian woman, was prostrated by seasickness. Violet Williams was looking after her mother, and the remaining women, apart from Dulcie Kendall, were middle-aged or elderly. Dulcie never lacked animation, and she regretted that her colleagues were not more companionable. She learned little or nothing about them and failed to achieve any level of intimacy with them. They were all wrapped up in themselves, and she did not exclude herself from this disapprobation; for many days Colin had absorbed her completely. Now he had quietened down, but she feared it was more languor than submission. He had found his lifejacket so uncomfortable that he had refused to wear it, so she discarded her own. If they met some further mischance she really couldn't see herself coping.

The two Russian men, incongruous with their overcoats and trilby hats amongst the half-clad Europeans and Indians, felt no obligation to demonstrate Marxist philosophies by sharing their property, as others had done, or, as workers of the world, to unite for the common weal. Their attitude was stolidly capitalist: their government had paid for their passage and it was up to the shipping company to get them to their destination. They promised to report Nutter to the British Government for not giving them enough food and drink.

On Sunday evening, 15th November, some of the company

attempted to sing a hymn. They could manage little more than a croak, but they did join in a prayer before settling down for the night. The Indians too began to pray each evening. Next morning, as visibility cleared, an Indian was found dead in the bottom of the boat. This first death had a depressing effect on them all, and Nutter was particularly upset as the man had been a friend. The Indians themselves showed little emotion, but Nutter conducted a short burial service, after which the body was lifted over the gunwale. As it floated gently away it offered a macabre reminder of their snail-like progress.

On the eleventh morning, two more Indians were found to be dead. Nutter still refused to give the sick extra rations, and as for the dying he took the hard line that they were too far gone to be saved, and that extra water was wasted on them.

Vic Chambers wondered how long the rest of them could last. He was convinced that a stubborn and unreasonable determination to survive was going to be decisive, and with the intolerance of youth he had little compassion for those whose lack of resolve spoilt their chances. Dying in these circumstances was too easy, requiring no effort. This, he imagined, was why the Indians, with the fatalism of their faith, were the first to succumb. His own motivation, at 22, was a strong desire to live rather than any fear of dying. But if the time ever came, he would simply drop over the side, quench his thirst, and drift away. That would be preferable to enduring a slow death tortured by want of water.

In daylight his mind ran wild in search of an explanation for their suffering, but all attempts at rationalization failed. Was there a God? Was this some sort of test or punishment? Sometimes he offered a silent prayer, promising good behaviour in the future if the opportunity were afforded him. He was almost glad when night came and he took his place at the helm, where his mind was fully occupied and he had no time for morbid thoughts.

Hopes of finding St Helena were fading. Even assuming zero progress on the first two days, ten days at an average of 50 miles a day, which was what Nutter was estimating, should have brought them within sight of the island. What had happened to Britt? Surely he would have stirred up the locals by now.

Later that day they sighted a piece of driftwood, fanning the embers of their optimism. Land, or the shipping lanes, must be close. Violet Williams actually fancied she saw an island, and Nutter too was deceived for a time. It was just another of the countless mirages they all saw day after day. Three birds that flew by towards dusk, however – two gulls and another bosun bird – rekindled their hopes. But with still no sign of land as darkness fell, Nutter faced a dilemma. Had they missed the island? Were they already heading out into the trackless void beyond? Had they miscalculated, or were their estimates approximately right? Should they start a square search for the island?

Eventually Nutter decided that they were more likely to have exaggerated their progress than under-estimated it. Very probably they were still some way, perhaps a long way, from the island. Should he therefore cut down the rations, legislating for a longer voyage? This would give the few who survived a better chance of making a landfall. But having not the slightest notion of how much longer they might be adrift he resolved not to do it. Such action could precipitate a paradox for which his lifeboat training had warned him: people dying of thirst in the midst of comparative plenty.

To some extent this was happening already, and the pressure on Nutter to increase the ration intensified as two more Indians fell into a coma. There was no doctor on board, and Nutter could not tell whether these men were alive or dead. The absence of a pulse was not necessarily conclusive, and not until *rigor mortis* set in did he pronounce life extinct. He had done his best, the first time, to conduct some sort of ritual, but as the deaths mounted the bodies were heaved over the side without ceremony.

The state of some Europeans was hardly less desperate, and some were delirious, but their resources, in the battle of attrition, were taking longer to exhaust. Nutter judged that the majority, Asians and Europeans alike, would last a few more days. So, at the present rate of consumption, would the water. How glad he was that he had stood out from the start against all imprecations and entreaties for more! There was nothing for it now but to keep doggedly on.

*

Nutter had indeed exaggerated his daily rate of progress in Boat 6; Boundy and Rogerson, with the advantage of being able to fix their position by sextant, reckoned they were advancing on St Helena at 35 to 40 miles a day. They had settled down on a north-easterly course which when allowing for drift took them almost due north. But astro-observation from a lifeboat tossing in the swell could scarcely be counted on for accuracy, and there were doubts too about Rogerson's watch. Boundy's confidence in his readings, however, never wavered, and on the ninth day, Sunday 15th November, the day Green and Whyte separated (and the day of the first death in Nutter's boat), he pinpointed the two leading boats, Nos 5 and 7, as 220 miles from their goal.

If Boundy was right they had covered not less than 260 miles since the sinking, a rate of approximately 30 miles a day. At the slightly better rate they were now making they could expect to sight St Helena within six days. Rogerson, however, felt bound to take a pessimistic view, and he believed that even another six days would severely test their powers of endurance.

Of most immediate concern to him was the deterioration of Francis McQuone. Unable to eat, and getting progressively weaker, McQuone lay all day in the bows of the boat. Despite his sufferings he remained an uncomplaining patient, determined to give as little trouble as possible, but he was urgently in need of specialist medical attention. Others giving cause for concern in Rogerson's boat included Herbert Shenton, a 48-year-old engineer with the British India company, and supernumerary engineer John McFarland, one of the so-called 'distressed British seamen'. Shenton was a cheery soul who had taken charge of the hand-pump at an early stage; whenever it jammed through corrosion, Shenton always coaxed it back to serviceability. He and McFarland sat together on the water-tanks to guard them, and they were left with little room for movement, so that after a week they were both suffering from numbness of the legs. The massage administered by Douglas Quantrill and Gladys Usher went some way to restoring circulation, and both men were philosophical. When Gladys Usher told Shenton how sorry she was he simply shrugged and said: 'It'll all come out in the wash.'

Another man who seemed to be suffering more than most was Lawrence McGaffney, 36, travelling with his wife Catherine (who was pregnant) and their two small daughters. McGaffney, a strong, athletic type, and a genial extrovert, was the man who had played the violin on the *Cairo*. Quantrill was surprised at his aggression over the water ration: he was clearly not himself, and he continually requested more. The dissension that resulted aroused the Asians, who thought they should have more as well. Quantrill tried to treat everyone fairly while still favouring the workers, but the Asians always suspected they weren't getting their whack. As they exerted themselves little they were probably right. Quantrill was fortunate in having the support of the deck *serang*, an imposing figure who kept his compatriots under control.

Rogerson tended to let quarrels take their course, on the principle that they provided a safety-valve, but with the death of the old Indian cook the previous day, and the general signs of a growing debility, he felt the time had come to make use of the only means of acceleration available to them. After a consultation with Boundy it was agreed that Boundy should tow Rogerson's boat at intervals until they were within 50 miles of St Helena, when they would come within range of the patrols they hoped would have been alerted by Britt. They would still conserve sufficient fuel for a final dash into port.

Thus it was that Sunday, 15 November, a day of trauma and crisis for the three boats left behind, brought a fresh impetus in all senses for the occupants of Boats 5 and 7. 'We're getting somewhere at last!' said Allan Tempest as they bowled along, and they made excellent progress until, towards evening, a bearing sheared in the motor and towing had to be abandoned for the night. Engineer Bob Gerner had suffered a collapse that looked like heart trouble, but a young supernumerary engineer, Leslie Mountain, another distressed British seaman, took on the repair work. Previously 'Mr Mountain,' as everyone called him, most of them unaware that it was his real name – he was as solid as it implied – had been remarkable only for his astonishing capacity to sleep at all times and in all postures when not actually on duty.

Now the discomfort to those seated round the engine caused by his unwonted burst of activity was cheerfully accepted. In his waking moments Mountain was a first-class mechanic, and next morning Boundy was able to catch up with Rogerson and again take him in tow. There was further rejoicing when Boundy's noon sight revealed that they had covered 73 miles in the previous 24 hours.

CHAPTER 9

Mutiny in Boat 8

Bringing up the rear of the scattered flotilla, without hope of overtaking the others, Tommy Green and the occupants of Boat 8 sorely needed a psychological spur. While the other five boats, as it seemed to them, sailed purposefully ahead for St Helena, they had been left with a defective mast and a Girl Guide's compass to cope as best they could, and they felt isolated and abandoned. Green's unfailing good humour was supported by the two quartermasters Campbell and McKelvie and by the Millers, but something was urgently needed if despondency was not to take a firm hold. The incentive seemed to come on that second Sunday morning when, ahead of them and a little to starboard, a purple rain-cloud began emptying its burden into the sea.

Rain! For nine days they had prayed for it, and now their prayers were answered. A slight change of course and they were heading straight for the squall. The hood that they spread over the boat at night for protection was carefully arranged as the main catchment area, so placed that they could funnel the water straight into the casks. All empty provision tins were feverishly sought, so that everyone could gather a personal supply. But the more progress they made, the more distant the cloud became. The squall was moving away from them.

There were no curses adequate to relieve their frustration, and when they eventually rolled up the tarpaulin and put down their tins it was in a silence more eloquent than any blasphemy. In an effort to revive their faith Donald Miller conducted a special service that afternoon. Choosing passages from the prayer book with which he judged most of the Europeans were familiar, and a psalm which he discovered the Almond boys had memorized at school, he intoned the Confession, the Lord's Prayer, and the Creed, but even the memories of the missionaries let them down so badly that they floundered, and Miller fumbled over phrases he could have sworn were engraved on his memory. Few minds were crystal clear. Prompted haltingly from the congregation, Miller somehow got through, then offered a few special prayers. In these, to the accompaniment of piteous cries from the three-year-old Esther, Miller remembered their loved ones at a distance, the issues on which the war that had caused their suffering was being fought, and the soldiers, sailors, airmen and civilians who were fighting it. The effort of remembering others gave them a curious comfort, as though they in turn were being remembered in prayers elsewhere. Whatever the reason, they no longer felt quite so desolate.

The spiritual uplift, however, was quickly engulfed in physical suffering. Swollen and sore limbs were universal, ease was unobtainable, and thirst dominated their thoughts. Hardly anyone was able to eat, but the craving for water was intense. 'Pani, sahib, water, sahib,' pleaded the Indians, whose condition was worsening, and Miller moved freely among them in the well amidships, giving the sick men swabs of brandy on cotton wool, or sal volatile, or an extra sip of water. For these errands of mercy, lest he stumble on the mesh of arms, legs and heads entwined at his feet, he took off his shoes. Knowing how quickly personal items disappeared, he had the presence of mind to store them safely in a locker.

Rough seas and a heavy swell that night swamped the boat, and the wind swung them round on to a reciprocal course, so that they suddenly realized they were sailing back over distance grudgingly gained. Rousing the men to row, and extracting the oars from the well, where people were lying on them, took minutes, and although they eventually got back on course, Green realized the men were becoming too weak to row. As the wind stiffened, threatening a repetition, he daren't take down the sail in case they lacked the strength to hoist it again.

The old engineer Lewis Scaife felt himself a liability, taking up more than his share of the seating, and only with difficulty was he restrained from throwing himself overboard. Eileen Simms, too, was driven to distraction by the incessant cries of young Esther (to whom she gave much of her rations). Marvellous with all the children, not merely her own, she was painfully aware of the curses that were heaped on both her and the child for the disturbance they caused, and she felt so strong a compunction that in a moment of hysteria she would have sacrificed herself and the child for the sanity of others had she not been prevented. Eventually Donald Miller convinced her that none of their lives was more precious than that of the youngest. The presence of the children, indeed, proved a steadying influence, demanding from the adults an example which, in this boat at least, they mostly provided.

If the Europeans sometimes felt they were sailing aimlessly on into oblivion, the Asians were convinced of it, and as in other boats they started to drink salt water. The Europeans watched them with morbid fascination. Like alcohol, it seemed to stimulate. 'When are we going to reach land?' they demanded. 'When are we going to be rescued? Water! We want more water.' The behaviour of the professional Lascar seamen remained well disciplined, but they were in a minority, and others, resenting Green as an interloper who had no right to give orders, and objecting to the authority he continued to vest in Dr Miller, became aggressive.

One English-speaking Goanese steward, a Roman Catholic, stood by the mast and declaimed to high heaven his frenzied anger that God did not save him. Green, a Roman Catholic himself, rebuked him. 'But for His mercy,' he said, 'God would strike you dead.' His words had their effect and the crisis passed. Another Goanese became demented, peering about him wildly and uncannily, eyes bulging and pupils dilated, leering balefully at his companions. Both these men had been drinking salt water. But the first man to die was neither of these. This man, a stoker, sat silent and immobile, refusing to drink sea water and troubling no one. May Almond, watching him, suspected he was willing his own death and was deeply moved. She had heard in India of such a phenomenon and realized she was witnessing it at first hand. On the eleventh morning, without lamentation or fuss, he just faded away. His Moslem colleagues composed his features and intoned a prayer, and then his body was cast overboard. Accepting the inevitable, he had died with dignity.

Soon afterwards the Goanese steward with the staring eyes died, and his body too was lifted over the gunwale. Of the Europeans only Scaife seemed near death, but many were dangerously comatose. Tommy Green and his principal lieutenants – the two quartermasters who shared watches with him at the tiller – were also showing symptoms of exhaustion, and Marjorie Miller, recognizing that survival for everyone depended on the stamina of these three men, surreptitiously gave them extra water.

That night some of the Indians, suspecting this, bored a hole in a cask to quench their thirst. When this was discovered next morning the racial antipathy and tension that had been building up for days finally erupted. Naturally non-violent, the Indians were numerous enough to usurp their appointed leaders if they were roused. And as it happened there were two agitators on board – the two men whom Rogerson had transferred to Green early on because of their subversive influence in Boat 5. He had thought to cauterize the infection by separating them from their cronies. Now they so inflamed the others that Green found himself confronted by a mutinous mob.

Green tried to reason with them, but they advanced on him menacingly, their purpose abundantly clear. 'He's no good! Throw him overboard!'

Physically and psychologically Green was at a disadvantage, first because of his injured hand, which was still heavily bandaged, and second because of his lack of a uniform. Seeing boldness as the best means of reasserting his authority he handed the tiller to Campbell and jumped down to confront his accusers. In seconds he would have been overwhelmed, but before that could happen another man of non-violence intervened. Thrusting his slight body between Green and the mutineers, Donald Miller addressed them in a language they could understand.

'Stop! He's the only man who can save us! He's a qualified officer and he's doing his best for us!'

It was the spontaneous courage of Miller's action, rather than what he said, that outfaced the Indians. More than anyone else on board, Miller had befriended them, and they hadn't forgotten it. Shocked back to their senses, they rejected their ringleaders and allowed themselves to be pacified.

After the drama, the monotony of hour upon hour of vacuity returned. To relieve her boredom, May Almond day-dreamed of an English spring, with new-born lambs, fresh green leaves, and a cherry tree in bloom against a pale blue sky – and wondered if she would ever see them again. But if days and nights seemed interminable to the grown-ups, to the children they seemed to last for ever. Yet everyone was proud of the way the children behaved. They talked about what they would do when they were rescued, what they would eat and drink, what they would do to Hitler. Mary Simms kept her water ration in her pemmican tin and took a sip now and then. She found this such a good idea that at night, lying in the after well, she kept the tin beside her and whenever she woke up took a sip. By sliding back the panels of the lockers the smaller children could get their heads inside for shelter, but this was where the cat pawed Susan. It was still too timid to come out and had to be fed by putting food and water in the locker.

For Susan the days merged into a blur. Odd things were happening around her, she knew that, yet somehow they didn't seem odd at all. She simply accepted them. She didn't want to do anything, and didn't want to think about anything except herself. She had become as self-centred as the grown-ups. But she did not doubt for one moment she would be rescued. People were dying all round her, but it didn't occur to her that she might die herself. It was only grown-ups who died.

Lewis Scaife seemed a little better, but the gunner with the damaged back lay under a tarpaulin, unable to move. Another Indian died during the night, and another began a crooning chant to Allah the all-merciful. Lisa Simms, the frailest of the children, drooped like a faded spring flower.

Delhi missionary Evelyn Ashdown thought most about places and people she knew and loved. Of the people, there seemed to be no distinction between the living and the dead. If anything she felt closer to the latter. She did not fear death, but she did fear that the circumstances of it might be unpleasant. Above all she feared being a trouble to others. Prostrated for two days by fever, she seriously considered, as others had done, whether it might soon be her duty to slip overboard quietly at night.

Sitting next to Evelyn Ashdown's colleague Cecilia Norris, Donald Miller reminded her of a conversation they had had on the ship about Christian community life, the surrender of individual freedom, and the shedding of personal possessions, during which he had quoted the poet Tagore's 'Renunciation is not for me'. With 27 crates gone to the bottom, the Millers had lost their all, and Cecilia Norris, too, had lost much of intrinsic as well as sentimental value. 'We've all things in common now,' said Miller, 'what little there are of them. Moth and rust have corrupted with a vengeance.' They looked at each other and laughed. They laughed, too, at Marjorie Miller in her torn evening jacket, with her cropped auburn hair blowing in the wind, and she grinned and grimaced back. What she had lost her husband had gained. 'I never thought I was going to have a husband with a beard!'

Miller found that his attitudes hadn't changed. To renounce God's gifts was an impoverishment. Given the opportunity he would simply try to use those that were granted to him less selfishly than in the past. His resolve was not fundamentally different from the promises that were being made by most of those who had survived this far. Get me out of this, God, and I'll lead a better life.

Survival, though, seemed less and less likely, and when Green took a careful timing of the sunset that evening, with the help of Evelyn Ashdown (whose fever had left her), they discussed the situation privately and agreed they must still be at least 200 miles from St Helena. 'We don't really know where we are,' Green admitted to Miller. 'We've no means of telling how far we've drifted and we're all getting weaker. I don't know how long we can last, but many more will die soon if I don't give them more water.

Yet that's something I dare not do. Will you say another prayer for us, Donald, before nightfall?'

Throughout the ardent prayer that Miller offered, the crying of Esther provided a poignant descant. Miller began as a suppliant, confessing his utter dependence on God's grace, power, and mercy. But as he prayed he became like a man possessed. Presuming to remind God of the young lives at stake, he asked that God in his goodness and omnipotence should bring deliverance, or sure evidence of it, *the very next day*. He knew they needed this degree of encouragement to fortify them against despair, and these were the words that emerged from his lips. So fervent was his appeal that no one could mistake that he was talking to God, and the Moslems and Hindus kept a reverent silence.

When Miller finished he experienced a glow of spiritual exaltation. Twenty years in a leper colony had taught him to believe in miracles. Perhaps it was the crying of the child that had penetrated, and not his arrogant prayer. But he *knew* that God had heard, and would answer.

That night he reclaimed his shoes. 'What do you want those for?' someone demanded irritably. 'I shall want them tomorrow,' said Miller.

CHAPTER 10

'Ship Ahoy!'

Rogerson and Boundy in Boats 5 and 7, although still trailing Britt in Boat 1, were meanwhile drawing farther and farther ahead of the others; but their dramatic progress on the tenth day, assisted by the use of the motor, was not maintained on the eleventh. Nevertheless the effects of a short period of towing were reflected in Boundy's mid-day sight, which showed them another 46 miles nearer the island. According to his calculations they had actually over-corrected for westerly drift and on a course of 350 degrees they had another 115 miles to go.

How reliable were Boundy's figures? Everyone wanted to believe them, but even master mariners like Bob Skea, who had checked and re-checked Boundy's calculations from the start, felt the odds were against them. There were so many imponderables. The possibility of cumulative error in the navigation tables and of personal error in the use of the sextant, and the lack of a chronometer, not to mention the inaccuracies of dead reckoning and a frequently overcast sky, were all factors militating against precision. The emptiness of ocean became more and more oppressive, while evidence of physical deterioration continued to grow.

Despite the extremes of temperature no one caught cold, but hypothermia, even more than thirst, was the enemy. A crustaceous scab that formed on and around the lips, together with a weeping from nose and mouth, were the most repellent symptoms, and it was clear to Captain Rogerson that there would be many more deaths if they didn't sight the island soon.

A sudden attack of malaria prostrated the Belgian Pierre Jaspar, in the course of which he too tried to throw himself overboard. He was in such a pitiable state that Janine Jaspar pleaded on his behalf for two exceptional favours: first, that he be allowed to lie under the benches, and second, that he be granted a supplementary ration of water. Boundy gave him a half-dipper, and he lay wallowing in the bottom of the waterlogged boat for the next two hours, after which the fever miraculously left him. It had weakened him so much, however, that he was no longer able to play an active part in the bailing and rowing.

Concern was transferred at once to the Jaspars' six-year-old son Michel, who collapsed like his father in the bottom of the boat and lay there, silent and immobile, for the rest of the day. Life, it seemed, was leaving him. That evening he pronounced one word: 'Water.' Soon afterwards the ration was distributed, and when the dipper reached Michel he grabbed at it so avidly that he upset it. Seeing what he had done he fainted. Despite the pleas of his parents, Boundy refused to refill the dipper for him and passed on to the next in line. The Jaspars thought this a pitiless act, but they came to accept that Boundy in his intransigence was right. He knew, as they did, that they had it in their gift to compensate by giving the boy half of their own ration. If more were needed, Boundy decided, he could think again. As it happened, the sacrifice of the parents revived the boy and, they believed, saved his life.

All the infants except Ferdy cried repeatedly for water, none more loudly than Qunk. Freda Bullen and Joan Redl were sitting together in Boat 5 next to Quantrill, who issued the water ration almost under their noses, and Qunk always screamed at the sight of the dipper, whether it was his turn or not. Quantrill resisted on the grounds that the boy still had the strongest lungs in the boat. Dieckhaus was disdainful of the English parents, who failed in his view to discipline their children, even where both parents were present. When Ferdy asked for more water Dieckhaus answered him shortly. 'You can't have more water. Keep quiet.' 'O.K., Daddy,' Ferdy would say.

The Davies children, Ann and Janet, cried for water in Welsh or Hindustani. Born in India, they spoke no English other than the smattering they had picked up from other children on the boat. 15th November was Ann's fourth birthday, and she talked maddeningly of the cake that had been specially made for her on the *Cairo* but which she was never to taste. Both girls were so thirsty they sucked their thumbs continually, until the skin turned brown and started peeling. Janet, two-and-a-half years old, had a high, melodious voice, and the lilt of it, during the night watches, nearly drove Bob Skea mad. He forgave the child when Padre Davies, though a sick man, lent him his greatcoat for the night. That, he appreciated, was an act of rare Christian sacrifice.

Skea had admired those who gave up their water ration, or some of it, to the children early on, but such acts became rarer as time passed. They had reached the stage where they all expected to die – and what was the point, thought Skea, of noble acts of self-denial if no one was left alive to tell the tale? What did the world matter if one was not in it?

Two Indians died in Boat 5 that day and one in Boat 7, and it became more and more of a struggle to lift bodies from the well of the boats over the side. Jaspar, recovering slowly, felt the Asians knew as well as the Europeans that drinking salt water was dangerous, but that their resistance was less, and that once they had drunk it they could not control their desire to slake their thirst. At the same time he wondered if the Europeans clung to life more tenaciously because they had more to live for, or because they had a greater fear of death. Certainly they were less accustomed, in normal life, to the reality of it.

Were the threats of the Europeans to jump overboard merely anguished cries for help, as in so many attempted suicides? It did not appear to be so with the Asians. That day an Indian jumped overboard without warning, and they went back for him. When darkness came he tried it again and was not missed till morning. The live bait brought an escort of sharks that tailed them unceasingly.

Another curiosity that appealed to Jaspar was that whereas the Europeans repeatedly saw mirages, often of a bizarre and ludicrous nature, the Asians apparently did not.

The power they had always assumed lay behind creation suddenly seemed merciless, and they were appalled at their own insignificance. Was there nothing to come? That question occupied many minds, to the exclusion of speech. What happened to them when they stopped breathing? The knowledge that their lives were slowly ebbing away did much to concentrate thought.

Skea and Boundy were sitting astride one of the last kegs of water, and the rule in the stern was that everyone periodically swapped seats, which resulted in keen competition amongst the women to claim it was their turn to sit next to the men at the tiller. Why such popularity, wondered Skea? 'It's not for our looks,' he assured Boundy, with his usual mocking grin. 'It's simply that they think we might be able to slip them a drink.'

Slipping someone a drink was becoming an obsession with Skea, especially slipping one for himself. He was sorely tempted to urge Boundy to adopt the same policy as in the accompanying boat, where Rogerson had ordained that the specialist workers be sustained at all costs. Silently he rehearsed the arguments. 'These people will never get to land without Boundy and me, so it's essential we get enough water to keep us alive.' Boundy had been adamant in opposing this. How could he snatch a quick drink? In the darkness he shifted his bottom, turned to look aft to cover his actions, and imagined himself dropping the dipper in the cask and then pulling it up and drinking from it, using his body as a shield. With those around him dozing, the temptation was real. But he couldn't do it, and he put the idea out of his mind. It was the brain making excuses for the body.

'If you get us out of this,' Jaspar promised him, 'I'll see you get the *croix de guerre*.' Jaspar's brother had been Minister of Health in the Belgian Government and had escaped to London to continue the fight. 'You'll be far too busy', answered Skea with a twinkle, 'getting one for yourself.'

Condemned to stay seated, crushed against one another, virtually deprived of nourishment and sleep, they became more and more introspective, and meaner and more spiteful in their treatment of each other. In their misery, words were rarely uttered. For days Pierre and Janine Jaspar sat next to each other without speaking. Only the infectious cheerfulness and confidence of Les Boundy and the barbed wit of Bob Skea protected them all from despair.

One man who Skea had thought wouldn't last was a frail 65-year-old Irish Presbyterian missionary named Robert Dickey, who had been invalided home. Taciturn and morose at the best of times, Dickey surprised Skea by his resilience. The longer the ordeal went on the better his mental state, and although he showed an irritating solicitude for his wife, who was travelling with him, he never asked for anything and never complained. That night he whispered to Skea: 'Have we missed St Helena, Bob? Where are we heading for now?' Skea judged his audience correctly. 'We're heading for one of three places. We're either going to heaven, to hell, or to St Helena.' As he had expected, Dickey relished the joke.

The ship's carpenter, a 47-year-old Highlander, reported to Boundy: 'Och Sassenach, I've got a dead Indian here, and his pals will do nothing about it.' 'All right,' said Boundy, 'I'll help you get him over the side.' When the job was done the 'chippie' came the old soldier. 'I feel queer,' he said. 'That man's skin was cold against mine. You've got some brandy there somewhere, and you know what the rule is at sea.' The carpenter was referring to the tradition that the 'chippie', having sewn up a dead body in a sack for burial, was entitled to a 'peg'. 'O.K., Chippie,' said Boundy, 'I'll give you a snort.'

In Boat 5, too, their first task next morning, the twelfth since the sinking, was to commit to the deep the bodies of the Indians who had died in the night. They had now lost five from each boat. If the remaining Indians suffered less discomfort as a result it wasn't apparent, and as for the Europeans, their situation worsened as more room had to be found for invalids to lie down. The atmosphere in the two boats was one of glum expectancy: very soon they would know the worst. A gentle south-east breeze, a low swell and a slight sea meant that progress towards the island must bring them within striking distance soon – but only if their heading was right. Boundy's noon sight disclosed a day's run of 50 miles, leaving, by his estimate, 66 miles to go.

Many expected to do no more than hold on until those miles

were covered; they would not survive another disappointment. Allan Tempest, like several others, was feverish, and in his delirium he recited chunks not only from his studies but also from his sub-conscious: he was explaining how to play croquet, and quoting 'Page five paragraph six' of some croquet manual, although he had never played croquet in his life. At noon he was in a blacked-out Tube train, his ear-drums reacting to the displacement of air in the tunnel; next moment he was seeing all the colours of the rainbow. Quantrill tried a left hook to the jaw, as Silcock had done with Dieckhaus, and Tempest came to. Quantrill gave him sal volatile, pushed him forward near the mast amongst the Asians, and gave him an extra dipper of water.

Gladys Usher was most worried about Francis McQuone. She feared he was dying. Shenton, too, looked unlikely to last. This man who had helped so energetically with the bailing was at the end of his strength. Soon he fell from the bench beside her into the bottom of the boat, and no one could move him. Freda Bullen, so stoical and uncomplaining, was also distressingly weak, and Gladys Usher sat with the twins on her lap. There was very little brandy left but the few drops that remained were given to Shenton and McQuone.

In Boundy's boat a worrying casualty was Bob Skea. No one in either boat had taken so much out of himself. He had been on duty almost continuously and apart from an occasional doze had never slept. Until now his lean, wiry fitness and equable, puckish temperament had stood the strain, but now he became light-headed. Eventually Betty Birchman prevailed on him to lie down. Of the others, engineer Bob Gerner could no longer take a turn at the tiller. He too was nursed by Betty Birchman. His trick at the tiller was shared between Arnold Silcock and Billie Rooksby.

'If my calculations are correct,' announced Boundy that evening, 'we shall see St Helena tomorrow at dawn.' But he added, for the benefit of the few: 'I have based this on my watch in conjunction with Captain Rogerson's. Every minute fast or slow corresponds to a difference of fifteen miles. But there's high ground on St Helena going up to nearly three thousand feet. We must look out for it in the morning.'

Few could believe their ordeal could be ending, and excitement was muted. Impatient to prove or disprove Boundy's forecast, they urged him to start the engine. But Boundy refused. 'If I take you in tow tonight,' he told Rogerson, 'we might pass the island in darkness. I suggest we continue under sail, without tying up but taking care to keep in contact. We've no torches left now.' Rogerson agreed. Passing the island without sighting it was his greatest fear.

At dusk three birds flew past, and Jim Chapman, an amateur ornithologist, gave Boundy qualified support. 'We can't be more than a hundred miles from the island.'

Pierre Jaspar was one who had confidence in Boundy and felt immensely reassured. Without some such fillip he felt he couldn't have lasted. But the stimulus came too late for one of the best-loved of the *Cairo*'s crew. *'Purser McQuone passed away during the night,'* recorded Stubbs in his log. *'Body committed to the deep.'* If Boundy was right, McQuone had died when almost in sight of the island. He would never swallow the anchor now.

Unlike the corpses of the Indians, which sank quickly, McQuone's body floated on the surface, clearly visible in the moonlight. It was watched sadly by his shipmates until it drifted out of sight.

It was a beautiful night, calmer than it had been for days, and Gladys Usher, still with the twins on her lap and trying to keep them warm, felt the impersonal aspect of nature; it was a perfect night for a sail. Tomorrow they might all be saved, but in stark contrast was the untimely death of Mr McQuone.

Allan Tempest lay propped up on an oar against the bow thwart, at an angle of thirty degrees, head down in the bilges, feet over the gunwale. Someone threw a blanket over him, but then he fell into the bilges on top of the Indians. Unable to extricate himself, he sank lower and lower. When he tried to stand up the Indians pushed him down. He finished up sitting in six inches of filthy bilge-water, and he actually slept for a time. He awoke to see McQuone's body being put overboard.

During the night both Rogerson and Boundy fired flares, partly to keep in touch with each other and partly in the hope that they might be seen by short-range patrols from the island. Then towards morning they saw what looked like Very lights on the horizon *to the south*. Could they have passed the island already?

It was a searching test of Boundy's self-confidence, but he refused to panic. St Helena, he insisted, lay to the north. 'They're British recognition lights,' said a woman's voice in Rogerson's boat, and Rogerson broke in at once. 'Who said that?' The answer came from Sybil Chapman. 'It's Mrs Chapman speaking. I know they're recognition lights. I've seen them before.' Half a lifetime in British India had educated her in such matters. But Rogerson was dubious. They could be lights fired by one of the boats left behind, trying to make contact; or they could come from an enemy vessel. 'Keep your eyes open and your heads down,' he said. 'It may be a German submarine.'

The flares had not come from an enemy vessel. They had been fired from George Nutter's boat, No. 6, which was still trailing the leaders.

Nutter and Chambers remained uncertain whether or not they had missed their landfall. For them this thirteenth night, for all its moonlit beauty, was the darkest so far. When daylight came they would have to reconsider their strategy. Somewhere they must have gone wrong; they had nothing to fix their position, but they believed they should have seen St Helena by now. Tomorrow if they failed to sight the island they would have to make an informed guess at a new course to steer. So much depended on this decision that Nutter began to think in terms of a consensus, explaining the situation, perhaps recommending a course of action and putting it to the vote.

This would be the last night, too, on which they could sail: the lifejacket batteries were exhausted. Nutter was using his torch for a periodic check on the compass, but the strain on Vic Chambers was becoming insupportable. They would have to ride to a sea anchor at night, sailing only in daylight.

A babble of angry voices interrupted his reverie. Some of the Europeans had been tapping one of the casks, and the Asians had seen them. With an ugly fracas developing, Nutter saw that his only chance of acting justly and seeming to do so was to issue an extra ration all round. Once the Asians realized this they were mollified.

In this boat, too, several people were suffering from a form of delirium. Violet Williams' parents were among them, and during the night her father, resigning himself to his own and his wife's demise, sought Nutter's protection for his daughter. 'Look after her for us, won't you?' he murmured, and he handed Nutter a slip of paper. Nutter put it in his pocket without looking at it, thinking perhaps it was an address. Later he discovered it was a £1 note. Clearly Williams had been rambling, and the tactful Nutter decided not to embarrass him by returning it. Plenty of time to do so if they were rescued.

If they were rescued. There had been no organized prayer in Nutter's boat, but during the night he heard some of the most profane characters punctuating their curses with prayers.

At precisely 04.30 that morning the Russian journalist Vassili Kariakin shouted that there was something on the horizon, at no great distance. To Nutter it looked like a freighter, and at once he began flashing with the torch he had saved for this moment. *'SOS Help. SOS Help.'* Others were feverishly preparing the two remaining flares, while everyone prayed that this time there were no duds. Fervent thanks were offered to God when they both produced star shells and thick clouds of smoke. These pyrotechnics, they knew, were their last throw.

These were the flares that were seen and identified by Sybil Chapman. But had they been seen by the freighter?

On board the *SS Clan Alpine, en route* for St Helena, the chief officer reported to the captain that a morse lamp was flashing 'SOS Help.' Then he saw the flares. Meanwhile Nutter was signalling in more detail. 'SOS ex *City of Cairo*, torpedoed 6th November, 50 people here, will you help us?'

Captain Charles W. Banbury, master of the *Clan Alpine*, was a cautious man. The message might be a decoy. He was inclined to accept it, and he sent a single flash of his Aldis lamp in acknowledgement; but for safety he decided to circle till dawn.

For the next thirty minutes the occupants of Boat 6 were almost choked with suspense. The question 'Have they seen us?' was asked again and again. At dawn, in a tidal wave of emotion, they saw the freighter steaming towards them, and they hugged each other and cried with an inexpressible joy. They were saved!

'Ship ahoy! Ship ahoy!'

While waiting for the ship to come in close they treated themselves to a supplementary ration of water. Of his 36 gallons of water, Nutter found he had about six gallons left.

'Stand by to come alongside. Please down sails.'

Making a lee for the lifeboat, the *Clan Alpine* unfurled rope-ladders and manoeuvred skilfully into position, and efforts were made to get people aboard. Most were too weak even to be helped up the rope ladders, but fortunately the accommodation ladder had been rigged and this was lowered and rescue effected. Laughing and crying with relief, they were helped aboard, but even then they lacked the strength to stand unaided. When the lifeboat, too, had been lifted clear of the water, the *Clan Alpine* continued.

Hot tea was quickly provided as a thirst quencher and restorative, and Vic Chambers, gulping it greedily before letting it cool, scalded his mouth and throat. Oranges, which were part of the cargo, were generously distributed, and these were devoured almost whole.

'Where are you bound for?' they asked.

'St Helena.'

'St Helena! How far is it?'

The gesture that followed was almost dismissive. 'It's just over there.'

Just over there! So they had almost reached the island! 'When do we get there?'

'About noon. But you were lucky we saw you. We were about to change course for the island.'

In spite of Nutter's corrections to allow for the south-east trades, they had drifted marginally to the west. But the island was little more than 50 miles distant. With Diana's Peak, the highest point, rising to 2,685 feet, they would almost certainly have sighted it later that day or the following morning.

'There are other boats ahead of us,' Nutter told Captain Banbury. 'They may not all have reached the island. Will you be sure and look out for them?' His boat had been the first to lose touch, and he was unaware that there were two boats behind him: boats the *Clan Alpine* had not seen.

Among the survivors were Dulcie Kendall and Colin, Peggy Marr, the Williams family, Minnie Clark, George Blagrave-Dean, George Racher, Randolph Godlieb, and the Russians. Four Asians had died. Beds of a kind, in bunks and on benches and floors, were found for everyone, and they collapsed gratefully on to them, none sleeping more soundly than Vic Chambers and the sunblistered George Nutter.

In Boats 5 and 7, another sleepless night was terminated by a cold, leaden dawn, with clouds hanging low on the northern horizon. In that direction, fine on the starboard bow, some fancied they saw a faint blotch sandwiched between the grey of the cloud and the grey of the sea. It was the sort of speck they had seen a hundred times but which had always proved to be cloud. If the shape changed, as it always did, it was cloud. If it remained constant, it would be fairly safe to assume it was land.

For half an hour their gaze was riveted on the small black dot that they prayed might be their haven. As the light became stronger the long-sighted maintained that the outline was constant, and even the sceptical had to admit that the shape didn't seem to have changed. Standing at the mast, alternately looking away from the shape and then back to re-focus, was Douglas Quantrill. 'It might be cloud, it might be land,' he said, 'but I *think* it's land.'

Rogerson, roused from a doze, asked a single question. 'What shape is it? Has it got two peaks?'

Quantrill did not speak at first, and the seconds ticked away. Then his answer came in a hoarse crescendo. 'It has. . . . *It has!*'

Boundy in Boat 7 nodded agreement. 'I think that's the island.' For him, more than for anyone, it was a moment of triumph. Some raised a cheer, but many, having rehearsed this moment a thousand times, were too spent to rejoice. Pierre Jaspar, lips and tongue almost paralysed with thirst, spoke to his wife for the first time for three days. 'Janine – St Helena.' She did not raise her head.

Bob Skea dragged himself up to take a look and recognized Diana's Peak. Betty Birchman gave him a teaspoon of brandy to revive him and he was immediately drunk.

In a surge of exuberance they fired several flares, but with no reply from the island, Rogerson and Boundy were reluctant to issue more than a token celebratory ration of water. Land was still 30 miles distant, and there were known hazards ahead. Boundy, however, started his motor and took the captain's boat in tow, and although the wind was light, the silhouette of the island hardened perceptibly.

Two hours later, in the opposite direction, heading towards them from the south, they sighted a ship, and it was very soon plain that the ship had seen them. The irony, after thirteen days of distress, privation and death, of being presented with two chances of salvation simultaneously, struck them with such force that they almost doubted the reality of either. But amidst the tears of thankfulness neither Rogerson nor Boundy could any longer resist the clamour for water.

Quantrill, measuring out the water, found when he had finished that his own empty pemmican tin was missing. Seizing a catheta from his medical bag, he drank through that. It was the most marvellous drink he had ever had.

On the *Clan Alpine* the second officer was reporting that two more boats were in sight. The time was 08.20, just under four hours after the first sighting of George Nutter's flashlight S.O.S. By nine o'clock the ship was alongside Boat 7, taking aboard the Dieckhaus family, the Jaspars, the Davieses, the Rooksbys, the Dickeys, Betty Birchman, Arnold Silcock, Bob Gerner, Bob Skea (still half drunk), Leslie Mountain (now fully awake), Les Boundy and many others, among them fifteen Asians. Five had been lost.

Boundy was still wearing his striped pyjama jacket and service cap.

The most volatile of the children, in more ways than one, was Ferdy. Captain Banbury, having unwisely picked him up, set him down again rather more rapidly and went off to change his jacket.

Then it was the turn of Boat 5. As with Boat 7, many had to be assisted or carried up the accommodation ladder. Among these were Bert Shenton, John McFarland, Lawrence McGaffney, Allan Tempest, and Jim Chapman. The casualties in this boat were five Asians and two Europeans – Kate Richardson and Francis McQuone. The surviving women and children were Freda Bullen and the twins, Joan Redl and Qunk, Catherine McGaffney and her two daughters, Flossie Gavin and Sheila, Gladys Usher, and Cynthia Saunders. Others in good heart were George Waters, Bill Stubbs, Douglas Quantrill, and Captain Rogerson. '*These boats were also full,*' noted Captain Banbury in his log, '*and the people in them were slowly taken aboard.*' So, afterwards, were the lifeboats. Captain Banbury and his crew counted 150 survivors, '*the majority*', they noted, '*in a weak and emaciated condition.*'

The *Clan Alpine* was now so overloaded that the survivors from Boats 5 and 7 had to be accommodated on deck. They too were showered with oranges, and most people simply stuck their thumbs in them and sucked.

Of the 166 souls who had embarked in these three boats or been transferred to them subsequently, 16 had been lost, 14 Asians and two Europeans. 66 Asians and 84 Europeans had survived the ordeal. Everything possible was done for them on the *Clan Alpine*, but some were past saving, and during the morning two more Asians died.

'There are other boats on this ocean,' Boundy told Captain Banbury. 'We've got to round them up.' Banbury posted extra look-outs in the hope of sighting one or more of the missing boats, but nothing was seen.

Joan Redl, after staggering on board, was 'delivered into the hands of the ship's carpenter, who made me gloriously drunk on brandy and filled me up with the most wonderful oranges'. It was a pleasant surprise, too, to find that George Nutter's boat-load were already on board. The immensity of Nutter's achievement, superior even to that of Boundy (Nutter had had no sextant, no motor, no specialist navigator, no ship's officer, and no company for the last six days), was not fully appreciated until later.

By signalling the plight of the survivors visually from a distance, Captain Banbury ensured that, in addition to preparations for their reception being begun, a sizeable proportion of the three-thousand-odd islanders were on the quayside at the port of Jamestown to welcome them when, at 13.15, the *Clan Alpine* cast anchor off-shore. Simultaneously with her arrival an armada of small boats hurried alongside, and in a surprisingly short time the survivors were tendered ashore. The only hiccup came when Padre Davies's two children, Ann and Janet, their previous experience of small boats all too fresh in their minds, threw a tantrum and refused to budge from the ship. It was some time before they could be pacified. Few were able to walk unassisted, and those who tried found the ground rolling beneath their feet. They were taken to one or other of the two hospitals, one civil, one military, overlooking Jamestown harbour.

'All crews in boats were very distressed after thirteen days' exposure,' reported Captain Rogerson, and George Blagrave-Dean ('Ruggles') summed up their emaciation hoarsely but succinctly. 'When I tried to sit on the lavatory,' he said, 'all I had was a hole.'

Captain Rogerson estimated the distance covered by the two leading lifeboats as 670 miles. As for navigation, Boundy's calculations had been soundly based. 'My watch,' wrote Rogerson in his official report, 'previously set at G.M.T. and used for navigation, was 15 seconds out in a fortnight.'

The discovery that the jewellery stacked in the stern peak of Boat 5 by Captain Rogerson for safe keeping was missing led to an overt act of discrimination. The Asians, many of whom had been moved one at a time into the stern peak during the voyage to give the stern a better grip on the water, were searched before leaving the ship. Nothing was found. The Europeans were not subjected to this indignity.

In the civil hospital, the women were accommodated on the ground floor and the men on the first. Segregation however appears to have been lax, if attempted at all. Ferdinand and Avis Dieckhaus increased their family on 19th August 1943, nine months to the day after landing on St Helena.

Only a handful of the survivors were seriously ill, and most were discharged from hospital within a week and billeted in private homes and business accommodation in various parts of the island. Inevitably, though, there were some, like Francis McQuone before them, for whom rescue came too late. First to die, on the day after arrival, was the British India engineer Bert Shenton; he too had been an exemplary patient, but he had been desperately ill for those last few days. More of a shock was the sudden death of Lawrence McGaffney, the BP engineer from Abadan; he was sitting up in bed next to Pierre Jaspar, about to have a meal, when he collapsed. In the hospital, as in the boat, they hadn't realized how ill he was.

How was it that the hospitals were able to cope with the unscheduled arrival of 148 survivors? According to Mona Rooksby, for many months the Governor's wife had been pleading with the Commonwealth Office to send beds and bedding in case a ship was sunk near St Helena and survivors were landed. Finally the items were delivered by destroyer and volunteers carried out a 'dummy run' as an exercise, erecting the beds in the two hospitals. They were so exhausted afterwards that the dismantling was delayed for 48 hours. Next day the *Clan Alpine* arrived.

Janine Jaspar, visiting her husband in hospital, asked him: 'Why are you all grey?' Jaspar didn't understand the question until Janine handed him a mirror; his hair had changed colour. Jaspar survived, but two more Asians died. John McFarland, who had sat so long with Bert Shenton on the water-tank in Boat 5, had a leg amputated.

In the months that followed before repatriation was possible, the islanders, whose spartan lives were already aggravated by the problems of war transport, made sacrifices and showed a friendship which none of the survivors would ever forget, and in recognition of this the survivors clubbed together to present a memorial gift to the civil and military hospitals.[1] Long before these events, however – indeed on arrival – they suffered a shock which seemed incomprehensible. Nothing had been seen or heard of the group they had all envied so much – Chief Officer Sidney Britt and the occupants of Boat 1.

There had been 54 people in that boat when Britt set off on his own, and most of those who had reached the island had friends or acquaintances among them. Names recalled most readily included Dr Tasker, Tiny Watts, Angus MacDonald, Jack Edmead, Bob Ironside, Marshall Crichton, and the three women, Annie Crouch, Ada Taggart, and Diana Jarman. What could have happened to them? There were few who, dominated as they were on the island by Diana's Peak, did not think first and foremost of Diana.

Then there was Knocker Whyte's boat (Boat 4), and Tommy Green's (Boat 8). News of the latter, at least, was forthcoming.

[1] See Appendices I and II.

CHAPTER 11

An Answer to Prayer

On the thirteenth night, forerunner of the thirteenth day, the wind assaulted Tommy Green's group in Boat 8 in icy, spume-laden gusts, and they huddled together for protection and warmth. 200 miles from St Helena, and 150 miles behind the straggler of the first three boats, they were caught in a squall too far south to be visible to the leaders. In the darkness and confusion the rolling of the boat forced them to reef in the sail, and the oars had to be manned to maintain the boat's heading into wind. Exhausted by their endeavours, which increased their thirst, they were further disheartened by a chill, sunless dawn.

A growing awareness of the remoteness of rescue rendered faces pale and downcast. The children too were affected by the general malaise, and the grown-ups guiltily avoided their gaze. Eyes that had become bulbous in emaciated faces seemed already to contemplate death. Such was their corporate weakness that instead of waiting until eight o'clock to issue the morning's rations, Tommy Green decided to break with routine and distribute them straight away. The enamel dipper was filled and passed from hand to hand, the drips from the dipper as it emerged from the bung-holes being caught and preserved, as had become customary, for the cat. Faces brightened, but only Donald Miller displayed any real buoyancy. 'My shoes!' he said. 'Give me my shoes! Didn't I say I'd need them today?'

His salt-bleached shoes were handed up to him, and he was lacing them up, soon after eight o'clock that morning, when a shout came from the bows.

'A ship! A ship!'

Those in the bows had a clear view of a vessel steaming towards them on an opposite course, but in the stern the view forward was blocked by the sail and they couldn't believe it was true. Mary Simms, in the after-well with the other children, was about to take a sip from her pemmican tin when the hubbub reached her, but the pressure of people struggling to their feet above her and fighting to get a glimpse forward was at first impenetrable. Had they been seen? Hastily Evelyn Ashdown produced matches, and while those in the bows hardly dared breathe in case the ship turned away, Green prepared to fire flares.

'She's coming! She's coming!'

The vessel that was approaching was the 8,500-ton *Bendoran*, an old coal-driven cargo carrier of the Ben Line which would have been scrapped before this but for war losses in the company's fleet. She had started out from Scotland for Simon's Bay, Cape Town, in convoy seven weeks earlier, but through mechanical trouble she had fallen behind. Her master, Captain William C. Wilson, was scanning the object in the water through a telescope, focusing on what looked to him, from the brown skins of the occupants, like an African fishing vessel, presumably blown out to sea. The unlikelihood of this made him suspicious, but he concluded that they must be either Africans or Asiatics. Wary of diverting for what might be a decoy, he ordered the opposite action.

'She's turning away!' At this point Green fired the flares.

Without escort in dangerous waters, Captain Wilson's duty was not to hazard his ship. The Admiralty had given him a diversion that morning, so almost certainly there were U-boats about. Meanwhile some of the younger castaways in the after-well of the boat had wormed their way through to the top of the pile, and Captain Wilson was focusing not on the brown bodies of grown men but on children.

'She's turning back!'

Euphoria in Boat 8 thus coincided almost exactly with the rejoicing that same morning in Boats 5, 6 and 7. And it brought the same irresistible demands for water; they could drink their fill now with impunity. The remaining cask and a half were freely distributed, they recovered their voices, and they all talked at once, listening to no one yet conscious of the joyous cries of the children. But as the ship came nearer, and figures could be seen running about on deck, uneasiness returned. Were they British, or Dutch, or perhaps Scandinavian? Or were they German? Please God, don't let them be German.

Among the first to be reassured was May Almond. A round, rustic, rubicund face peering over the rail stood out from the others and convinced her it could only be British.

The rusted iron precipice of the ship's hull towered above them like a fortress, offering a temporary lee and, once negotiated, a permanent shelter. But first it presented a formidable barrier. As cadaverous oarsmen mustered the energy to row the boat alongside, ropes were secured and scrambling nets lowered. The entire ship's company had assembled to receive them, and a selected few hastened down the nets to their aid.

Yelling with excitement, some of the Indians could not resist swarming up the nets, and Green made a virtue of necessity by ordering them all to go first. Soon a stretcher was lowered for Scaife. Of the women the first to attempt the climb was Evelyn Ashdown. One of the ship's officers accompanied her to give her confidence, and she kept her gaze firmly fixed on the side of the ship at eye level, determined not to look down. When she reached the top she was too weak to climb over the rail, but a Scottish quartermaster lifted her over and carried her like a baby to the saloon, where she collapsed on the floor. 'She's fainted,' said Captain Wilson. 'What shall I do?' The middle-aged missionary waved an arm feebly and managed to say she was only giddy, and a Chinese steward brought her a mug of hot sweetened milky coffee. She had never tasted anything so delicious.

May Almond would have sworn she could never have been persuaded to climb a perpendicular ladder up a ship's side, even in her younger days, let alone a scrambling net. But if Evelyn Ashdown could do it at 54, so could she at 49. It was marvellous, she reflected afterwards, what one could do when death lay behind one and life lay ahead.

The children were carried up to the deck, but when they got there they begged to be allowed to walk. They wobbled so uncertainly that they had to be carried to the saloon. The crew had been about to have breakfast, and the eyes of the children widened at the feast that lay before them – which had to be quickly removed. 'The poor kids couldn't understand why we wouldn't let them drink deeply,' wrote the second wireless officer, a married Bristolian named Clifford Smith whose own child had been evacuated to Canada. 'They tried to grab the cups and cried in weak painful sobs which were enough to break your heart. I don't think I'm unduly tender-hearted but the sight of the saloon crowded with these pitifully grateful people was too much for me.'

After seven weeks without sight of land the crew of the *Bendoran* were stale and homesick, and the children were smothered with affection as a heaven-sent reminder of family life. Heaven-sent was an expression that was also applied to the rescue. 'I was given my courses all the way to the Cape before leaving Scotland,' Captain Wilson told them, 'and then last night we received a wireless message from the Admiralty to change our course. That's the only reason we came to cross your path.'

Clifford Smith noted: 'When you consider the chances against any ship meeting any boat in the Atlantic it must seem, as it did to us, a remarkable piece of luck, if nothing more, that we happened to be there at the time.'

Many believed that it *was* something more. The lifeboat, as the occupants now discovered, although maintaining a correct course, was still 200 miles short of St Helena. If they had ever reached it, few would have been left alive. The Admiralty knew nothing of the sinking of the *Cairo* until a claim was made in an enemy broadcast on 18th November (the previous day), no position was given, and they had no information on the progress or location of any lifeboats that might have got away. Neither, of course, had the crew of the *Bendoran*. 'But God knew,' wrote Donald Miller, remembering his spiritual experience of the previous evening, 'and in this mysterious way our prayer was answered.' May Almond wrote in similar vein. 'It was really a wonderful example, we all felt, of a direct answer to prayer.'

Those who preferred to believe in luck cited the feline company they had enjoyed, if that was the word – the boorish ginger tom. Didn't a cat have nine lives? They had been right to spare and nourish the cat, yet in the excitement of rescue he had been forgotten. The *Bendoran*, unlike the *Clan Alpine*, had no facilities for hoisting the lifeboat on board, but before the crew sank it by gunfire as a potential beguiler of shipping they returned briefly to rescue the cat. It proved as intractable as ever. All efforts to coax or entice it out of its hiding-place failed, Captain Wilson could hazard his ship no longer, and the involuntary instrument, as some conjectured, of both their shipwreck and their rescue was drowned in the craft in which he had first sought refuge from man. There was regret, but sadly few tears, for the unfortunate but unsociable ginger tom.

Lewis Scaife died that afternoon. He had been in great pain for much of the time, but he had borne his misfortune bravely. For the rest of them – 47 out of the original complement of 55 – it was mostly sleep for the next two days, in cabins vacated for them by the crew, with drink after drink in their waking moments. Then the children, fragile and with little sense of balance at first but with brains and tongues accelerating rapidly into top gear, explored the ship and were welcomed everywhere. They discussed the deaths of the Indians, the loss overboard of Daniel McNeill and the illness and death of Lewis Scaife in a disarmingly calm and matter-of-fact manner, entirely without the horror and bated breath which such tragedies might have been expected to inspire in a child's mind. Vivid as their impressions were, their attitude was that they had had an interesting and probably unique adventure, to be bragged about later to their friends, but certainly not to be worried about now they were rescued. These conclusions were faithfully recorded by Clifford Smith. Fond of children, and missing his own child 'like hell', he fell particularly for the saucer-eyed Mary Simms. 'It seemed to me', he wrote, 'that she realized exactly what her rescue meant and what might have been.' He didn't think any of the children would suffer permanent harm, though Francis Almond wrote to his father: 'We are still frightened of bumps and bangs.'

The distance they had covered with so much toil and tribulation over a total of 13½ days was encompassed by the *Bendoran* in a single day, and in less than a week they were back in Cape Town, where they were received with equal kindness. Captain Wilson noted that the women and children seemed to convalesce much more quickly than the men, several of whom had to be assisted ashore. Some had to go into hospital, among them Sir John Dain.

Evelyn Ashdown and Cecilia Norris picked no more flowers on Table Mountain, but they did renew acquaintance with their hosts of a month earlier, whose reaction when the two refugees told them they had no hope of a ship for another six weeks (according to the shipping agents) is not recorded. Cecilia Norris, though, didn't believe it; she had a premonition they would go *that day*. So she was not surprised when the telephone call reached them while they and their hosts were at lunch.

The survivors of No. 8 Lifeboat, split up into groups, faced many dangers and vicissitudes in their several voyages home, but they all got there safely. They had heard on the *Bendoran* that three other boats had reached St Helena, but of the other two they still had no news.

CHAPTER 12

It Began with a Quarrel

For Chief Officer Sidney Britt and his complement of 54 (31 Asians and 23 Europeans) in Boat 1, the pioneering venture they had undertaken acted as a stimulant. No longer would they have to mark time with mounting impatience as other boats slowed them down or brought them to a halt. They were the outriders, with responsibility not only for themselves but also for sending help from St Helena for the unfortunate laggards behind. For Britt, as for several others, the adrenalin flowed.

Their first night alone, the night of Wednesday 11th/12th November, was the night when a rising wind brought tempestuous seas and the boats behind, nearly torn apart and in constant danger of collision, were finally forced to slip their connecting warps – the night of the sea anchors. Britt, too, put out a sea anchor, while several took turns to steady the boat's heading with a steering oar. Three times during the night gigantic breakers almost engulfed them, and being so deeply loaded they were perpetually soaked to the skin. 'Keep bailing!' shouted Britt, and although there were eager helpers, some ignored Britt's remonstrance that there were no passengers in a lifeboat and left the bulk of the work to the few.

'Boy – bring me coffee!'

There were others whose lack of response to Britt's urgings was traceable to injury or sickness, among them Ada Taggart and Bob Ironside. To add to their number was Burma Oil Company doctor Ronald Tasker, who was failing both mentally and physically and had temporarily lost orientation. As a measure of his befuddlement, he had opened the first-aid box in search of drugs and drunk from a bottle of iodine, which was hardly likely to improve his condition. That evening his voice tailed away to a murmur, but during the night, his power of speech returning, he called loudly for coffee, and later for beer. With the recovery of his voice he became more physically active, but at first his restlessness was put down to the discomfort and insomnia that plagued them all. Then quartermaster Angus MacDonald noticed him trying to fit a piece of cloth over a rip in his trousers.

Surreptitiously, as MacDonald discovered, the doctor had cut a piece of cloth from the trouser leg of engine-room storekeeper Frank Stobbart while the latter was dozing, and he was trying to use this to patch his own. Stobbart had woken up and noticed the incision, and although he had not yet discovered the culprit, he was bent on making an example of him when he did. Before the tragi-comedy could develop into a punch-up or worse, MacDonald pacified the doctor, took away his knife – it was a small silver knife with a whisky advertisement on the side – and returned the patch to the aggrieved Stobbart, promising to sew it back for him next day.

As understanding returned, the doctor apologized and asked for water, and Britt told Jack Edmead, whom he had put in charge of the rations, to give him a small extra measure.

As in other boats, the majority of Britt's Asians were cooks, stewards and cabin staff, and they were no more capable as seamen than their fellows. Britt's compassion towards Dr Tasker did not escape them. 'Pani, sahib, pani, sahib,' they chorused; but Britt was lucky in having as one of his stalwarts the old engine-room serang Budroodin Baba, from Ratnagiri, on the coast 130 miles south of Bombay. Although 61, he was strong and active, and he got the best out of the Lascar seamen, encouraging them or keeping them quiescent as necessary. He had as his chief lieutenant a fireman from Zanzibar who was almost as good.

By noon next day the wind had abated, MacDonald reset the sails, and they resumed their northerly course, the navigation being in the hands of Britt and a 44-year-old master mariner named Thomas McCall, captain of a cable-laying ship operated by Cable and Wireless. Well clear of the other boats now, they confidently expected to sight St Helena within five or six days.

Nevertheless, believing that their S.O.S. had been acknowledged, they still thought they might see some sign of a rescue ship or reconnaissance plane, and one man was always posted as look-out.

That night Dr Tasker slumped heavily against MacDonald, who sensed at once he was dead. At dawn Britt recited the Lord's Prayer and they lifted his body overboard. They had nothing with which to weight it, and as the body floated face down just below the surface the sharks converged. This was the first death in Britt's boat and the unexpectedness of it cast a gloom over them all. Furtively they glanced at each other. They knew the doctor was ailing, but they had not suspected for one moment that he might die. The fact that death could come so quickly and so stealthily doubled the shock. They wondered nervously who might be next.

Later that day MacDonald crawled aft to have a yarn with his injured shipmate Bob Ironside. Ironside, from Aberdeen, was 30, about the same age as MacDonald, but whereas MacDonald was a confirmed bachelor Ironside had recently married and had the added anxiety of a young baby. Finding that Ironside couldn't sit up, MacDonald feared he had seriously damaged his spine. 'Do you think we've got a chance, Angus?' asked Ironside, and MacDonald was reassuring. 'Of course we have. Everything will be all right, Bob, and we'll get you to hospital. Either we'll get to St Helena or we'll be picked up beforehand.'

Continuous bailing was still necessary, but under Britt's confident leadership all tasks were enthusiastically undertaken and the climate of optimism and expectancy that their lone voyage had begun with prevailed. But on their fifth day alone – the tenth since the sinking – for no obvious reason the atmosphere changed.

It began with a quarrel between Britt and MacDonald. Britt was setting the course to steer daily in consultation with McCall, and once or twice MacDonald, who had been responsible for the sails and running gear from the start, suggested, from his station in the bows, an additional correction to starboard to compensate for the westerly drift. To MacDonald's astonishment Britt bridled at his interference. Normally these two men understood and admired each other, MacDonald especially almost hero-worshipping Britt as the kind of man he would like to have been. But a clash between Britt's autocratic self-assurance and MacDonald's dour obduracy was perhaps always conceivable.

Britt was giving his orders in a peremptory manner, understandable when he was dealing with the less co-operative amongst his complement but inappropriate to MacDonald. Jack Edmead, although loyal to Britt, and aware of the strain he must be under, sympathized with MacDonald. Britt needed to be tough, especially with anyone prepared to argue, but MacDonald was his right-hand man, and anything MacDonald had to say should surely be given consideration.

Britt, perhaps, feared a loss of control; navigation by committee would be fatal. He became more and more imperious and unapproachable, and when he began reorganizing the watches MacDonald, who had arranged them, lost patience. 'I've had enough of you, Britt,' he muttered, but Britt heard him and responded with a threat. 'I'll get you, MacDonald, when we get ashore.'

From noon until six o'clock that evening the sun beat down relentlessly and with no wind it was impossible to keep cool. Tempers under these conditions were easily lost. Edmead tore up an old flag and distributed a scrap to everyone who lacked a head covering, but the relief was minimal, and several people showed symptoms of sunstroke. In the flat calm MacDonald lowered the sails and took up an oar. Among those still strong enough to row with him were serang Budroodin Baba, the fireman from Zanzibar, Jack Edmead, and the indefatigable Londoner Tiny Watts. They made little headway but it was something. MacDonald, for one, was determined to keep fit for whatever ordeal lay ahead; but there were some who saw the rowing as futile, and an admission of failure.

'Shouldn't we have seen the island by now?'

This, towards the end of that debilitating tenth day, was the question in everyone's mind, and it was inevitable that someone should voice it. Many of the passengers, not to mention other members of the *Cairo*'s crew, held strong views on the correctness of the course computed by Britt and McCall. In the absence of a sextant the heading could only be a matter of guesswork, and conjecture was rife. Those who were dissatisfied could not even agree amongst themselves, and an acrimonious discussion developed.

'Britt said we'd see the island in four or five days.' He had actually said five or six.

'The quartermaster was right. We're on the wrong course. I've said so all along.'

'What happens if we overrun St Helena? Where do we end up then?'

'Maybe we've overrun it already.' This was the dominant fear.

'The moment there was any doubt we should have turned back and joined the other boats.'

'The other boats? They're probably there by now.'

As the calumnies and recriminations multiplied, the disaffected conveniently forgot their own part in the unanimous decision to go it alone.

'The captain said we'd never find St Helena without a sextant.'

'We should have stuck together.'

'It was madness to charge off on our own.'

The accusing finger was pointed at one man: Sidney Britt. No one could guess that Britt had been right in anticipating a general fragmentation, and that they might in any case have finished up on their own. From being the most popular man on the *Cairo,* Britt faced something very near universal opprobrium. Despite their differences, MacDonald was not having this, and he spoke up at once, regarding denunciations of Britt and his leadership as despicable, especially when they came from men who had done little or nothing to help. 'Mr Britt's in charge here,' he reminded them. 'If you want to get to St Helena you'd better lend a hand. Look at Diana! She's been at the tiller for the last three hours, while some of you sit there like dummies. Are you going to let a girl show you up?'

It was not only the Europeans who were dispirited. The Asians were equally despondent. All that day, besides praying to Allah, they kept up a continual chant of 'Pani, sahib, pani, sahib,' and there was little Budroodin Baba could do to quieten them. Some of them, as in other boats, had begun to drink sea water, which aggravated their thirst. One was delirious, and Diana, who did most of the nursing, could do nothing for him. Yet they were all dismayed when they found, on the eleventh morning, that he had died in the night. Lacking any comparison with experience in other boats, they imagined that their losses were unique.

The Indians were especially troublesome at night, when they clustered together for warmth in what Edmead called 'bundles of ten', de-stabilizing the boat. Exhortations to break it up were in vain. 'Do as the sahib tells you,' implored banker Marshall Crichton. One of the kindest of men, he had spent 34 years in India and spoke their language. 'You'll capsize the boat if you don't.' Some of them moved, but eventually Edmead had to go amongst them and pull them apart, while MacDonald did the same in the bows. To improve stabilization MacDonald dispensed with the main sail and used only the jib sail forward, and this helped to keep the boat's head into wind.

That night was the coldest so far, and next morning the bodies of three more of the Indian crew were found in the sludge at the bottom of the boat. Why was this happening to them? It seemed like some kind of visitation. Budroodin Baba, his gnarled frame suggesting a greater age than the 61 years he admitted to, said a prayer for them and Watts helped MacDonald heave their bodies overboard.

Ada Taggart, the sick stewardess who had written so hopefully from Durban to her sister in Montrose, had been lying day after day in the same position, and her back was a mass of sores. Diana had nothing to dress them with except salt water, and although she applied this frequently the sores were beginning to fester. Tiny Watts seemed to know more about first aid than anyone, but he and Diana could do no more than pad her round with discarded lifejackets to make her comfortable. On the twelfth night she slid down into the bottom of the boat, as everyone seemed to do as they got weaker. There her limbs became entangled with those of a male passenger named Basil Watkins-Ball, a 28-year-old railway engineer from Calcutta. When Mac-

Donald straightened them out next morning both were dead.

Two more Indians died that night, and when they were buried at daybreak the sharks turned up in shoals, agitating the sea into a maelstrom as they writhed amongst the bodies. Even this ghastly spectacle did not rouse some from their lethargy. One young engineer sat with his head drooped on his chest, the picture of resignation and misery. 'Pull yourself together!' urged MacDonald. 'You're young and strong – don't you want to live?'

'I don't care – leave me alone.'

'Take a lesson from Diana. Look at her – not half your strength! You ought to be ashamed, giving in like this. If you don't want to be tomorrow's breakfast for the sharks you'd better snap out of it.'

MacDonald's sermonizing had some effect. 'All right Angus – you win.' For an hour the lad helped with the bailing, but by nightfall he had withdrawn again into his shell.

Appetites for the unpalatable rations, mostly ship's biscuits and pemmican, had long since faded, and the water situation became graver daily, but no one was yet dying from hunger or thirst. The enemy, as in other boats, was exposure, coupled with an insidious moral malaise. People of all races simply lost heart and gave up.

Apart from the sick and injured, the first of the Europeans to show signs of failing were those who had done least to help. Edmead thought these infirmities were a question of cause and effect. Probably these people had suffered more than others when they were thrown into the water. MacDonald's conclusions were less charitable, but his chief concern was the leadership. Britt's attempt to ride roughshod over a trusted quartermaster was so uncharacteristic that it suggested some inner conflict. If Britt of all people began to have doubts they were lost. In an effort to bolster Britt's confidence, MacDonald appealed again to the Europeans to back him up.

Annie Crouch, the stewardess who had gone back to sea at 64 to escape the bombing, had more excuse than most, with her injured leg, for despondency. But she was holding up well. MacDonald kept an eye on her, and several times he lifted her out of the well of the boat, where she was sitting in water, and propped her up in a dry spot in the bows. She was always apologetic, just as she had been over her brandy and soda, but she persistently slipped down again, and her feet and legs became so swollen that MacDonald knew she could not last. Her death on the thirteenth day left Diana the only woman in the boat. Diana was as energetic as ever, helping others where she could but spending most of her time at the tiller, where she had become expert at steering a course.

Jack Edmead was keeping a diary of events, and he and MacDonald relieved the dead bodies of their effects before burial and recorded them, Diana keeping all they collected in her emergency bag in the stern. Edmead, lacking MacDonald's pre-occupation with sailing the boat, learned to live within himself, using his own thoughts and fantasies to keep him going. He noted a peculiar circumstance about the burial of the women as opposed to the men, one that he puzzled over for days. Whereas the bodies of the women floated face uppermost, the men turned on their fronts.

This was the day – Thursday 19th November – on which four of the *Cairo*'s boats were picked up, with close on 200 survivors; but in Britt's boat they knew nothing of this. Nevertheless, they were tormented by the thought that the other boats, emulating the tortoise as opposed to the hare, must by now have reached port.

MacDonald continued to perform his duties with his usual taciturn efficiency, but his concern for the leadership – and the navigation – grew. Twice he caught Britt mumbling absent-mindedly to himself, and when MacDonald asked him a question about the course he answered in a vague and perfunctory manner. Britt, like Rogerson, had been dragged down with the ship, and MacDonald feared that the experience of being half-drowned, coupled with the terrible responsibility he had assumed in Boat 1, had affected his mind. This, if it were so, would be the worst catastrophe of all.

Next day Britt was unable to sit up, but he retained control of the navigation, and he was punctilious in maintaining a log of their progress. He was laid alongside Bob Ironside in the stern, where

MacDonald visited him. Edmead gave Britt an extra ration of water in the hope he would soon recover.

Meanwhile MacDonald was questioned by Bob Ironside. 'Do you think there's still a chance, Angus?'

'Of course there is. Don't you be giving up hope, Bob. We'll be home soon enough.'

'I can't hold out much longer, Angus. Will you take off my ring and send it home to my wife? That's if you get back?'

'Of course I will, Bob. But we *will* get back. Both of us.' MacDonald did not give the ring to Diana but stored it carefully in his pocket, making himself personally responsible for it.

Both Britt and Ironside seemed perfectly rational that evening. But during the night, in a demented state, they turned on each other. Too weak to raise themselves even into a sitting position, they fought at full stretch, the only destructive weapons available to them being their teeth. Neither man knew what he was doing, but next morning their faces were covered in blood. Diana cleansed the bites in salt water, and the two men were separated. Responsibility for the navigation passed to Captain McCall.

As though the collapse of Sidney Britt were not shocking enough, MacDonald was further depressed next morning to find that Tiny Watts, his right-hand man in the bows, was dead. Watts hadn't complained of any illness and overnight had seemed as strong and as willing as ever. His death held disturbing implications for them all. It wasn't only those who gave up who died.

'Pani, sahib, pani, sahib.'

There were seven corpses in the boat that morning, five Asians and two Europeans (storekeeper Stobbart was the second), and they had to dispose of the bodies. But instinct had drawn the dying men to seek what privacy and security they could in the deepest and most sheltered parts of the boat. Lifting them out, first on to the thwarts, then the gunwales, and finally toppling them over, was almost beyond the strength of those remaining. Several times during this grisly operation MacDonald and others had to stop and lie down.

Efforts to maintain a proper reverence deteriorated into blasphemous curses as bodies stubbornly resisted their shaky manhandling, sliding back off thwarts and gunwales in maddening convulsions. Ridding themselves of the mourned but massive frame of Tiny Watts left them totally exhausted.

Of the able-bodied Europeans remaining, most were in their forties and fifties, and a powerful man like Tiny Watts was irreplaceable. The same could be said of Britt; but at dawn on the fifteenth morning both he and Bob Ironside were dead. Captain McCall remained at the tiller with Diana, but he too was failing, and that night he died, leaving no one with any navigational qualifications in the boat.

Captain Rogerson and the leaders of the other boats had all feared that another two or three days adrift would have brought many more deaths, and in Boat 1 the truth of this apprehension was being tragically proved. Three more Europeans died that night, among them the banker Marshall Crichton, and three more dead Lascars brought the total for burial to eight. The task was almost too much for the remainder, and with their diminishing numbers the time was approaching when it might be more than they could manage to dispose of their dead.

Sorting through the effects of the men who had died, the survivors emptied the pockets of a patent waistcoat of Marshall Crichton's which contained many personal treasures. Among them was a representation in jade of the three wise monkeys – see no evil, hear no evil, speak no evil – an ornament, and a philosophy, that the kindly banker had valued. There was also a silver brandy flask, disappointingly empty. All the items were put with the other valuables in Diana's bag.

Reduced in numbers to less than half, they needed a new leader. The survivors, recognizing MacDonald as a man apart, uncommunicative but selfless and dedicated, voted that he take over command and try even at this late stage to get them to St Helena.

The normally imperturbable MacDonald was appalled at the situation that confronted him. On checking through Britt's papers he found that the estimated distances for each day's run, the courses steered, and the computed positions reached had been meticulously entered up to the tenth day. After that they tailed off until they became a mass of indecipherable scribbles and symbols. McCall had done no better. In taking over the navigation, MacDonald was starting from an unknown point.

Next he consulted Edmead on the water supply, to find that none of the tanks had proper gauges but that Edmead reckoned they had sufficient for only a few more days. Nothing but rain or early rescue could save them. MacDonald decided to cut down the ration to a single issue daily, one tablespoon each night after sundown.

There were plenty of biscuits and malted milk tablets, but the lack of lubrication made swallowing or dissolving them impossible. The biscuits could only be ground into a waxen powder which slowly poured out of the corner of the mouth, while people with dentures suffered agonies of discomfort as biscuits and tablets stuck in a doughy mess to their teeth. Nearly everyone had a sore throat. Some gargled with sea water, others tried a mixture of salt water and iodine from the first-aid kit, but the soreness only got worse.

The condition of the Indians was pitiful, and one of the firemen, calling to Edmead in a harsh croak, said he would throw himself overboard if he wasn't given more water. Edmead resisted, as he was bound to do, and the man made good his threat. Whenever bodies were tipped overboard the sharks thrashed around them, but Edmead had not actually seen them devour corpses. The fireman omitted to take off his lifejacket, those who remained did not have the strength to turn the boat round to recover him, and in a flurry of turbulence the sharks got him before he could drown.

As the boat steadily regurgitated its human cargo it grew lighter and rode higher, raising more of the planking – and therefore more of the leaks – above the waterline. This brought a noticeable loss of stability, but although they still had to bail regularly the boat was much drier. It was also more comfortable, and at least they could sleep.

In the middle of the seventeenth night MacDonald awoke to find that the boat was steady and still, its stability miraculously restored. Then he heard a shout from Diana at the far end of the boat. 'What's happening? We're full of water.'

Jumping up to investigate, MacDonald found that the boat was half full of water. Edmead, sitting amidships, could see the plug-hole glittering beneath him like a phosphorescent blue light, and he too shouted to MacDonald. Somehow the plug must have come out. Or could someone have removed it? A man was lying half-immersed near the plug-hole but he was taking no interest in the flooding.

MacDonald found a spare plug and inserted it, then set to work with Edmead and others to bail the boat out. When they had reduced the level sufficiently they went back to sleep. Half an hour later the boat began filling again, and this time MacDonald was sure someone must have removed the plug.

He found the missing plug and reinserted it, then lay back with one eye open. Sure enough, after a few minutes he saw a hand reach down and grope for the plug. He grasped the hand and traced it to its source. It belonged to a young European.

'What the hell do you think you're doing?'

Meeting the man's gaze in the half-light, MacDonald saw his eyes glint with a cunning that bordered on madness.

'Why shouldn't I? I'm going to die, so why not? We might as well all go together.'

MacDonald moved him to the fore part of the boat and the others took turns to watch him. Even then he managed to grab the first-aid box and throw it overboard. But this was his last gesture of destruction, and on the nineteenth day he died.

There was not much talk as the days passed, but such as it was it ceased abruptly each evening when Edmead issued the water ration. In complete silence it was possible to gauge, from the hollow sound as the dipper clattered against the sides of the tank, the level of the water. As their last tank began to empty, Edmead wrapped lifejackets round the tank to muffle the sound.

At the end of that third week there were only eight left alive of the 54 who had set out with Britt. All were robust types, either physically or mentally or both, though now they were bearded and haggard. There were four members of the *Cairo*'s crew – Mac-

Donald, Edmead, Budroodin Baba, and the fireman from Zanzibar. And there were four passengers, three men and Diana. The men were all middle-aged, even elderly. All had been working on contracts in India, and all were among those who had done what they could to help from the start. 'We'll stand you a champagne supper', they promised, 'when we get home.'

Jack Oakley, 57, powerfully built and remarkably fit for his age, was a bridge construction engineer from Birmingham; he had been engineer-in-charge of the construction of Calcutta's Howrah Bridge, the bridge across the Hooghly River. Bob Little, 61, from Hamilton in Lanarkshire, was the man who had saved Sybil Chapman during the sinking. Joe Green, from Wigan, the oldest of the three at 64, was a cotton mill manager. But for all Edmead's camouflage, they knew very well that the last tank was nearly empty and that they could hardly last out much longer. Rain seemed the only hope. They had lost count of the days, yet the fourth week advanced and all were alive.

One night, as they lay dozing, the boat lurched and cavorted as though in a storm. Yet the sea was like glass. MacDonald thought they had run aground, perhaps on an island, and he roused himself to find that a sizeable fish, three feet long and of substantial bulk, had landed in the boat and was thrashing about wildly in perplexity and fury. Grabbing an axe from its stowage, he swung it at the fish with the blunt side and delivered a few firm cracks to the head. Here was a heaven-sent meal, juicy and nutritious. But the skin of the fish was so unyielding that the axe rebounded as though bouncing off rubber.

During his frenzied efforts to quieten the fish MacDonald gashed a finger against the creature's teeth. But at last it lay still, and he tied a length of rope to its tail and suspended it from the mast. It was all he could do to lift it.

At daybreak he surveyed the catch and identified it as a dog-fish. He had heard of people drinking blood and he thought they might get some from the carcase. The flesh was incredibly tough, but he cut into it with Dr Tasker's knife and managed to extract a few teaspoonsful of viscous, reddish-black liquid. Then he cut a few slices of flesh and removed the liver and heart.

The others were awake now and although they were almost too weak to move they were impatient to try the meal MacDonald was preparing. He gave the first spoonful of blood to Diana but she spat it out. 'Horrible! It tastes horrible!' They all tried it in turn, but one by one they shuddered and grimaced. 'It's vile, it's vile!' MacDonald was the last to try it, but he could get very little of it down, and even having it in his mouth made his tongue swell. They chewed for a long time on the flesh, but few could swallow it and eventually they spat it out into the sea.

MacDonald's arm swelled up from the gash on the finger and Diana diagnosed blood poisoning. She herself was suffering from a throat so raw she had difficulty in speaking, and the first-aid box had gone, but she advised him what to do. 'Let your hand drag in the water.' After he had done this for about two hours she squeezed the wound and it suppurated freely. 'Now put your hand back in the water.' At intervals she squeezed his arm from the shoulder down and gradually the swelling subsided.

As the fourth week ended, the shipping company began notifying the next of kin of those missing. Meanwhile in Boat 1 they lost three more of their number – Jack Oakley, Bob Little and the Zanzibar fireman. All three kept up their courage to the end. Yet instinctively they lay at the last in the bottom of the boat, and it took the rest of them many hours, with breaks in between, to drag them up and roll them overboard. When they had finished and Edmead had issued the ration of water, it was more than he could do to mask the emptiness of the tank. There was scarcely one ration each remaining.

The deaths of these three men affected the five who survived them more deeply than any that had gone before. They had hoped and believed that they might all come through; yet still they hadn't lost hope altogether. Joe Green was incoherent at times, and the serang was barely conscious, but they still did what they could for each other. They bailed out the boat twice a day, and they drank the last of the water. They were all suffering from a thick, yellow catarrhal discharge, due, they thought, to continual dampness in the waterlogged boat. Even MacDonald was too feeble to contribute much towards their progress, and the sails were left down.

For days most of them had been throwing an occasional gulp of sea water down their parched throats and had felt none the worse for it. They had seen what had happened to those who overdid it, but soon there would be no alternative. Now, as they discussed how they might manage to keep alive, Diana came up with another idea.

'Let's spend a penny and drink it.'

They were all constipated, but they were still passing water regularly, and MacDonald volunteered to be the guinea pig. He urinated into a hand-bailer, then strained the muddy, repulsive liquid through a piece of cloth. He tried a mouthful, but he couldn't bring himself to swallow it. Immediately he felt his tongue swelling up and he thought it would choke him. He had to rinse his mouth out many times with sea water to take away the taste. No one else attempted it.

They still talked of rescue, and of the celebration they would have when they got home. But that night Joe Green told Edmead: 'You know, Jack, I'm afraid I'll never have that champagne supper with you. But I'll try to give you as little trouble as possible.' With that he dragged himself forward, wedged his emaciated body, still an appreciable weight, into the fork of the bows, and refused MacDonald's pleas to lie elsewhere in comfort. 'I won't last the night,' he said, 'and if I lie down there I'll finish up in the bilges and you'll never be able to lift me out.'

The life of the serang, too, was reduced to no more than a flicker, but his wasted body would give them less trouble. Next morning both these brave old men were dead.

There wasn't a drop of water left in any of the tanks and the three survivors lay in a state of limbo, drifting aimlessly, halfway between life and death. Diana moved to the bows because it was drier there. Edmead was amidships, and MacDonald was still at the mast, though all he was doing now was dreaming and hallucinating. In one vivid dream he was walking up the pierhead at Liverpool with Diana and Jack, and when he awoke he really believed it would happen. He related the dream to them and swore it could only mean that one day it must come true.

Twice MacDonald tried putting up the jib again, but they simply went round in circles and he took it down. For thirty days they had kept on sailing, in the direction of St Helena as they thought, but they knew now they must have gone past it. Yet every morning Edmead assured Diana they were bound to be picked up that day, and she would smile back at him and give him encouragement. 'We still have a chance if we could get some rain.'

Their dreams were mostly of water, of cool, translucent streams they had swum in as children, of cascades of foaming liquid, of jets of water sprayed around with reckless prodigality. So real were these dreams, too, that they believed them, waking up with a sense of physical joy.

'Rain! Rain!'

They only half-believed MacDonald's shout, but they roused themselves to discover that either they were still dreaming or rain was falling. Edmead was too feeble to react at first but Diana crawled back to help MacDonald spread the main-sail to catch the water, scarcely daring to believe that what was happening was real.

It was no more than a shower, but it was heavy, and they collected several pints in the main-sail and more in the hand-bailer and in tins, cracks and crevices. Careful not to waste a drop, they funnelled all they could into one of the tanks, then sucked the droplets from the sail and the woodwork. Everything was impregnated with salt, but they lapped up the moisture like nectar. They felt much better for the extra water, and MacDonald, with the aid of the massage oil, had his first bowel movement since the sinking.

Diana's throat was so swollen she could hardly swallow, but as water trickled down her throat the relief was intense. MacDonald mixed a solution of pemmican and water to restore their strength and they each managed a few spoonfuls. The two men showered in sea water in the well of the boat to reinvigorate themselves, then gave Diana a strip wash. Although speaking mostly in whispers, her voice was stronger and she still radiated the conviction that they would soon be picked up. She talked to them of her home in Hertfordshire, of seaside holidays at Hove as a schoolgirl, and of how she had played tennis and ridden horses in the country and would one day do so again. 'You must come down and visit us when all this is over,' she said.

They still had to ration their water, but for a day or so they drank more freely. Diana was better, but the two men were disappointed that their strength did not return. Edmead lay poised between sleeping and waking for most of the time, oblivious to whether it was day or night, and MacDonald, having set the jib again, found he still lacked the strength to handle the mainsail. Instead he spread it out and used it as a bed and had his best sleep for a month.

It was out of a similar sleep, shortly before dawn several days later, that Diana roused him.

'*Listen, listen. . . .*' The whisper, loud and breathy in his ear, reached him as though from the far end of a long corridor. 'Can you hear a plane?'

There was a noise like engines all right, and it did sound like a plane. Stumbling aft in the darkness, MacDonald grabbed one of the hand flares and ignited it. It blinded him completely as the flame pierced the dawn.

'All right – put that light out!'

Edmead, struggling to raise himself above the level of the gunwale, discerned the dim silhouette of a towering vessel not a hundred yards distant. The noise they had heard was her diesels.

'Can you come alongside?'

Were they still dreaming? Was it an illusion? Emotionally drained, they reacted mechanically. While Diana crawled to the tiller, MacDonald caught and held the line that was thrown and made it fast. But he had no strength to row. Edmead, although realising there was a ship very close, could do no more than lie back in the lifeboat and wait.

A pilot ladder was lowered, and two sailors came down to the boat. They fashioned a small rope sling in which Diana was hoisted aboard. MacDonald climbed up unaided, and then Edmead too went up in the sling.

Edmead's impression was that it was an American ship, but MacDonald recognized the Dutch flag painted across the hatch cover. That was good enough. All they cared about for the moment was a drink. They were given bottles of sugared water, but as they were drinking someone leaned over the side of the bridge – it looked like the captain – and called to them: *'Langsam! Langsam!'*

MacDonald understood the word perfectly; he had been apprenticed in Holland on leaving school and knew that the word, in Dutch as in German, meant 'slowly'. Drink slowly. But the word puzzled Edmead.

'This *is* an American ship, isn't it?'

'No. This is a German ship. But don't let that disturb you.'

The conflict of emotions that this aroused in MacDonald and Edmead was quickly resolved by the girl. 'It doesn't matter what nationality it is, so long as it's a ship!'

They were helped down to the doctor's cabin, where Diana was laid on a couch. The doctor began attending to her, and then the officer who had called to them from the bridge reappeared. 'I am Captain Jacobs. My ship is the *Rhakotis.* What happened to you? How long have you been in that lifeboat?'

MacDonald related how they had been torpedoed 480 miles south of St Helena on 6th November, and how they had set out to sail to the island. 'We must have been in the lifeboat over a month but we've lost all count of the days.' 'It's now December 12th,' said Captain Jacobs. So they'd been in the lifeboat 36 days. 'You've come a long way past St Helena. Five hundred miles to the north-west,' continued the German captain. 'But you'll be well looked after on the *Rhakotis*, and we shall put you ashore at our first port of call.'

Suddenly MacDonald remembered the bag of valuables. The ship was still stopped with the lifeboat alongside, and the crew were clearing it before sinking it as a hazard to shipping. MacDonald went back on deck with the chief officer to explain where the bag was hidden – behind one of the water-tanks. The bag was found and handed up and taken to Captain Jacobs. 'I'll put this in my safe,' he said.

MacDonald and Edmead were led away to be bathed by a medical attendant, and after being dressed in Japanese-style silk nightshirts and borrowed carpet slippers they were brought back to the doctor's cabin and given sweetened coffee and an injection. The two men were put to bed on couches while Diana slept in the bunk. 'Now we're going to turn the lights out and leave you to rest,' said the doctor. 'I'll come in again in about five hours' time.'

When they had gone Diana, with much of her old exuberance, bounced up and down on the springs of the bunk. 'This is better', she said, 'than lying in that wet boat!' But as they were soon to learn, the *Rhakotis*, a HAPAG freighter of 6,753 tons, was running the Allied blockade. She had set sail from Yokohama, Japan ten weeks earlier, on 27th September, and after loading at various Asian ports she had headed for home with one of the most valuable cargoes of the war.[1] It included 4,000 tons of rubber – enough to equip four armoured divisions with all their needs for a year – a substantial quantity of other goods in short supply, and a consignment of cultured pearls valued at 50,000 yen for the Japanese Embassy in Berlin, where it would be converted into foreign currency for war purchases. Altogether the cargo was worth six million marks.

The Germans would do all they could to protect the *Rhakotis* from enemy action, while the Allies, who were anticipating a blockade runner, though they did not know which, would do all they could to sink her. With more than 5,000 sea miles to cover before reaching the port of Bordeaux, the *Rhakotis* had no more than an even chance of escaping destruction.

[1] She had been stranded on the west coast of South America when the war started, and she had crossed the Pacific to Yokohama in June 1941 to be fitted out for a blockade-running attempt.

CHAPTER 13

Target Brazil

When the Australian Margaret Gordon returned to Jimmy 'Knocker' Whyte's boat from her brief sojourn in Boat 8, she was able, as she had expected, to perform many minor services for her companions that they wouldn't have bothered to do for themselves. She trailed their clothes over the side during the day to clean them before hanging them out to dry, and she made moccasins out of the canvas sail cover for men who had no shoes. She massaged their legs with whale oil, she used her cold cream to treat cases of sunburn, and with the aid of her mirror and Freddie Powell's comb they smartened themselves up to boost their morale.

Sparkie Humphries had a jaunty white cap to protect him from the sun, and Whyte had a pair of thick cotton underpants which covered his head and kept the sun off the back of his neck, but for the others Margaret made rakish, brigand-like hats out of the sail cover, sewing them with lengths of binder twine. Like Diana in Boat 1, she had to insist on being addressed informally. 'For heaven's sake call me Margaret.' Whereas Diana was the youngest in her boat, Margaret was the oldest, a year or so older than 'Solly' Solomon, the senior of the returning glider men, and although the other Europeans complied with her request, Knocker, the youngest, could not bring himself to do so. The result was that, through shyness, he did not give her a name at all.

The days were warm, without much wind, the water was crystal clear, they had seen no sharks for some time, and after posting look-outs they took turns to slip over the side in their underclothes, and they felt wonderfully refreshed, as though their bodies might have absorbed some of the moisture. This applied only to the Europeans, of whom there were seven: crew-members Knocker Whyte, Sparkie Humphries and engineer Bill Pirrie, and passengers Margaret Gordon, Solly Solomon, Bill McGregor and Freddie Powell. The Asians, of whom there were ten, showed no inclination to bath. While Whyte, McGregor and Pirrie, all of whom had small-boat experience, shared watches at the helm, the others provided eager hands to assist in bailing, rowing and adjusting the sails. They were exclusively a volunteer crew: all had come from other boats to help out.

The fact that they were now sailing alone seemed to have a demoralizing effect on the Indians. The rain they were all hoping for did not come, and under the day-long glare of the sun their thirsts became raging. Whyte was firmly opposed to the drinking of sea water, and he and Margaret did their best to stop the Indians, but as in other boats they were the first to succumb. Margaret felt extremely sorry for them, caught up in a war that few of them could understand, in a situation beyond their comprehension. 'Memsahib, where are we going?' they asked plaintively, and she tried to explain to them, in her halting Hindustani, that they expected to reach land soon. She did the same for them as for the Europeans, but she could not rouse more than a few of them from their submissive state. The most resilient were the captain's serang, two of the stewards, and a very old man with no teeth and no clothes who was the best of the lot. A fine seaman, he was always willing to row.

On Wednesday 18th November, on the eve of the safe arrival of the three boat-loads at St Helena, the first of the Indians died. After being comatose the previous day he became delirious during the night, and he died of what Whyte diagnosed as salt-water fever. His death seemed to take much of the stuffing out of the remainder. Another died after a similar sequence next day, and a third on the 20th. Yet their faith in the next world never faltered, and nor did their comradeship. Even when to the Europeans it seemed clear that life was extinct, the surviving Asians, many of them near death themselves, squandered their precious water ration in irrigating the mouths and nostrils of corpses in the vain hope of reviving them.

Diana Jarman.

Dulcie Kendall and Colin.

Eileen Simms, with Mary and Esther (left) and Lisa and David.

Five of the children who reached St Helena, still showing the effects of their experience. From left to right: Sheila Gavin, Michael Bullen, David Redl ("Qunk"), Ferdinand Diekhaus junior ("Ferdy") and Peter Bullen.

Dr Margaret Miller with one of the children at Purulia.

A group of survivors on St Helena. From left to right: (standing) Andy Green, Thomas Parkinson, Leslie Mountain, George Blagrave-Dean ("Ruggles"), Bob Skea, Charlie McKechnie; (middle row) George Nutter, Roland Dodds, Victor Chambers, Ted Elliott; (front row) John Cullinane, Allan Tempest, James Turner, Charlie Williams.

Whyte wished he could have shared their faith, but he couldn't bring himself even to pray. He hadn't prayed when things were going well and he didn't think it was fair to start now. He drew his strength from confidence in his stamina and seamanship. That short, stocky figure held physical reserves of which its owner, for one, was not unaware.

He was calculating the distance they travelled each day, and on 20th November he announced that if they were going to strike St Helena they should see it soon. Anxiously they scanned the northern horizon, but heavy clouds descending to sea level consistently baulked their view. Somewhere beyond that horizon lay the island, and they peered for it until their vision blurred. Even in moderate visibility they might be within a few miles of the island and not see it.

They had no means of knowing that three boats had already reached the island, but they imagined that most of them must have done so, and this gave them false hope. They could not know, either, that Captain Rogerson had discovered on landing on St Helena that sailing in the island's coastal waters was notoriously difficult and that there were no local craft available for a search. Bob Skea had put forward the theory – correct, as it happened – that Whyte had never received Boundy's change of course on the day he dropped out, and that it was possible to calculate from this where Whyte's boat might be. Boundy's boat with its engine might have been requisitioned for a search, but there was no one fit enough to man it.

Within a few days all Whyte's Asians were dead bar one. The exception was the captain's serang. It could not be long, Margaret realized, before there would be deaths among the Europeans, and she resolved to write down the name and address of her husband's relatives in Scotland and of her mother in Sandringham, Victoria, in case others survived and she didn't. She mentioned this and they all gave their names and addresses, from which she compiled a list. Sparkie had a 1941 diary, in which Margaret was already crossing off the days on the 1942 sheet. The diary had many blank pages, and Margaret tore one out and wrote down the eight names and addresses in pencil, no one possessing a pen. They kept the diary in a plastic bag to preserve it. All but one asked that if they were survived by someone else in the boat, someone should communicate with their next of kin and tell them what had happened. The exception was the bachelor Bill Pirrie; for him, notification of his death would be enough. In contrast, Humphries spoke freely of his mother in South Wales and his fiancée, a nurse called Sheelagh Bray who was working at a hospital in Wiltshire.

Next day their numbers were reduced to seven in a most poignant manner when the captain's serang, depressed at being the last of his race left alive, threw himself overboard. He had removed his lifejacket and he disappeared at once, drowning before they could reach him.

Whyte now faced a classic navigational dilemma: should he continue to search for St Helena, or should he cut his losses and aim for South America? For a young man of 25 it was an awful responsibility, and for two days, beating as much to the east as possible, and with a rota of look-outs standing at the mast, they kept up the search. Whyte still had his sketch map, on which he kept a plot, and like Rogerson he had a Rolex 'Oyster' which enabled him to work out his approximate longitude, though without a sextant he could not fix his position. His own inclination was to abandon the search and turn west, sailing with the wind for a coastline that although more than 1500 miles distant must eventually materialize if they could keep going long enough. Their water situation, although improved by the deaths of the Asians, would become desperate long before then, but surely in the meantime they would get some rain. Another point was that although they might never reach South America they would be sailing towards the shipping lanes rather than wandering about in the no-man's-land of the South Atlantic.

Some of the men, all older than Whyte, were inclined to argue; not all of them had adapted easily to Whyte's somewhat single-minded leadership. But, as the only deck officer present, his judgement on this issue could not be seriously challenged. On Monday 23rd November they gave up the search for the island and turned west-north-west for the bulge of South America.

If Whyte had a fault it was that he was not very good at explaining things and that he was inclined to be impatient of the ineptness of others. Perhaps because of his own expertise in small boats he was not very good at delegating. He could do everything himself so quickly and efficiently that he saved himself much time and trouble if he just got on with it. This left his companions with too little to do.

The exception to this was Margaret. Whyte was very unsure of himself in dealing with women. Leaving school at 16, he had concentrated all his energies on his career, and there had been few women in his life apart from his mother, a capable and accomplished person whom he worshipped. In Margaret, however, he had the perfect foil. There was no stronger character in the boat than Margaret, yet in what she accepted as a man's world she was prepared to be dominated by a man. She wasn't critical, as some of the men were, she didn't complain, she didn't answer back; she just did as she was told. Whyte did not find her any more approachable than he found most women, but he admired her for her composure and adaptability, and he found her, in his own vernacular, easy on the eye. More and more he came to rely on her.

As for Margaret, she had lost her husband and all her possessions. What more could happen to her? She had told Mona Rooksby that she didn't care whether she survived or not. But as a descendant of a long line of survivors, going back to the nineteenth-century immigrants to Australia, she retained an instinctive will to live. If Knocker thought they could get to South America she was going to give it a go. With nothing to lose, she wouldn't worry about anything except the task in hand.

Once the decision was taken there was no turning back. But some of the men, having done their mental arithmetic, began to grasp the immensity of the venture, and to lose heart. Even Whyte for a time seemed half-stunned at the prospect. But he soon roused himself to action. 'I'm going to sail this bloody boat to South America,' he swore to them, 'if I die in the attempt.' Some of his companions found the alternative too likely for comfort; but

Whyte was in his element, attempting something he had been trained for since boyhood.

Margaret kept the boat clean and tidy and attended as best she could to their domestic needs. Whyte's trousers were falling apart and Margaret had a needle, but she had no cotton thread so she tried sewing them together with a length of binder twine. The repair didn't last. The men spent all day making a spinner out of empty pemmican tins to catch fish, a variation to their diet that had consistently eluded them, but the only spare piece of rope they could find for a line proved to be rotten, and the first fish that bit took line, spinner and all.

McGregor and Pirrie were still taking turns at the tiller, but they were palpably weaker, as was Humphries, though he kept cheerful and gave no trouble. The other men kept asking for brandy and sal volatile, which Margaret felt was probably not good for them, but with Whyte's agreement she doled it out until it was gone. She kept the brandy in her own small bottle in case anything happened to Knocker.

'Do you think it would help if we drank our own urine?' one of them suggested. Margaret's answer was that since it was already a waste product of the body, she didn't think there was much point. Everyone was constipated, and this too worried some of them, but Margaret was again dismissive. 'We're existing on survival rations, which ought not to contain much waste material. No wonder we're constipated. It's nothing to worry about.'

Bill McGregor, after months in hospital on a liquid diet following multiple burns, suffered more than anyone from lack of fluid. The burned area, extending to the top of his thighs and over his back, as Margaret found when she massaged him, was only partially healed, and the cold nights were torture for him. Yet he resolutely refused to drink sea water. The boat was little more than a rowing boat, lacking the deep well of the lifeboats, but there was a small well aft of the stern thwart which was the warmest place in the boat. This was where the two Almond boys had slept before they were reunited with the rest of the family, and it was where Margaret slept now. McGregor joined her there to get some warmth, and they talked. She found him one of the most good-natured and sympathetic of men, and she fully understood why Diana had been attracted to him. He still talked of his 'wifey' and child back in Leith, but she feared very much he wouldn't last long enough to return to them.

Another man who had scarcely had time to recuperate, in his case from the effects of an earlier torpedoing, was Freddie Powell, and this contributed to his low metabolism now. Nothing could take away from him the unselfishness of his action in joining Whyte's boat, the last one to do so, at a time when the danger was plain; but he was undergoing the same sort of personality change that had affected so many. He did not always take notice of Whyte, he ignored warnings about drinking sea water, and he became agitated and inclined to be violent. On 25th November, after two days of delirium, he died. 'Poor Fred', as he had called himself, seemed to have had a premonition that, like the thoughtful gifts that had gone down with the *Cairo*, he might not get back to the celebration his family were preparing. But by an odd quirk of fate the first batch of gifts he had sent home many months earlier, hitherto written off as lost at sea, had turned up at Romsey.

Before they buried Powell, Whyte rather shamefacedly appropriated his trousers. When he saw the disapproving looks of the others he made them a promise. 'I won't do this to anyone else. It's a case of necessity.'

The death of the likeable Powell cast a gloom over them all, and Whyte, who treated Margaret as though she was indestructible, chose her as his confidant. 'These fellows', he said, 'are not going to last. We'll have to increase the water ration. We can afford to do it, at least for a time. There's no point in conserving it if they're all going to die.' She found his reliance on her stimulating: she would not let him down. In addition to a dipper (two ounces) per person morning and night, they agreed on a dipper at midday to revive them.

Despite the increase, McGregor kept asking for water, and he became more and more difficult to handle. He too showed signs of agitation, and he could no longer take his turn at the tiller. Whyte moved him to the bows, where he lay alongside Humphries under a boat cover. On Saturday 28th November, the twenty-third day since the sinking, he demanded a drink in mid-morning, which Whyte refused. 'You can't have a drink until lunchtime. We're drinking three times a day already. If we drink in between we'll soon have none left.'

'If you won't give me a drink, I'll jump overboard.'

Whyte interpreted this as an idle threat. 'Do what you like. You can't have any more water till lunchtime.'

Perhaps the mental disorder already displayed, first by the Asians and then by Powell, should have warned Whyte of some serious blackmail attempt. Before anyone could get to him McGregor went overboard, just as he was, with no lifejacket.

'Throw him a rope!'

Margaret threw him a lifejacket, but it drifted away from him, and Whyte tried to throw him a rope. The boat was so unwieldy that by the time they got near enough to help him he'd gone.

Whether McGregor would have survived if he had stayed with Britt in Boat 1 is doubtful. But Margaret was sure he had only thrown himself overboard with the idea of pressurizing Knocker into giving him a drink; he was much too attached to his 'wifey' and child to have killed himself in his right mind. Grieved as she was, she consoled herself with the thought that he couldn't have lasted much longer. In his semi-invalid state it was remarkable he had lasted so long.

One of Whyte's regular tasks was to patch the sail, which was eroded and perished, and that night, after he had lowered it to repair it, it ripped down the centre. Only by dint of exceptional perseverance did he manage to patch it, and in doing so he used all the twine that remained. As an insurance he hoisted a second sail, which he made from half the boat cover nailed to an oar. It was tricky to handle but it didn't disintegrate, and it made the most of the wind. Margaret watched him in amazement. While the others were reduced to lying about exhausted and helpless, Knocker could still summon the strength to work miracles.

With McGregor gone and Bill Pirrie complaining of double vision and even blindness, some relief was needed at the tiller. Solly Solomon was a qualified engineer and he had made himself useful throughout, but he too was running a fever, and the only alternative was Margaret. 'I'm going to have to teach you how to steer,' he told her. He showed her how to get the feel of the rudder and how to keep to a compass course, and to Whyte's delight she showed she had quite a flair for it.

That night she was roused by a shout from Knocker. 'What's happening?' Bill Pirrie had been doing his best at the tiller, but he had fallen asleep. The wind had filled the sails on the wrong side while he slept, and the boat had turned flat aback. Despite his almost churlish exterior, Pirrie had been utterly reliable all through, but he had reached the end of his strength and his patience. When Whyte upbraided him he exploded. 'That's it. I'm finished. What the hell's the point of it anyway? We'll never get anywhere.' With that he stalked off into the bows.

Whyte's anger was understandable: he had to get the oars out and row the boat round, an arduous task and a heavy tax on his diminishing strength. Everything seemed to be going wrong for him. To give himself a rest for the night he put out the sea anchor, but it broke away and was lost. He spent all next day fashioning a replacement, only to lose it the following night.

Solomon's fever, too, degenerated into dementia, and after lying around semi-conscious all day he became violent at night. In his delirium he jumped into the cockpit and nearly overturned the boat. It was all that Whyte and Margaret could do to restrain him. Two days later, on 4th December, he died, leaving just the four of them: Sparkie Humphries and Bill Pirrie under the cover up front, Knocker Whyte and Margaret Gordon running the boat.

Next day, 5th December, was the day on which the Hall Line, writing from their offices in Liverpool, informed the next of kin of all those already reported missing that their relatives 'do not appear in the list of survivors received up to the present. Should any further news come to hand we will immediately inform you.'

Some of the relatives dreaded the confirmation that they felt must come, others remained optimistic. Among the latter was Jim Coles, Whyte's instructor with the 3rd Erith Sea Scouts. 'You need have no fear', he told Whyte's parents, 'that he won't come through.'

*

Whyte's determination to survive extended equally to his shipmates, and he did all he could to sustain them. On the assumption that they might be at least another two weeks at sea he decided they must go back on short rations of water, two ounces at breakfast and two ounces at night, with no more than a moistening of the lips at midday. He talked to his shipmates about it and explained it to them, and he did all he could to encourage them to eat, mixing pemmican with drinking water into a soup to give them nourishment, without reducing their water ration. He and Margaret *made* themselves eat. 'I *must* keep up my strength,' said Whyte.

After eating and before drinking their water ration they rinsed their mouths out with salt water, as had been the practice in most other boats, but they tried not to swallow a drop. Twice flying fish landed in the boat and they cut them up and ate them with relish, but otherwise fish still refused to be caught. Margaret abandoned all squeamishness about her tooth brush and went forward daily to brush Sparkie's teeth. Bill Pirrie, still fiercely independent, did not avail himself of a similar offer.

There was plenty of room to move about now, and by taking out some of the side-boards and laying them across the thwarts they made comfortable places to sleep, and they had a stack of lifejackets for bedding. Margaret was so thin that she couldn't sit without two or three lifejackets under her rump.

She and Knocker kept the boat sailing throughout the 24 hours, which was roughly half day and half night, alternating frequently in the heat of the day but keeping three-hour watches at night. Their course was taking them well up into the tropics and during the day they repeatedly threw salt water over their clothes and dipped the wet rags they tied round their heads. Water still leaked into the boat, making bouts of bailing essential, and there were always repair jobs to do. But they rested whenever they could.

After chatting with the sick men and making them comfortable for the night, Whyte took the first watch at sunset, setting the boat on what he considered the right course. He had used up the torches first, saving the compass oil, but the many swampings they had sustained had soaked their matches, they were unable to re-light the wick, and they were steering now by the stars. At ten o'clock Whyte woke Margaret, and if it was a clear night he gave her a star or a group of stars to navigate by and she settled down confidently enough. Only once did she fail him, when like Bill Pirrie before her she fell into a doze and eased her grip on the tiller, so that for a second time the boat turned right round and Whyte had to row them back on course. This exhausted him, and he could not hide his vexation. Until he recovered she felt a tremendous burden of guilt.

Despite their peril there were compensations. The clear tropical nights were sublime in their beauty, and the boat seemed to Margaret to scud along much faster in darkness than daylight. At these times Sirius, the dog-star, shone with pale brilliance astern, and there were entrancing hours when they sailed directly into the path of the moon. As the only living creature awake on the dark surface of ocean Margaret felt a solitude so intense as to be soothing and uplifting. Like so many lone travellers before her, she sensed some invisible power at her shoulder, guiding and protecting her on her way.

Her watch had rusted and stopped, but when she estimated she had been at the tiller for three hours she woke Knocker, and he in turn woke her at four. After the low physical ebb of the night hours it was therapeutic to see the light seeping under the serried banks of cloud to the east. If Knocker wasn't already awake she would call him, and he would check with his watch and try to calculate their progress westwards. Margaret would cross the date off the calendar, and Whyte would make up his log. This was the pattern in the early days of December; but on the 12th, when Britt's boat, Boat 1, with its three half-dead occupants, drifted into the arms of the *Rhakotis*, Boat 4 was still many hundreds of miles from the Brazilian coast.

Each day they continued to make a point of washing, combing their hair, and tidying the boat. Whyte was fond of admiring his beard in Margaret's mirror, and to Margaret he looked like a genuine Elizabethan sea-dog. He insisted on caring for his two shipmates himself whenever he could. Conversation was never more than spasmodic, but slowly Margaret learned more about her companion.

Whyte's paternal grandfather had been an engine fitter in a Govan shipyard; his children had had a sound Scottish education. Whyte's father went to sea as a lad and worked his way up to chief steward and purser on a small cargo liner, but he lost his job during the Thirties' depression. Whyte's maternal grandfather was the son of a Kentish yeoman farmer who harvested too well on the hops he grew and fell on hard times, leaving his son to make his way in the world as a gardener. The son graduated to superintendent of the Erith municipal cemetery, where the family lived in the cemetery lodge, and it was here that grandchildren James Allister and his younger brother Eric were born. 'Except when there was a funeral,' Whyte told her, 'the cemetery was our playground.'

His father eventually got back to sea as a cabin steward; meanwhile his mother, formerly a schoolteacher, returned to teaching. 'She's still teaching now,' said Whyte. Both boys won scholarships to Erith County Secondary School, but Knocker was always obsessed with the sea. His favourite reading was Percy F. Westerman, but he also loved poetry, favouring those poets who wrote about real life and the sea. He was familiar, though, with some of the nobler epics, and one day in the lifeboat he and Margaret recited between them the whole of Gray's *Elegy*.

He was always sturdily built, his mother noting that 'Eric has the brains, Jimmy the brawn'. At the age of 20, with Eric a year or so younger, he could grab his brother by the seat of his trousers and lift him off his feet one-handed. Yet he was short in the leg and had stopped growing at about five feet four.

Shy with Margaret even after a month of close contact, so that he still could not give her a name, he affected to have no interest in women. When he told her he wasn't married she asked: 'Haven't you a girl friend?' The answer he gave was: 'No, I'm a misogynist.' The stories he told about the temptations women passengers put in his way always ended with him saying good-night to them at their cabin door. The only woman he had ever loved, he told Margaret, was his mother. Nevertheless, he had once confided to his brother that a niece of Jim Coles, Joan Coles (she had been 'the girl next door' in Erith) 'would make him a marvellous wife'. In this as in other things he was the kind of chap who knew what he wanted and quietly went about getting it.

So their strange existence continued. Their bodies were becoming cadaverous, their nails turned brown, their eyesight grew weaker, and they were getting increasingly deaf, so that they had to shout to make themselves heard. Yet they remained mentally alert. Humphries and Pirrie lay day after day in the bows, unable to move, still refusing to eat. Whyte and Margaret continued to bail and do any routine jobs that were necessary.

On 16th December, their fortieth day, disaster struck. Whyte was hoisting the sail to catch a fresh breeze when the pulley at the top of the mast jammed. Nothing he did would move it. 'If we take the mast down to repair it,' he said, 'we'll never get it up again. We shan't have the strength.' The boat would be virtually uncontrollable and they would never reach South America. Laboriously, in that moment of crisis, Bill Pirrie crawled from his bed, dragged himself up the mast, freed the pulley, and dropped down again. In an extraordinary feat of will-power he had given them all a reprieve. He went back to his bed afterwards and never moved again.

Margaret had seen how patient Knocker could be in performing routine tasks in the boat, but she was seeing a new side of him in his care and concern for his shipmates. Sparkie he was especially fond of. Sparkie had been the first to volunteer to join him, and he could not bear to think it might cost the little radio officer his life. Sparkie was lapsing at times into delirium, but he managed to write a last message in his diary. A gold bracelet he was carrying was to go to his fiancée, and there was a final word for his mother. 'I have made my peace with God.' A week before the Christmas they had all hoped to spend in England he died. Bill Pirrie followed him two days later. Whyte's strength was just sufficient to get the two bodies over the side.

They were on their last tank of water, but with only two to drink it Whyte thought it might last another seven days. He believed they were within 200 miles of the Brazilian coast, and he urged Margaret, during her sessions on watch, to look out for shipping. With their vision impaired it would have to come close.

A further setback assailed them when the patched sail finally disintegrated, but this was something Whyte could cope with. He tacked two blankets together and hoisted them as a substitute, and to Margaret they seemed to blow along rather faster than before. The strong breeze and the towering breakers that now overtook them terrified Margaret as she strove to hold the tiller against them, but Knocker could hardly contain his excitement, feeling that at last they were getting somewhere. The calm day with no breeze that followed made him restless and despondent, and it was Margaret who revived his flagging spirits. Surely they would not fail now.

All the way they had seen an occasional sea bird, and that night while Margaret was steering a black bosun bird perched on the blade of an oar and rode with them till morning. When it was Whyte's turn at the tiller Margaret woke him and indicated the bird. It did not impress him. 'We must be a hell of a long way from land for a bird to come and perch here all night for a rest.'

On 21st December they sailed into a huge patch of muddy water that stretched for miles. Whyte wondered if they could conceivably have sailed too far north, as far as the equator even, and be crossing the Amazon outfall. That was what it looked like to him. But it was an illusion. On closer examination the patch proved to be fish spawn, and eventually they emerged once again into clear water.

Next day a large wooden crate floated past them, and on the following day the branch of a tree. They must be near the shipping lanes. On Christmas Day they toasted each other in the last of Margaret's brandy and wished each other 'Many Happy Christmasses to come.'

That afternoon a familiar roaring noise burst on their ears and they looked up to see an aeroplane flying fast and low directly towards them. Whyte seized a smoke flare and threw it over the side, but he was much too late, and despite their frantic waving and shouting the plane flashed past and was gone. Shattering as the disappointment was, the plane was an encouraging sign. Whyte estimated next morning that they could not be more than a hundred miles from the coast.

During Boxing Night Whyte woke Margaret to look at an evanescent gleam that was piercing the darkness. Some distance away, it resembled a coastal beacon, flashing intermittently as though as a warning. But as they turned north to head towards it, it vanished. They were seeing things all the time now, but this light had been so strong that Whyte thought it must have been caused by an electric storm.

They saw nothing more of the light, but Whyte's interpretation was confirmed at dawn on the 27th when Margaret, glancing astern, saw a beetling indigo cloud precipitating in a thick curtain that was advancing rapidly towards them. She woke Knocker and he jumped up and adjusted the sails so they could steer more towards it. It overtook them with the speed and force of an avalanche and they were deluged – their first rain for more than seven weeks. They collected all the tins they had saved over a period of 51 days for just this eventuality, rinsed out the salt that had corroded inside them, and drank. They spread the jib to catch more, though that too had to be scrubbed down first to remove the salt. They sat there in the early dawn, drenched and shivering, intoxicated with happiness, drinking their fill. All too soon the storm passed, but they were able to replenish the last of their tanks with the surplus they had collected. They were good now for another few days, long enough, surely, to get them to land.

From a sensual pleasure akin to ecstasy they were assailed almost at once by a new trepidation: the boat was flooding and sinking. The rain accounted for some of the flooding, but it was much more than that. 'For God's sake!' shouted Whyte. 'What's happened? Quick – we'll have to bail!' They worked feverishly but the boat remained waterlogged. 'It's not getting any less,' said Whyte. 'It's still coming in.' Feeling for the plug, he found it had gone. He could only imagine that the sudden accumulation of rain water had somehow altered the pressure inside the boat and loosened the plug. Quickly he improvised a substitute, and their bailing began to reduce the level.

After these extreme fluctuations of emotion Margaret felt drained, and as it was her turn to rest she lay down on a mattress of lifejackets and slept. This time it was Whyte's turn to shout a reveille.

'Ships, ships, ships!'

A fleet of ships was crossing the horizon, and to Margaret's impaired vision they seemed uniform in size but ragged in formation, jerking about like puppets but retaining their image.

'Get the flares!'

Margaret jumped down to the forward locker and threw three flares up to Whyte. The first two fizzled out, but the last one spewed a billowing cloud of scarlet smoke. As the smoke cleared they watched breathlessly for some sign that they had been seen. Their horizon was severely limited, but the ships were not far away. Soon one of the escort vessels detached itself from the convoy and came bustling over. After standing off for a while it edged closer, and someone shouted at them from the bridge. The language sounded like Portuguese.

'We're British!'

The vessel approaching was the *Caravellas*, a corvette of the Brazilian Navy, part of a convoy heading southwards down the coast towards Rio. It lay some distance off so as not to swamp the lifeboat, and the crew shouted 'Row over.' Margaret could barely lift the oars into the rowlocks, and how Whyte found the strength to row she couldn't imagine, but soon they were alongside and a rope ladder was lowered. They sat for a moment silent and undemonstrative, physically and emotionally ravaged, only their eyes meeting in a thankful but impalpable embrace.

'Go on,' said Whyte, 'you go first.' But her knees wouldn't support her. Above her the rail was lined with smiling, friendly faces, and soon a Portuguese seaman came down the ladder and helped her up.

Whyte followed, and they were seated in chairs on the deck. 'What would you like?' Margaret was asked. All she craved was a hot drink.

They were a long way south of their intended landfall, but they had got to within 80 miles of the coast. With the benison of the cloud-burst they would certainly have reached it. When the convoy duty was completed they would be landed at Recife – the port for which they had sailed from Cape Town nearly two months earlier. Since setting off on their own on 13th November they had covered over 2,000 miles.

Washing in sea water for so many weeks had removed none of the grime on their bodies, and they stank of the whale oil they had used in their massage, so they were soon taken below for a shower. Sitting in a wooden chair under the sprinkler, Margaret was luxuriating in the sensation of soap and running water when there was an urgent tapping at the door. It was Whyte. 'Don't take too much water,' he called. 'It's their drinking water.' Whyte replaced her under the shower, and a cabin was cleared for them.

The intimacy of 51 days in a small open boat, where no secrets were possible, did not lessen Whyte's shyness and embarrassment at sharing a cabin for the next few days with his fellow survivor.

CHAPTER 14

On Board the Blockade-Runner

After their first night on the *Rhakotis,* Angus MacDonald and Jack Edmead were moved to the ship's sick bay, leaving Diana in the doctor's cabin. When they looked in a mirror they didn't recognize themselves. MacDonald, with his red beard and fleshless face and body, and Edmead, with his black beard, hollow cheeks and accentuated angularity, resembled nothing more closely than the typical castaways of illustrated fiction. They were given an injection and put to bed, MacDonald in the top bunk and Edmead below. Against doctor's orders MacDonald got one of the crew to bring him a bottle of water, which he drank before going to sleep. The two men slept for many hours, and when MacDonald awoke he found he had soaked not only his own bunk but Edmead's as well. He woke Edmead to apologize, but Edmead's sense of humour was equal to the insult and he laughed. They showered, and a steward came in and with similar tolerance changed the bedding.

The *Rhakotis* had sailed from Batavia (Djakarta) for Bordeaux on 5th November – the day before the sinking of the *City of Cairo.* After crossing the Pacific she had rounded Cape Horn and kept to mid-Atlantic on the homeward run, a course that had taken her within a few miles of the lifeboat. During the night of 11th/12th December she had stopped for five hours with engine trouble, and she had only just re-started her engines when the lifeboat drifted by. But for that fortuitous halt the paths of freighter and lifeboat would never have crossed, the three survivors would never have been rescued, and nothing would ever have been known of the tragic events in Britt's boat.

The best chance the *Rhakotis* had of successfully running the

Allied blockade lay in evasion; whereas for the Allied navies the protection of trans-oceanic trade was a prime function, the German merchant service could expect little help from the *Kriegsmarine.* Germany relied far less heavily on seaborne supplies, and adequate escort forces could not be maintained for the occasional blockade-runner. The best that could normally be hoped for was some distraction or diversion to keep hostile forces pre-occupied elsewhere when the most vulnerable section of a return passage was reached. Special efforts, however, were being made for the *Rhakotis* in view of her cargo. An escort of three U-boats was to rendezvous with her 400 miles north-west of the Azores, where she would turn due east for the final run of some 1,500 miles into Bordeaux. Aircraft and torpedo boats would provide short-range escort for the last few hundred miles into Bordeaux, where she was due to dock on New Year's Day. But these precautions were unlikely to save her if she was spotted by the British in time, and her best hope lay in a spell of bad weather.

MacDonald with his compact figure recovered the use of his legs more quickly than Edmead, and soon he was given the run of the ship, save that he wasn't allowed to visit Diana. This after 36 days together was something he felt as a cruel deprivation, but Captain Jacobs came to the sick bay and gave them bulletins daily. Diana, he explained, needed complete rest. She couldn't swallow any food as yet and was being fed by injections, and the doctor feared that her recovery would be slow.

In his rambles about the ship MacDonald found the crew touchingly concerned for the welfare of 'the English *fraulein*'. Few German merchant seamen were members of the Nazi party, and no doubt this was why, in most ships, one or more crew-men were appointed to maintain the political zeal of their comrades. Attached to the *Rhakotis* were a *Kriegsmarine* officer and ratings whose task it was to man the ship's defensive armament, and it was only from these men that MacDonald met any antagonism. Their attitude was 'correct' but stiff and cold. In theory the senior *Kriegsmarine* officer present was in charge of the ship, but German masters always insisted that the traditions of the sea gave them overall responsibility and command, and Captain Jacobs was no exception. This, thought MacDonald, might be important in a crisis.

A week after their rescue, on 19th December, Captain Jacobs visited them in the sick bay accompanied by the doctor. Their expressions were grave. 'The English girl hasn't been able to eat,' said the captain, 'and she can't go on living on injections alone. The tissues of her throat have collapsed and the doctor wants to perform a tracheostomy. I shall need your permission. The doctor says the operation has only a limited chance of success.'

'And if he doesn't operate?'

'She can't live.'

The two men glanced at each other. 'If you think the operation is essential,' said MacDonald, 'then you have our permission. All we want is to see her well again.'

'Would you like to see her now?'

They responded eagerly to the invitation, and Edmead, who could still scarcely walk, was carried to the cabin. They found Diana bright and well-groomed, her hair had been washed, and at first glance she seemed almost normal. 'I'm being very well looked after,' she told them. But she still talked in a whisper. 'You'll soon be better, Diana,' they said, and squeezed her hand. They could not bring themselves to mention the operation.

It was late that evening before the captain visited them again, and they recoiled from the look on his face. 'I have bad news for you. Will you come with me, please? The English girl has died.'

Diana lay on the couch with a bandage round her throat. A tiny spot of blood had seeped through. She looked utterly peaceful, as though she was sleeping, and they could scarcely believe she was dead.

'The operation was a success,' said Captain Jacobs, 'but her heart wasn't strong enough to stand the anaesthetic. She will be buried at sea tomorrow.'

Broken-hearted, blinded with tears, MacDonald and Edmead turned away, unable to speak. This lovable girl had shared all their sufferings and had never let them lose heart. Both felt they owed their lives to her, and back in the sick bay they cried inconsolably. The unemotional MacDonald admitted to Edmead next day that he had cried like a baby most of the night, and Edmead was no less affected. It was beyond all enduring that she should have come through those 36 terrible days with such courage only to die after rescue.

At six o'clock next morning, 20th December, the ship stopped for the funeral and they were taken up to the fore-deck, where the crew were paraded in uniform. Balanced on the fo'c's'le rail was a plank, over which was draped a Union Jack. Outlined under the flag was the wasted body of Diana Jarman, sewn into a canvas bag and weighted down with fire-bars. Overwhelmed with grief, the two men bit back the tears.

Captain Jacobs gave a short address in German, then spoke in English, 'for the benefit', he said, 'of this unfortunate girl's comrades – this brave English girl who has lost her life as a result of the *krieg*.' He turned to MacDonald and Edmead. 'A very plucky girl. She did not deserve to die.'

The plank on the rail was tilted seawards and the crew stood to attention bare-headed. As the canvas sack splashed into the water Captain Jacobs saluted. 'Diana,' he said, 'I greet you for the last time.' Many of the Germans, Captain Jacobs among them, had tears in their eyes, and for MacDonald and Edmead the fiercest clenching of mouth and teeth could not hold back the flow. They resolved that one day, if they survived, they would tell the story of Diana Jarman.

When they were well enough MacDonald and Edmead were moved into the forward hold, where they joined at least a dozen other prisoners, Norwegian and Danish seamen who had been captured at sea and were being repatriated. MacDonald had already learned from the crew the importance of the ship's cargo, to which he reacted with mixed feelings. What he earnestly wished for was that the *Rhakotis* would be sunk or captured by an Allied ship which would take the German crew prisoner and recapture the Norwegians, the Danes and themselves. But there was nothing he or Edmead could do to advance such an objective.

Christmas on the *Rhakotis*, for crew and prisoners alike, was a festive occasion. MacDonald and Edmead had regained their normal appetites, the butcher killed two of the four pigs that were in a pen on the after-deck, and everyone had as much roast pork as they could eat. 'We're having a better Christmas here', MacDonald remarked to Edmead, 'than they'll be having on many British ships.' But a day or so after Christmas, as the time for the rendezvous with the U-boats approached, the atmosphere on board changed to one of extreme tension and vigilance.

The three submarines ordered by Flag Officer U-boats to keep the rendezvous 400 miles north-west of the Azores were U410, U621 and U409; U621 made contact on December 27th and U410 on the 28th, and although the third boat failed to appear through a radar failure U659 was substituted and made the rendezvous on the 29th. The *Rhakotis* stopped at seven o'clock that evening, and the first two U-boat commanders boarded her. Nobody prevented MacDonald and Edmead from watching. After spending half an hour with Captain Jacobs the two submariners returned to their craft and the *Rhakotis* continued under U-boat escort. U410 positioned herself 40 sea miles ahead of the blockade-runner, with the other two U-boats a similar distance on her flanks.

Air reconnaissance by three long-range Focke-Wulf Condors began at dawn next day, 30th December. These four-engined aircraft were not suitable for combat, but they would sweep the area, warn of Allied surface activity, and co-operate with the U-boats, leading them to any suitable target. Combat aircraft and torpedo boats were preparing to mount short-range escort for the last 400 miles into Bordeaux.

The portents for the *Rhakotis* were good, judging from the confidence – indeed the elation – of the crew. And although the British had reason to anticipate a blockade-runner, they knew few details. They didn't know the name of the ship, nor did they know which of the Biscay ports it was making for. Most favourable augury of all for the *Rhakotis* was the weather forecast, which promised a rapid deterioration.

On 31st December British Intelligence accurately estimated that the blockade-runner might be approaching the entrance to the Bay on an easterly course by the evening of the following day,

1st January, 1943. If that were so, her position by dawn on the 2nd would be so far into the Bay as to come under close escort, making interception by surface vessels impossible and by strike aircraft uncertain. Only if the vessel could be picked up on the night of 31st December, or early on 1st January, and shadowed from then on, was there much chance of intercepting her before she disappeared into the clutches of the close escort. The weather forecast for the vital night was as bad as it could be.

Yet if only the *Rhakotis* could be found, the British had a trump card to play. The cruiser *HMS Scylla* (Captain I. A. P. MacIntyre), returning from the 'Torch' landings in North Africa, had left Gibraltar the previous evening on passage for Greenock to join a Russian convoy. Whether this was a fortunate coincidence or a swift reaction to intercepted enemy signals is not officially recorded, but the fact was that, with no more than a minor diversion, the *Scylla* could be in just about the right place at just about the right time, dawn on 1st January. Despite forecasts of a low cloud base and limited visibility, a comprehensive air search was laid on for the night of 31st December/1st January.

At four o'clock on the morning of New Year's Day the guns of the *Rhakotis* went into action and the sky above the vessel was brilliantly illuminated. 'Look at that yellow light!' shouted Edmead to MacDonald. Rushing up from the hold, they were just in time to see an incandescent flare suspended overhead and hear the drone of aircraft engines before being ordered back into the hold.

'What's happening?'

'We're being attacked by British aircraft. They've got away undamaged. Get back into the hold.'

Two R.A.F. Whitleys had taken off from their Devon airfield either side of midnight to patrol the approaches to the Bay. The weather at their bases was so bad that they would not normally have been despatched, and they soon found the forecast only too accurate, dense cloud covering the area from 3,000 feet down to 400. Their search had to be carried out above cloud using radar, and, greatly to the credit of the two crews, both obtained radar contacts at a distance of 15 to 20 miles. After breaking cloud they sighted the wake of a ship, and the flares seen by Edmead disclosed the blockade-runner.

Despite the pessimistic report by the *Rhakotis* crew, the first Whitley had in fact been hit on its approach run, and with its hydraulics put out of action it was forced to return to base. The pilot of the second Whitley, Flying Officer A. Hodgson, made several runs over the target, but visibility was so poor that his bomb-aimer was unable to release his bombs. However by the light of flares Hodgson and his crew correctly estimated the ship's tonnage, course, and speed. At present she was clearly making for Bordeaux. A bombing attack by an R.A.F. Wellington two hours later failed to inflict any serious damage, however, and contact was afterwards lost. It remained to relocate the vessel in daylight and bring forward *HMS Scylla.*

Alerted by Hodgson's signal the *Scylla*'s officers worked out an interception course. The diversion was not exactly welcomed. Not only would it delay their arrival at Greenock (and the crew were due for leave), it would also involve penetration into U-boat-infested waters – the passages in and out of the Bay. The crew prayed for a quick sighting, a clean kill, and bad weather in which to escape.

As the crew tumbled out of their bunks on that New Year's morning, the urgent thrust of the ship's screws indicated a purposeful increase in speed. 'We should sight a blockade-runner some time in the First Dog Watch,' announced a voice on the amplifiers. 'Ship will go to Action Stations at 15.00.'

The chances of sighting an enemy vessel at the end of a 200-mile dash such as this were no more than modest. Air contact had not been re-established, and meanwhile the *Rhakotis* was making full speed for Bordeaux. But during the night two Sunderland flying-boats had been despatched to find and shadow the blockade-runner and home the cruiser on to the target, and that afternoon one of the Sunderlands sighted the approaching *Scylla.* The crew then went off in search of the blockade-runner. At 16.30 they sighted the *Rhakotis*, and although their endurance was up, by using smoke floats they laid a trail to the target for the *Scylla.*

Despite having reached crisis point the crew of the *Rhakotis* were not denied a special New Year's Day dinner, and nor were the prisoners, many of whom were still in the Mess Room amidships when the first salvoes were heard.

'What's happening?'

'British cruiser!'

As the alarm bells started ringing, armed *Kriegsmarine* guards ordered all prisoners down an alley-way and back into the forward hold. They could hear gunfire plainly now, and as the ship sustained its first hits the racket was ear-splitting. Some of the prisoners tried to break for it up the alley-way, but they were pushed back at gunpoint by the *Kriegsmarine* guards. These men were tearing off their uniform jackets (just as Captain Rogerson and others had done eight weeks earlier), and preparing to pose as merchant seamen in case of capture.

Two machine-guns were mounted in the alley-way on tripods to control the prisoners, and to Edmead it seemed certain that if the ship sank the prisoners were to be eliminated. He feared that in the eyes of the marines they had learnt far too much about the movement of German blockade-runners and their U-boat escorts for their recapture by a British cruiser to be contemplated.

'To the boats!'

The call came from the chief officer of the *Rhakotis.* The prisoners heard him shouting at the marine officer: Captain Jacobs' orders were that the prisoners were to be allowed on deck to take their chance. The chief officer kicked away the tripod supports of the machine-guns, the marines disappeared, and the prisoners, cheered beyond measure, raced for the deck.

MacDonald saw some of the crew preparing scuttling charges, set to explode after they got clear; the *Rhakotis* had no chance against a cruiser, and Captain Jacobs would not risk his ship falling into enemy hands. The charges were scarcely required: the first torpedo missed astern after breaking the surface, but the second hit the vessel forward. By the time crew and prisoners reached the boats the ship was on fire.

Neither MacDonald nor Edmead knew for certain from which side the shells and torpedoes were coming, but as Edmead accompanied the chief officer to a boat on the starboard side, MacDonald, ever the loner, made for one on the port side. Edmead knew he wouldn't have survived this far without MacDonald, but in that moment he allowed himself the reflection that the durable Scots quartermaster was hardly the most companionable of men.

No sooner had MacDonald reached one of the port boat stations than he sighted the cruiser. She was still firing salvoes and he could see the flashes and hear the shells screaming past. He slid down a lifeline into the boat and helped push it clear with a boat-hook. He was sure the cruiser would stop to check the lifeboats for survivors. The boat had just got away when there was a shout from the deck of the blazing vessel and two more men could be seen silhouetted against the flames. The ship was listing and sinking and the scuttling charges must detonate soon, but the boat was turned back. The men jumped into the water and were dragged aboard. The cruiser didn't stop firing until the *Rhakotis* was on her beam ends, when she turned away full speed ahead and quickly receded.

Had the sinking occurred in mid-ocean Captain MacIntyre would have stopped, but in these waters it was far too risky. Unlike Captain Merten he had no time for apologies. Bitterly disappointed, MacDonald remembered the escorting U-boats, which must still be around, and understood.

As the *Rhakotis* rolled over and sank, MacDonald's companions in the lifeboat took off their hats and waved them and gave her three cheers. Lost with the ship, in the captain's safe, were all the valuables, trinkets and keepsakes that had been collected in the *Cairo*'s lifeboat, together with Britt's log and Edmead's diary of events – everything that had been preserved with such care. All MacDonald had retained was the signet ring given him by Bob Ironside and Dr Tasker's silver knife. One day, perhaps, he would be able to deliver the ring to Bob's wife.

The total complement of the *Rhakotis*, numbering 155, got away in four boats without loss.[1] In view of the source from which

[1] Another report gives the figure as 152 but confirms there was no loss of life.

shipwreck had come the two survivors of the *Cairo* feared further hostility and perhaps worse from elements of the German crew, but their minds were soon set at rest. The Germans took their sinking as a natural hazard of war, and they bore their enemy counterparts no ill-will.

The three U-boats, frustrated in their efforts to attack the *Scylla*, were ordered to search for survivors, and one of them, U410 under Korvettenkapitän Kurt Sturm, picked up 80 survivors from two of the boats on the following afternoon, 2nd January. Among them was Angus MacDonald. The other two boats, in the charge of Captain Jacobs and the chief officer respectively, were missed by the U-boats, probably because, taking advantage of a westerly wind, they set course at once for Spain. 38 survivors were landed at Corunna from the captain's boat on 3rd January and another 37 from the chief officer's boat – among them Jack Edmead – on the 4th. Edmead wanted to pull his weight in the lifeboat but the chief officer would not allow him to exert himself. When news of Edmead's arrival in Corunna reached the British Consul, arrangements were made to send him by train to Madrid and thence to Gibraltar and home.

U410, a Type VII U-boat of 517 tons, was meanwhile heading on the surface for St Nazaire with three times her normal complement, unable to submerge for more than short periods and thus extremely vulnerable to air attack. To ensure seaworthiness and diving capacity some of the torpedoes were jettisoned. An announcement over the loudspeaker in English warned that anyone touching the equipment or machinery would be thrown overboard, but MacDonald was treated with consideration by the hirsute commander and his bearded crew. As soon as the survivors were taken below, each man was given a hot cup of coffee laced with rum, shown the spot where he was to lie, and ordered to keep still. With 80 extra bodies in a small submarine the sardine-tin simile was never more apt, and the crew mostly slept at their posts. MacDonald's main trouble was his bladder, which he still could not control. On explaining his problem he was taken amidships to Captain Sturm, who arranged to have a crate of empty bottles placed within his reach for use when needed.

At 04.30 next morning the alarm bell sounded and U410 dipped and crash-dived. Within seconds MacDonald heard three shattering explosions. The first shook them up, the second was worse and the third was so close that the whole submarine shuddered and they were all thrown about. MacDonald, who was sharing a bunk with another man, fell to the deck, where he landed on two spare torpedoes. The engines were stopped and they were told not to speak or move.

Above them the crew of an R.A.F. Wellington bomber, after picking up a radar contact, had sighted the bow wave (or the wake) of a submarine, switched on their Leigh Light searchlight, and dived to the attack. The crew dropped four depth charges, one of which apparently failed to explode. So steep was the aircraft's dive that the depth charges fell in a salvo from low level. They hit the water close to the submarine's hull, while the tail gunner fired 200 rounds at the conning tower. U410, although shaken up, escaped damage. No further sighting was made by the Wellington crew and twenty minutes later, reaching the limit of endurance, they turned for home. U410 had been located, however, she could not stay submerged for long, and a further attack seemed certain.

It came, this time from a Whitley, just before noon that same day, 3rd January, the day Edmead landed at Corunna. Captain Sturm had not abandoned offensive action, and he was stalking an Allied vessel on the surface, to MacDonald's intense disquiet (he had enquired what was afoot), when the alarm bell clanged again, the nose of the submarine tilted down, and she crash-dived at such an angle that to MacDonald she seemed to be standing on her head. The disorientation was terrifying, and even the faces of the German crew seemed distorted and anxious. Then came the first depth charge, and the submarine, still descending steeply, rocked with vibration. She was coming up to an even keel when a second and third explosion followed almost simultaneously, throwing the interior into a contortion of bodies and limbs. U410 rolled over on her side, the lights went out, and compartment doors were hurriedly closed. Seconds later there was a bump and MacDonald guessed they were on the bottom.

There wasn't a sound in MacDonald's compartment, until a voice reached him out of the darkness: 'Lie still, don't speak and don't move. All movement uses up air.' Stretched uncomfortably across two spare torpedoes, with a bulky German submariner slumped across his legs, MacDonald was sweating with claustrophobia, but he dared not move. There seemed to be no water seeping into his compartment, but they got no enlightenment from the loudspeaker. In fact the area affected was mostly astern, and it included the rudder, the after hydroplane, and the main battery system.

Drops of moisture were falling now from the deck-head, presumably condensation, and every minute the air became more foul. All around him MacDonald could hear harsh and heavy breathing, and he himself was panting, half-choked by the fetid air. What a way to end after all he'd come through, suffocated in pitch darkness on the sea bottom! But the Germans – and the other prisoners – were suffering in silence, and if they could so could he.

The drips of condensation continued, and he lost all notion of time. It seemed they had been on the sea bed for hours, and he didn't think, in his weakened state, that he would remain conscious much longer. Suddenly he heard tapping from the far side of the bulkhead. One of the crew tapped back in answer, the watertight door was opened, and a crewman came through with a torch. Captain Sturm spoke on the loudspeaker system and told everyone to stay calm and that the damage was being repaired. MacDonald could hear hammering astern, and at length U410 got under way and rose to the surface. The hatch was thrown open and fresh air gushed in.

Surviving members of U410's crew do not remember this episode as being of particular peril, nor do they recall the boat grounding or any malfunctioning of the air supply. But memories may be faulty, and Captain Sturm's log clearly records the air attacks (confirmed by R.A.F. crew reports and remarkably accurate damage assessments), and lists the damage already referred to. MacDonald's unfamiliarity with the experience of being depth-charged would account for a reaction of heightened anxiety, and, as one crew-member recently observed, 'the Englishman was particularly exhausted' when brought on board. (He was, of course, a Scot.) But MacDonald was not one to embellish a story – very much the reverse.

There were no more incidents, and the following afternoon, 4th January, U410 limped into the submarine pens at St Nazaire. A large contingent of Storm Troops, S.S. and S.A., were formed up on the pier, and the welcoming party was led by high-ranking officers and supported by a military band. The presence of the S.S. and S.A., however, so alarmed Captain Sturm that he enquired, before docking, how his supernumeraries were going to be treated. Dissatisfied with the reply, he signalled that he would refuse to dock until he got an assurance that any shipwrecked enemy subjects in his complement would be properly respected as prisoners of war. Not until the S.S. and S.A. withdrew did he finally dock.

The prisoners were then lined up on deck, and they watched the U-boat crew step triumphantly ashore, to the accompaniment of a stirring crescendo of martial music and a chorus of acclaim. So far as MacDonald was concerned they deserved it. Then, to the astonishment of the assembled company, a long column of *Rhakotis* survivors poured on to the quay.

Separated from the other prisoners as the only enemy seaman among them, MacDonald was taken ashore for interrogation, still the lone, unassuming figure he had been throughout. Kept in solitary confinement that night, he was taken by truck to Nantes next day and thence by train to Wilhelmshaven and captivity.

CHAPTER 15

Postscripts and Superstitions

Angus MacDonald spent the next two-and-a-half-years in the Merchant Navy section of Marlag and Milag Nord Prisoner of War camp at Westertimke. When the camp was overrun by the Guards Armoured Division in May 1945, Bob Ironside's brother F. P. Ironside was one of the men who cut their way through the wire. Hearing that a survivor of the *City of Cairo* was one of the prisoners, Guardsman Ironside sought the man out. MacDonald still had his quartermaster friend's signet ring in safe keeping, and he gave it to Ironside, who recognized it at once and sent it home.

MacDonald had also retained Dr Tasker's silver knife, the one stamped with the whisky advertisement, but he lost it while serving in another Ellerman ship after the war.

After being repatriated, Jack Edmead spent several weeks visiting relatives on behalf of Ellermans before undertaking a nine-month nationwide tour of munitions factories and industrial centres for the Ministry of Information, inspiring war workers with his story of the privations endured by merchant seamen. (Mona Rooksby, who could have used her 'high canteen voice', was invited first, but she declined for domestic reasons.) Both MacDonald and Edmead were awarded the British Empire Medal for 'outstanding courage and fortitude throughout their severe and protracted ordeal'.

Is it really feasible that the column of sulphurous smoke produced by Dr Quantrill's fumigating candle could have led U68 to her prey? Unlikely as it seems, there is no evidence that the *City of Cairo* was making smoke that evening, the timing was right, and the unusual nature of the smoke that was sighted was referred to again many years later by German writer Jochen Brennecke in

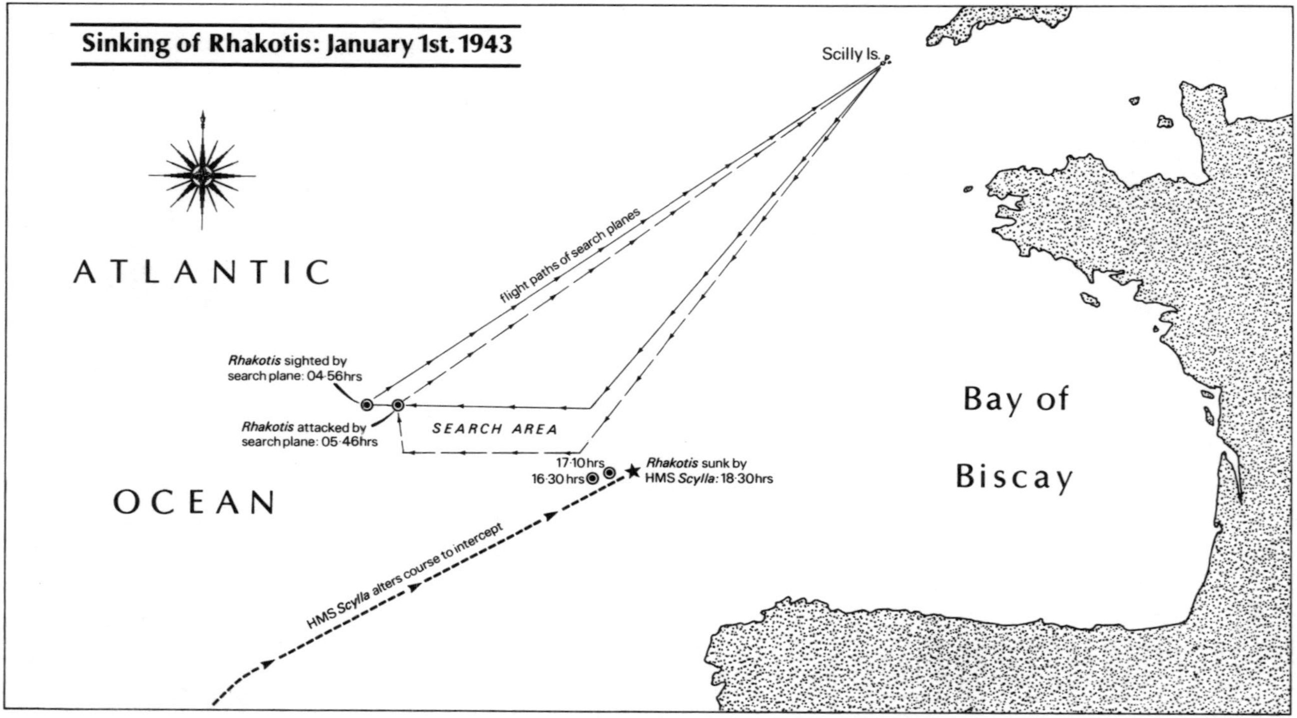
Sinking of Rhakotis: January 1st. 1943
Scilly Is.
ATLANTIC
OCEAN
Bay of
Biscay
flight paths of search planes
Rhakotis sighted by search plane: 04·56hrs
Rhakotis attacked by search plane: 05·46hrs
SEARCH AREA
17·10hrs
16·30hrs
Rhakotis sunk by HMS *Scylla*: 18·30hrs
HMS *Scylla* alters course to intercept

his book *The Hunters and the Hunted.*[1]. 'It was shortly after sunset', he wrote, 'that the look-out noticed a most peculiar cloud.' Brennecke knew nothing of the burning of the fumigating candle.

Of the 148 survivors who were landed on the Crown Colony of St Helena (84 Europeans and 64 Asians), two Europeans and two Asians died, leaving a total of 144. Of the crew, all but eight of the Europeans resumed their journey within a month, thanks to the arrival of the French ship *Chantilly,* and most of the Lascars, when they were well enough, were returned to India via Cape Town. But of the passengers, all but two who managed to get special priority (the Rooksbys) were obliged to remain on St Helena for the next three months. Thanks to the hospitality of the people of this volcanic island (once the possession of the East India Company), recuperation, for the 63 people remaining, in the delightful and healthy climate the island enjoys, was swift and complete. More than one ship that was intended to collect the survivors was sunk in transit, but at last, on 19th February 1943, they boarded the *TSS Nestor.* Their homeward voyage, via Freetown in Sierra Leone and thence in convoy, was a ghastly nightmare of sinkings, more terrifying than anything they had endured earlier, but the *Nestor* got through. They reached their homes about 5th April, 'just in time', as Bob Skea noted wryly, 'to pay my income tax'.

When Margaret Gordon went ashore in Recife she told the third officer of another Ellerman Lines vessel, the *City of Bombay* (which had arrived there five days earlier), 'You're not going to get me out of this country till the war's over!' After recuperation, however, first in hospital and then amongst the British community in Recife, she relented to the extent of sailing in March 1943 to New York, where she lived with an aunt and worked for a time as a librarian and information aid for the Australian Trade Commission. Meanwhile she applied to join the WRNS, and it was as a Wren that she attended the reception in Washington a year later at which the British ambassador, Lord Halifax, presented her with the British Empire Medal for her 'exceptional qualities of

[1] Translated by R. H. Stevens and published in London by Burke in 1958.

fortitude and endurance', and for 'doing all that was possible to allay the sufferings of the other occupants of the lifeboat as they died'.

She did not forget her promise to Francis Almond, the boy who, with his brother David, was transferred – mercifully, as it turned out – to Boat 8; and from New York she sent him a replacement scout knife, with a covering note:

For Francis
with Best Wishes and
Many Thanks
from
Margaret Gordon

For good measure, she sent a scout knife to David Almond as well.

Knocker Whyte avoided hospital at first and was accommodated in a hotel. But he exerted himself too much and his legs swelled up so terribly that he too had to submit to hospitalisation. When he was well enough he was flown first to Miami on 30th January and thence to New York. Meanwhile news of his survival had reached Erith, confirming the faith expressed earlier by scoutmaster Jim Coles. 'Give him a boat, and something for a sail,' said Coles, 'and I always knew he'd sail home from anywhere. James had the finest navigational instinct of any lad I knew.' Soon he would be on his way home to take his master's ticket. Wartime rationing or no, a bumper Welcome Home party was being prepared for him by his mother.

After spending most of February being fêted in New York, Whyte embarked for Holyhead and Liverpool at the end of the month on the Ellerman Lines vessel *City of Pretoria* as a distressed British seaman. He was going home on a lucky ship, one that had borne a charmed life, surviving Malta convoys, fierce Japanese air attacks, and the North African landings, in addition to the daily hazards of the war at sea. Also she was sailing in convoy. This time, though, she was carrying munitions; and somewhere between New York and Holyhead she disappeared without trace.

Could Whyte have survived a second time? It was many months

Joan Redl.

Lady Almond.

The Almond children, taken some years earlier. From left to right: David, Susan, Basil, and Francis.

Jack Edmead.

Margaret Gordon in the uniform of the W.R.N.S.

before the mystery was solved, and then only from enemy records. On 4th March 1943, in position 42.39 North 36.30 West (roughly mid-Atlantic), the *City of Pretoria* was hit by two torpedoes fired by a U-boat, and she immediately blew up. Closing the position of the sinking, the U-boat commander found wreckage bearing the words 'Ellerman Ltd'. He believed he had sunk the *City of Manchester*, but that vessel had been lost thirteen months earlier. There is no doubt that the vessel that disappeared in mid-Atlantic on that March day in 1943 was the *City of Pretoria.*

There were 152 people on board, among them six other distressed British seamen besides Whyte; but there were no survivors. With Whyte went all the valuables and keepsakes that had been preserved from Boat 4.

The loss of Knocker Whyte after his epic 51-day voyage was almost as poignant as the death of Diana Jarman just when it seemed that she too had reached comparative safety. Like so many others who survived the actual sinking, these two heroic figures did not get home to celebrate their escape.

Captain Rogerson was awarded the O.B.E. and Les Boundy and Tommy Green the M.B.E. Awards of the British Empire Medal to Angus MacDonald, Jack Edmead and Margaret Gordon have already been mentioned. What of Knocker Whyte and Diana Jarman? Decorations for these two presented a problem, since the O.B.E., M.B.E. and B.E.M. were not awarded posthumously. In Whyte's case the strategem chosen was to back-date an award of the M.B.E. to the day before he was presumed to have been drowned at sea. The parallel award for Diana Jarman would have been the British Empire Medal, the same as for Margaret Gordon; but in her case no contrived back-dating was considered. In a citation of close on 1,000 words in the relevant *London Gazette* supplement Diana receives no mention, not even a commendation for brave conduct, though such commendations went to Sidney Britt, Chief Engineer Robert Faulds, Douglas Quantrill, and Gladys Usher. It was an omission that was never corrected. Bob Skea and the Millers were others for whom awards might have been made with justice.

No award was made initially to George Nutter, presumably

because he had not been placed officially in charge of his boat, but in his case the omission was eventually corrected. A letter to the shipping company from a grateful fellow passenger, forwarded to the right quarters, helped to stimulate this belated recognition. 'I would like to mention', wrote missionary worker Miss Ruby Cooke, 'the splendid way in which Mr George Nutter, one of the passengers, managed our lifeboat, No. 6, under great difficulties and brought us, under God's guidance, to safety. If it had not been for his cheerful common sense I am afraid we should have been lost.' On 9th January 1946 the award of an M.B.E. was gazetted.

Here was another missionary ascribing her survival to God. Certainly the saga of the *Cairo* had shown there were battles that the human spirit alone could not win; but was it conceivable that He had looked after His own?

Most of those rescued soon forgot their prayers and their promises and preferred to count themselves fortunate. But on the subject of chance, the superstition that missionaries on board ship were bad luck was not borne out in the lifeboats. Indeed the reverse was true. There were ordained or lay missionaries (or both) in all those boats – but *only* those boats – which reached a haven in time to save the bulk of their cargo.

ACKNOWLEDGEMENTS

The seed of this book was a letter from a Mrs Kathleen Aish to the Editor of the *Sunday Express* telling him of her cousin Mrs Sybil Chapman, an octogenarian living in Dorset, who, said Mrs Aish, had a remarkable story to tell of a wartime sinking by U-boat of a passenger liner, of which she was one of the survivors. This letter was passed to me to follow up, and I visited Sybil Chapman. It soon became apparent that her story was part of a vast jig-saw which, if all the pieces could be found and fitted together, would present a picture of absorbing interest.

Research and writing of a three-part series of articles for the *Sunday Express* followed, the material coming from many sources, official and unofficial, published and unpublished. Most of the published material was brief, but contact with one survivor often led to contact with another, and the ship's papers provided a fruitful source. The series was published on 2nd, 9th and 16th August 1981.

Publication brought many fresh contacts, and the limitations on length of the newspaper series (15,000 words maximum in this instance) encouraged me to feel, as I had from the start, that full justice to the story could best be done at book length. Collins agreed. The articles stimulated a detailed reply from the commander of the U-boat involved, and a promise of help with my book; and among the major discoveries at this point was that the sole survivor of one of the lifeboats, a woman who had refused to be interviewed at the time and whom I had been unable to trace for the newspaper series, was alive and well and living in Australia, where she agreed to my visiting her. This was Margaret Gordon, and finding her really set the seal on the book.

I have had invaluable help from the Naval Historical Branch of the Ministry of Defence, where Mr R. M. Coppock has provided many significant facts and figures from British and German documents; from the Public Record Office, Kew, and especially from Wing Commander F. F. Lambert, D.S.O., D.F.C., R.C.A.F. (Retd), and Mrs Kay Twyman-Musgrave; from the British Library, and especially from the Newspaper Library at Colindale; from the Guildhall Library; from the Imperial War Museum, and especially from Mr G. Clout; from the

National Maritime Museum; from the General Register and Record Office of Shipping and Seamen, Department of Trade, Cardiff, and from the Marine Survey Office in Seething Lane, London; from Ellerman Lines Ltd, and especially from Mr Richard Gaunt, now of Gaunt Spreckley Williams Ltd; from the High Commission of India, and especially from Captain P. S. Barve, First Secretary (Shipping); from the Universities of Glasgow and Hull (Archives); from the Government of St Helena; from Smit International of Rotterdam; and from Allan C. Crothall, of Exmar Limited.

Most important of all have been interviews and correspondence with survivors and with relatives and friends of survivors. I have listed these under individual lifeboats, together with other relevant help. I also include a list of Books, Articles, Documents etc. which I have consulted and used as source material.

Boat 1 – Mrs Jean Foster, sister of Angus MacDonald, who kindly lent me the original of her brother's handwritten account of his experience, together with many relevant letters and documents; John Nelson, Branch Secretary, National Union of Seamen, Salford, Manchester; the late John Cheetham-Edmead (Jack Edmead) and Mrs Ruth Cheetham-Edmead; F. P. Ironside, brother of Bob Ironside; Mrs Cynthia McCready, a first cousin of Diana Jarman; Miss N. L. Collins, a friend of Diana Jarman; Pauline A. Veale, daughter of Robert 'Tiny' Watts; Henry G. B. Tasker and Mary E. Tasker, son and daughter of Dr Ronald Tasker; India Office Library and Records (Military Department) and National Army Museum (Indian Section) for details of the careers of Lt-Col H. E. Tyrrell and Captain J. D. Jarman; R. D. Kennedy, Editor of the *Evening Telegraph and Post*, Dundee, for help in tracing relatives of Angus MacDonald; Doug Daykin, Diary Editor, *Evening Echo*, Bournemouth, for help in tracing relatives of Diana Jarman.

Boat 4 – John Pinkerton, of Dromana, Victoria, Australia, who found Margaret Gordon for me; Australian Information Service, Australian High Commission, London, who failed in the same quest 'after a good deal of research', for which, although abortive, I remain grateful; *Sydney Morning Herald*, who also failed in this quest, but whose paragraphs on Margaret Gordon's award of the British Empire Medal in 1943 gave essential clues; *Miami News* Library, *Miami Herald*, and the Miami-Dade Public Library; Eric Whyte, brother of James Allister Whyte; Dr

Philip Stones, school friend of Whyte; Len F. Clarke; Bernard Tull, District Commissioner, Erith and Crayford District Scout Council; Mrs Elsie Cooper, sister of Freddy Powell; Ralph Cooper (no relation), then third officer of the *City of Bombay*, who, torpedoed six weeks after the *City of Cairo*, arrived in Recife ahead of the *Cairo* survivors and was on the quayside to greet them; and not least Margaret Gordon. Accounts that she wrote (unpublished) and subsequently made available to me are listed below.

Boat 5 – Mrs Sybil A. Chapman; Dr Douglas Quantrill; Mrs E. L. Rogerson (widow of Captain Rogerson); William Stubbs; A. B. Tempest; Francis Redl, Mrs Joan Redl, and David Redl; Mrs Nancy McNair; Mrs Cynthia Grant (formerly Saunders); Mrs Freda Bullen; Anthony McQuone, son of Francis McQuone.

Boat 6 – George Nutter; Victor Chambers; Mrs Dulcie Kup (formerly Kendall); Mrs Violet Jayes (formerly Violet Williams); Mrs Betty Clark, daughter-in-law of Mrs Minnie Clark; John J. Cullinane.

Boat 7 – Captain Robert Skea; Reverend Robert Waddell; Mrs Jenny Davies; Miss Elizabeth Birchman; W. Ferdinand Dieckhaus; Michel Jaspar; Mrs Mona Rooksby.

Boat 8 – Basil G. Almond, Francis R. H. Almond, Dr David L. Almond, and Mrs Susan Nagle (formerly Susan Almond), also various accounts by Lady Almond, listed below; Mrs Eileen Simms, David Simms, and letters written by Mary and David Simms soon after their rescue; A. Donald Miller; D. A. McNeill, son of Daniel McNeill; Lambert E. Scaife, son of Lewis Scaife; and Clifford L. Smith, second wireless officer on the *Bendoran.*

U68 and Captain Merten. In addition to considerable correspondence on U68's last patrol under his command, Captain Merten has helped me to pursue my search for survivors of the *Rhakotis* and U410. I am also indebted to Eric Reed, of Godalming, for a tape of his personal interview with Captain Merten in October 1981. U68 was eventually sunk by Allied aircraft off Madeira on 10th April 1944, only the look-out surviving.

U410 was sunk in Toulon by American bombers on 11th March 1944, but in contrast to the fate of U68 only one crew member was killed. Those from U410 who helped me with reminiscences of the patrol on which they picked up half the crew and prisoners of the *Rhakotis* were Friedrich Rachner, Huge Dinges, and Friedrich Ufermann.

General. I am also indebted for help with general research to Douglas Wiltcher and J. M. Weir, and for their meticulous care in reading the manuscript to my brother the Rev. Peter Barker and to James Wright.

APPENDIX I

The Commemorative Scroll, placed in the Civilian Hospital on St Helena[1]

The *S.S. City of Cairo* Survivors

On November 6th, 1942 the *S.S. City of Cairo*, carrying three hundred and one passengers and crew, was 'en route' from Cape Town to Pernambuco, homeward-bound from Bombay to the United Kingdom. At night, unconvoyed, in the mid-South Atlantic, a thousand miles west of the African mainland, she was attacked without warning and sunk by two torpedoes fired from an enemy submarine. Two ships' lifeboats were shattered, and the remaining six – all overloaded and two of them severely damaged – containing two hundred and ninety-four survivors, made contact the following morning and set course for the Island of St Helena. Of these boats one containing fifty-four persons lost touch, but was happily rescued by a steam-ship which landed the survivors at Cape Town. Another and smaller boat, containing eighteen survivors, lost touch, and was picked up by a Brazilian minesweeper off that coast on December 27th: by which time – after fifty-one days at sea – only two were left alive. A third boat, containing fifty-four survivors, lost touch, and was never heard of again. A fourth boat, containing fifty-six survivors lost touch, after seven days and nights, but sailed on alone for a further six days, when she was rescued by the *S.S. Clan Alpine*, bound for St Helena. After a hazardous voyage extending over five hundred and ninety miles and enduring for thirteen days and nights, without sight of land, or ship, or aircraft, the remaining two of these six open boats sailed safely within sight of the Island at daybreak on November 19th. Later that morning they were sighted and picked up by the *S.S. Clan Alpine* and – during the afternoon – this ship landed the one hundred and fifty-one survivors. Of the one hundred and sixty-nine who had set

[1] Some of the facts and figures in the preamble are marginally incorrect.

out in these three boats eleven were children, all of whom arrived safely. But of the remainder, comprising various nationalities, one woman and three men – all British – and also seventeen Indian seamen died in the boats, or in hospital after being landed. Of the one hundred and forty-eight men, women, and children who survived, some were enabled, after a few weeks, to leave the Island. The others who remain believe that all would wish this inscription to fulfil the following three purposes: thankfully to record the marvellous feat of seamanship by means of which their ordeal was safely passed; sorrowfully to commemorate their companions who perished; and gratefully to express their thanks to those, both on ship and on shore, who welcomed them with generous kindness and hospitality.

List of the Survivors – W. A. Rogerson, Master, R. A. Faulds, Chief Engineer, R. H. Gerner, Second Engineer, D. W. Quantrill, Surgeon, L. Boundy, Second Officer, W. Stubbs, Fourth Officer, H. D. Broomby, Third Engineer, L. Mountain, Supernumerary Engineer, D. Dick, (Ditto), C. H. Williams, Second Steward, W. B. Ritchie, Cadet, M. Campbell, Carpenter, P. McNeil, Quartermaster, M. McLean, (Ditto), G. Norton, Steward, W. A. Edwards, Corporal-Gunner, R.N., A. Cockill, Gunner, R.A., J. Martin, Seaman Gunner, R.N., J. V. Morris, (Ditto), H. M. Porterfield, (Ditto), D. Skinner, (Ditto), Elizabeth Birchman, Freda Bullen and Michael and Peter, Victor Chambers, James and Sybil Chapman, Minnie Clark, Ruby Cooke, Lennard Codling, John Cullinane, David and Jenny Davies and Ann and Janet, Francis Blagrave-Dean, Alexander Day, Robert and Elizabeth Dickey, Wilhelm and Avis Dieckhaus and Ferdinand, Roland Dodds, Edward Elliott, Florence Gavin and Sheila, Randolph Godlieb, Andrew Green, Pierre and Janine Jaspar and Michel, Vasilli and Galina Kariakin, Dulcie Kendall and Colin, Gregore Krakovski, Margaret Marr, John McFarland, Lawrence McGaffney (dec'd.) and Catharine McGaffney and Catharine and Patricia, Charles McKechnie, George Nutter, Thomas Parkinson, Elsie Petrie, Alfred Racher, Joan Redl and David, William and Mona Rooksby, Cynthia Saunders, Herbert Shenton (dec'd.), Arnold Silcock, Robert Skea, Allan Tempest, James Turner, Gladys Usher, Robert Waddell, George Waters, David and Mary Williams and Violet Williams. In addition there were sixty-four Indian seamen two of whom – Sultan Khan and Punnoo – died in hospital.

As a memorial gift to the Island of St Helena the Survivors have presented a Radio Receiving Installation for the Civil and Military Hospitals at Jamestown – February 16th 1943.[1]

[1] The radio receiver is still in use (1984) in the hospital. The Information Officer of the Government of St Helena writes: 'Although not now in very good condition, it's able to receive our local radio station.'

APPENDIX II

St Helena Government Gazette, Notice No. 62, Page 10 of edition for January to December 1942:

Appreciation of Services re Survivors. His Excellency the Governor and Commander-in-Chief desires to express his appreciation of the valuable work done by Government officers and employees, members of the Garrison and the Civil Defence organisations, and many other persons who gave their services during the recent landing of survivors, or contributed to the Colony Comfort Fund in money or in kind.

S. N. Peters
Chief Clerk, Secretariat

(The Governor and Commander-in-Chief at the time was W. Bain Gray.)

APPENDIX III

Where are they now? – Some biographical details of survivors

The Almond Family. 'Miraculously,' wrote Lady Almond at the age of 81, 32 years after the sinking, 'here we all still are. All the family are married, with children. In fact I have 16 grandchildren in all. Susan has six of them.'

Dr David L. Almond writes: 'The experience has certainly left an effect on me as I never forget the anniversary of the sinking – conveniently the day after Guy Fawkes Day.'

Lady Almond died in 1978 in her eighty-fifth year.

Evelyn Ashdown and Cecilia Norris, the two middle-aged missionaries from Delhi, withstood the ordeal as well as any. The former lived to the age of 86, the latter to 85.

S.S. Bendoran, the rescue ship that would have been scrapped already but for the war, gave good service to the last. 'In March 1944,' says the official history of the Ben Line, 'this old vessel, which had served in two world wars, was acquired for use as a blockship on the beaches of Normandy, as part of the now famous Mulberry Port which played such a prominent part on D-Day in the great Allied invasion of Europe.'

Betty Birchman, now 69, admits to having suffered greatly as a result of 'that dreadful ordeal – not mentally but physically, and to be still suffering today'. However she adds: 'It taught me a great deal about the people around me – their strength and weakness – and it most certainly taught me a great deal about myself and the values in life. My own strength then has certainly helped me a great deal in the past 40 years, and I have been much more aware of the needs of others. It seems a strange thing to say but it was a worth-while experience, though not one I would want to repeat. Still less would I wish anyone else to go through it.' Miss Birchman, who served in Africa after the war, now lives in Canada.

Leslie Boundy had joined Ellerman Lines in 1929 at the age of 32 and taken his master's ticket in 1935. His last deep-sea voyage with Ellermans was in the *City of Cape Town* in 1952/3. He died in 1964, aged 67.

Freda Bullen still lives in the house to which she returned (it was her parents' home) in Shropshire in 1943. Neither of the twins, she says, remembers anything of the ordeal.

Victor Chambers was appointed Technical Assistant to the General Manager of De Havillands on his return to the U.K., where his task was to organize Mosquito production for optimum output regardless of obstacle or cost. He describes it as 'an exciting and unforgettable experience'. In 1952, looking as ever for a new challenge, he emigrated to Canada, where he is due to retire this year from an appointment in the Civil Engineering Division of the Fanshawe College of Art and Technology in London, Ontario.

Jim and Sybil Chapman took up market gardening on the family's smallholding near Truro and worked it for many years. Mrs Chapman lost her husband in 1972 – he was 87 – but she herself (her part in the conception of this book is recorded in the Acknowledgements), although now in a rest home, is still going strong at 87.

Minnie Clark made her home with her younger son in Yorkshire, as she had planned, and remained there till her death in 1948 at the age of 72. The lifeboat flag she was given to use as a shawl is still in the possession of her daughter-in-law.

Ruby Cooke. I have not been able to trace relatives of Ruby Cooke, but she is believed to have been engaged on missionary work in India prior to the sinking. Her letter in praise of George Nutter has already been recorded, and she kept in touch with him until shortly before her death in the 1970s.

Sir John Dain appears to have made an excellent recovery from the illness that kept him in hospital so long after rescue. He died at his home in Tonbridge in 1957, aged 74.

Jenny Davies lost her husband some years ago but she writes of the two children: 'Ann (who was four) can remember that the sea was glossy black the night we were sunk and that the lights of the lifejackets were reflected on its surface. Janet (who was two-and-a-half) can remember looking over the side and watching the fish. Each can still remember that the skin around their thumbs had turned brownish and was peeling by the time they reached St Helena.' They remember the island, too, but their most vivid memories are of the voyage home in the *Nestor.* 'During the day the convoy was bombarded by aeroplanes and during the night ships were torpedoed. Ann has nightmares about being attacked by planes coming from all directions even to this day.'

Rev. Robert Dickey was a changed man afterwards, according to his companions on St Helena. 'There was a more restful look in his eyes,' writes a correspondent, 'and he was ready to meet and go about in company in a way which he would never have done before.' He maintained the improvement and was in excellent form when the Rooksbys met him in India after the war.

W. Ferdinand Dieckhaus later became manager for K.L.M., the Royal Dutch Airline, in Bangkok. He is now retired and living with his wife Avis in New Zealand. 'Ferdy', too, is in New Zealand. On a recent holiday in Holland the elder Ferdinand made a special visit to London to help with research for this book.

Jack Edmead related his experience in documents that are listed under Acknowledgements, but my efforts to find him failed. The failure was explained when I read Angus MacDonald's account (also listed). 'Jack got home safely through Spain, was given another ship,' wrote MacDonald. 'It was lost with all hands.' This revelation was repeated in May 1954 in a radio adaptation of MacDonald's story. 'No,' said actor James McKechnie, playing MacDonald, 'I never saw Jack again. He was sent home from Spain, joined another ship. It was torpedoed and lost with all hands.'

My initial researches confirmed MacDonald's account. 'He (Edmead) promised to come and tell us about the terrible experiences they had had, but the poor chap was lost at sea on his next voyage,' wrote one correspondent. 'He said he would visit us at a later date, which he never did,' wrote another. 'It was some years later that we learned he had been lost at sea.'

None of these reports brought any traceable contradiction or denial, yet after my articles appeared in the *Sunday Express* in August 1981, in which I noted the early demise of Jack Edmead, I was summarily contradicted by a man of advanced years who was understandably aggrieved at my Mark Twain exaggeration. Because he signed himself John Cheetham-Edmead his identity was even then not immediately recognized, but on 19th August, three days after the 'news' of his death was repeated in my story, I noted in my diary 'Jack Edmead is alive!'

It was too late for the *Sunday Express* to publish more than a belated correction, but I visited Mr Edmead and his wife next day in Market Drayton, and learned that after the war he had spent some years in Kenya, where the false reports had escaped his attention. At our meeting I was able to produce documentary evidence which, although viewed by Mr Edmead and his wife with understandable scepticism, went some way to establishing my good faith. Mr Edmead then corrected me on other less distressing misconceptions in my account and added significantly to my knowledge of events on the *City of Cairo* and in Boat 1.

Sadly Jack Edmead did not long outlive my visit, or the correction, which came only just in time for him to see it. Three weeks later he was admitted to hospital, and after another three weeks, on 4th October 1981, he died. He was 76.

The source of the 'exaggeration' was almost certainly Angus MacDonald, who must have heard the report about Whyte and somehow confused it with Edmead. What is far more remarkable is how the report, repeated so often in various media, went unchallenged for so many years.

Margaret Gordon was as good as her word: she did not cross the Atlantic again until after the war, continuing to serve with the WRNS in the United States until the end of the war. Meanwhile she steadfastly refused to give any account of her traumatic experience. The loss of Jimmy Whyte thus meant that very few details were available of what happened in Boat 4. As I have noted under Acknowledgements, not until after the *Sunday Express* articles appeared was I able to trace her, and then it was only after many promising sources had failed. The man who found her for me was a correspondent of mine in Australia named John Pinkerton (see Acknowledgements), to whom I am eternally grateful. Margaret Gordon had married again, and although still preferring to avoid the limelight, she agreed to see me and I went to Australia to meet her. Needless to say her help was indispensable to any detailed description of events in Boat 4. At her charming seaside home I learned not only the details of her survival but also enough about the lady herself to make that survival credible.

Tommy Green was appointed to the command of a cargo liner with the British India Steamship Navigation Company in 1954 and so far as is known remained on the U.K.–India service until his retirement in 1961. He died in February 1972 at the age of 68.

Flying Officer A. Hodgson, who together with his crew from 502 Squadron, R.A.F. (Whitleys) was responsible for the accurate estimate of the course and speed of the *Rhakotis* which eventually led to her destruction, and who was awarded an immediate D.F.C. in recognition, converted soon afterwards from two-engined Whitleys to four-engined Halifaxes and was tragically killed with three of his original crew on 26th March 1943 when taking off on his first operational Halifax sortie.

Dulcie Kendall married again and was recently widowed a second time. She says that four years after the sinking, when Colin was about seven, he started waking up screaming in the night, a disturbing symptom which continued for about a year. She could not trace it directly to the experience in the lifeboat but could find no other cause.

Michel Jaspar records that his father Pierre was invalided out of the Belgian armed forces following his experience in the lifeboat. However, he served in the Belgian Government-in-exile in London and in 1947 was appointed Head of the Marshall Plan for Belgium. He and Janine were divorced in 1951. Janine died in 1969 and Pierre in 1973.

Angus MacDonald went back to sea after his release from 28 months in PoW camp and sailed out of Liverpool for the next twelve years, always earning the highest possible assessments of his character and ability. Finally at the end of 1957 he took a shore job as an official of the National Union of Seamen in Manchester, a task he performed with the same methodical care and tenacity he had shown in the lifeboat. 'He loved his job,' says a colleague, 'and loved being associated with seamen.' This was his life – he never married. He lost this absorbing interest when he was made redundant in 1974, and it may well be that this hastened his decline. He died in 1975 at the age of 62.

Captain Karl-Friedrich Merten joined the German Navy in 1926 and was 37 at the time of the sinking. He took command of U68 when she was commissioned and sank 29 Allied ships totalling 186,064 tons from his first patrol, beginning in September 1941, to 6th November 1942, when he sank the *City of Cairo*. This was his last sinking. After this patrol he was appointed to command a submarine flotilla, and this and various training appointments curtailed his operational career. Nevertheless, when the war ended he stood fourth in the table of U-boat commanders in terms of tonnage sunk, behind only Otto Kretschmer, Wolfgang Lüth and Erich Topp. He did not join the *Bundesmarine* after the war but made a new career in ship-building, retiring in 1974. Now 79, he is working on his memoirs.

A. Donald Miller was 90 in August 1983 and is spry as ever. His wife Marjorie died in 1972. His memory is perhaps not completely reliable on contemporary matters but of those days in the lifeboat he retains almost total recall.

George Nutter, who regretted in the lifeboat that he had stayed single, put this matter right soon afterwards. He retired in 1970 as Chief Radio Officer of the Bibby Line.

Dr Douglas Quantrill. When Captain Rogerson left St Helena he placed the remaining survivors in Quantrill's care. Resigning himself to spending the rest of the war on the island when it seemed that no more ships were likely to be diverted, Quantrill applied for the post of Island Medical Officer, which was about to become vacant. His application was being considered by the Colonial Office when he was repatriated with the other survivors on the *Nestor.* Later the Colonial Office offered him an appointment in West Africa, where he served for nine years. From 1963 until his retirement in 1977 he was Medical Officer of Health for the Isle of Wight. In 1982 he returned to St Helena as a locum and renewed a number of friendships.

Joan Redl's marriage ended in 1961 and she is now living with her daughter Lydia in Australia. Lydia was born during the war. 'My husband had leave in England,' she emphasizes, 'otherwise you might wonder how Lydia turned up.'

David Redl took some years to shake off the nickname 'Qunk', whose origin remains obscure. After leaving school he joined the Army, and like his father served with the Gurkhas. Later he began a career in industrial chemicals which took him to Germany, Kenya and Hong Kong. He remembers nothing of the *City of Cairo* experience, though for some time afterwards he is said to have screamed (not perhaps exclusively for his age) at the sight of a wash-basin or bath. But he has no hang-ups about the sinking or its perpetrators, and he married a German girl. They have two children, both at school in Hong Kong.

Captain Rogerson later became senior master of the Ellerman Lines fleet. He died on 12th March 1972 and at his own request his ashes were scattered at sea a month later – from an Ellerman Lines vessel in the Atlantic.

Billie and Mona Rooksby. Billie Rooksby died in 1974. Mona Rooksby now lives in Bournemouth.

Cynthia Saunders, like nearly all the surviving passengers, spent three months on St Helena before returning home on the *Nestor.* 'I am grateful to say', she writes, 'that out of the horrors of war came much happiness for me.' Her marriage did not survive the wartime separation, but an attachment begun on the island did. 'I returned to St Helena in 1947 and married Homfray Solomon, whose ancestors had been on the island during Napoleon's exile. [They had established themselves there in East India Company days.] We had a very happy life together until he died in 1960. Two years later I married a Colonel Grant, who has since died, and I am now a widow living alone in the peace and quiet of the Isle of Man.'

Arnold Silcock remained a practising architect, and at the time of his death on 2nd July 1953 at the age of 64 he was in Jersey working on a development scheme for the island of Herm. Meanwhile he had continued to collect and write about Chinese ceramics and to collect and compose humorous verse, publishing *A Background for Beauty* (Andrew Melrose) in 1951 and *Verse and Worse* (Faber) in 1952.

Eileen Simms, like Margaret Gordon, chose not to attempt any more wartime voyages and she and the four children stayed in South Africa until 1947. Her husband, Gerald Simms, left the Indian Civil Service in that year and became one of Ireland's best-known historians, retiring as Professor Simms, Lecturer in History at Trinity College Dublin. He died in 1979. Eileen Simms, now 82, lives in an old people's home in Dublin. All her children are married, all have children of their own, and all are living in or near Dublin.

Robert Skea was with the B.P. company for the last 30 years of his seagoing life and commanded one of their oil tankers for the last 16 of those years. Born in 1905, he admits to having been 'around for some time'. 'My younger (unmarried) daughter lives with me in Edinburgh,' he writes, 'plus two cats.' Of all the survivors I met, few helped me more than Bob Skea, and no one made me laugh as much.

Smit International, Risdon Beazley Marine, and Exmar Limited. The salvage of the *City of Cairo*'s cargo might seem an impossible dream, but it has attracted some interest. First the firm of Risdon Beazley Marine, of Southampton, started enquiries, followed by Smit International of Rotterdam, the stimulus obviously being the consignment of silver. Precise details of what the consignment contained, however, do not seem to have been made public. Captain Rogerson's statement to the Receiver of Wreck simply said that the cargo comprised cotton, East Indian produce, manganese ore, and 'a consignment of silver'. 'Regrettably,' wrote Smit International (17th September 1982), 'we do not avail of more details as owing to the great depth (circa 2700 fathoms) at which the wreck is supposed to be resting, no serious research has been undertaken.'

In May 1983 a third company, Exmar Limited of Southampton, wrote that they were preparing 'a feasibility study for the possible recovery of a consignment of about 100 tons of Silver Coin which is understood to have been loaded on the *City of Cairo*'. Among those contacted by these firms have been Douglas Quantrill and Bill Stubbs. One estimate puts the value of the silver at £20 million.

Bill Stubbs took a shore job after the war, joining the North Eastern Electricity Board in the accounts department and remaining there until he took voluntary redundancy in 1973 six months short of his 65th birthday. But he did not wholly sever his connections with the sea, serving for some years as Divisional Officer of the Stockton Sea Cadet Corps.

A. Bernard Tempest. Having lost all his books and taken over six months to get home, Bernard Tempest (he adopted Bernard as his first name rather than Allan soon after the sinking) inevitably failed the Dartmouth entry examination. Instead he joined the Fleet Air Arm as a pilot and had the consolation of completing his training in the United States. After the war he qualified as a chartered accountant and set up his own textile business in Yorkshire, retiring in 1982.

Of **Gladys Usher** Joan Redl writes: 'She was quite the most wonderful person, always ready to help anybody in need. If anyone should have been made a saint it was Miss Usher.' After the *City of Cairo* experience she returned to her evangelistic work in Berhampore, where she died suddenly on 21st March 1949, aged 63. She had served in India for 30 years and was to have retired at the end of the year.

Rev. Robert Waddell married his fiancée in Edinburgh in 1944, subsequently returning to India with her until 1955. Since then he has held two teaching appointments and run two parishes, eventually retiring from the Church of Walkerburn in the Borders in 1974. He and his wife have two sons.

Mrs. Pauline A. Veale, daughter of **Robert 'Tiny' Watts,** writes: 'As with many couples who are very close my parents at times experienced almost telepathic communication. Some time after she knew my father was missing, my mother experienced a vivid dream in which my father was in a boat with Indian seamen and he said to her: "It is precious little that we can give, but it is marvellous the faith they have." From that moment my mother was convinced that he had died and indeed it now seems to have been very close to that time.'

Of the **Williams** family, Violet writes to say that her father died some seven or eight years later at the age of 68 but that her mother, whose heart complaint had so worried Violet and was the reason for the family's return home, lived to 81. Violet herself (now Mrs Jayes) had already met her future husband before leaving India, though they did not marry until 1946, after he left the Army. They have one son and two granddaughters. She adds: 'A few years ago I met a student from St Helena and he told me that one of the lifeboats was left on the sea front at Jamestown and they used it as a meeting place when they arranged to meet a friend.' Sadly it has since disintegrated. Like all the survivors who reached St Helena she cannot speak too warmly of 'the kindness we were shown, which was truly wonderful'.

BOOKS, ARTICLES, DOCUMENTS, PERSONAL ACCOUNTS ETC.

Personal Accounts

'14 Days Adrift in a Solitary Boat,' by Lady Almond, *Sunday Express*, April 1943. Also original mss. of same. Also copy of a letter written to Sir James Almond, ICS, dated 26th November 1942. Also copy of an article written for a South African magazine in 1974 when she was 81.

'Evelyn Ashdown's Shipwreck 1942/43 (15 Days in an Open Boat)', available in the Imperial War Museum and at the United Society for the Propagation of the Gospel, 15 Tufton Street, London, SW1.

'The Amazing Story of John Edmead,' written by him and published in the *Sunday Express* on 28th February 1943; and 'Report of an Interview with Mr J. C. Edmead' on Admiralty File ADM 199/2143, pages 61–4, at the Public Record Office, Kew.

'The 52 Days' Journey of Lifeboat No. 4 from the *City of Cairo*,' '51 Days on the South Atlantic, a Chronicle of the Journey of Lifeboat No. 4 from the *City of Cairo*,' and the first three chapters of an unfinished book, all by Margaret Gordon.

An Account by Pierre Jaspar in the Belgian newspaper *La Cité Nouvelle*, date unknown (original manuscript provided by Michel Jaspar).

'Touching the Adventures . . . of Merchantmen in the Second World War,' edited by J. Lennox Kerr (Harrap, 1953), among whose contents (Chapter 3) is an original story by Angus MacDonald. Alan Villiers called it 'the classic open-boat story of World Wars 1 and 2'.

'Ordeal', an adaptation for radio by Martin Chisholm of Angus MacDonald's story in the above collection, first broadcast on 2nd May 1954.

A Ship! A Ship! by A. Donald Miller, a booklet published by the Mission to Lepers, London, 1943.

'Report by Captain W. A. Rogerson on the sinking of the *City of Cairo* by Enemy Action on 6th November 1942 in Position: Lat.23.30S Long.05.30W.' Also letter from Captain Rogerson to Hall Line Liverpool dated 22nd November written from St Helena reporting the loss. Also 'Examination on Oath instituted by the Receiver of Wreck at the Port of Liverpool of William Alexander Rogerson' (undated, probably March/April 1943).

Some who had Lost their All at Sea by Gladys F. M. Usher, a booklet published by the Council for World Mission, 11 Carteret Street, London, SW1, 1943.

Rev. R. Waddell's account of the voyage of the City of Cairo, her sinking in the South Atlantic on the 6th November 1942 and the 13 days by lifeboat to St Helena [unpublished]; and copy of a letter sent by Rev. Robert Waddell, MA (Santalia) to his sister, of date 8th December 1942, written from St Helena.

Books

Axis Blockade Runners of World War II by Martin H. Brice (Batsford, 1981).

Lascars: The Forgotten Seamen by Conrad Dixon. From *The Working Men who Got Wet.* (Proceedings of the 4th conference of the Atlantic Canada Shipping Project, Memorial University of Newfoundland, 1980).

The Ellerman Lines at War by Taffrail (Captain Henry Taprell Dorling, D.S.O.). Article in *The Navy*, Vol. III No. 12, 1947.

The Hunters and the Hunted by Jochen Brennecke, translated from the German and published by Burke in 1958 and Corgi in 1960.

The Muscles of Empire. Indian Seamen and the Raj, 1919–1939 by F. J. A. Broeze. From *Seamen in Society* (Proceedings of a conference of the International Commission for Maritime History, Bucharest, 1980).

Through the Waters by Robert Hughes (Kimber, 1956), also published in paperback as *Flagship to Murmansk* (Futura, 1975).

Lloyd's *Register of Steamers and Motorships.*

Manual of Seamanship, Admiralty, Volumes I and II (varied editions, HMSO).

Royal Air Force 1939–1945, Volume II, by Denis Richards and Hilary St G. Saunders (HMSO, 1954).

Documents

Official Log of the *SS Bendoran.*

Official Log of the *SS Clan Alpine.*

Supplement to the *London Gazette* of Friday 3rd December 1943, dated 7th December 1943, giving details of awards and citations for crew and passengers of the *City of Cairo.*

Various Public Record Office Files, including:

Admiralty ADM 53/116621 and 118504 (Log of *HMS Scylla*); ADM 199/1276, 2047 and 2143.

AIR 15/470, on 'Interception of the *Rhakotis*', from the *Coastal Command Review*; and squadron histories on AIR 27/152, 1105 and 1959.

Board of Trade BT 110/1204.

Translations

Mrs D. Dorrell; Sarah G. Barker.

Index

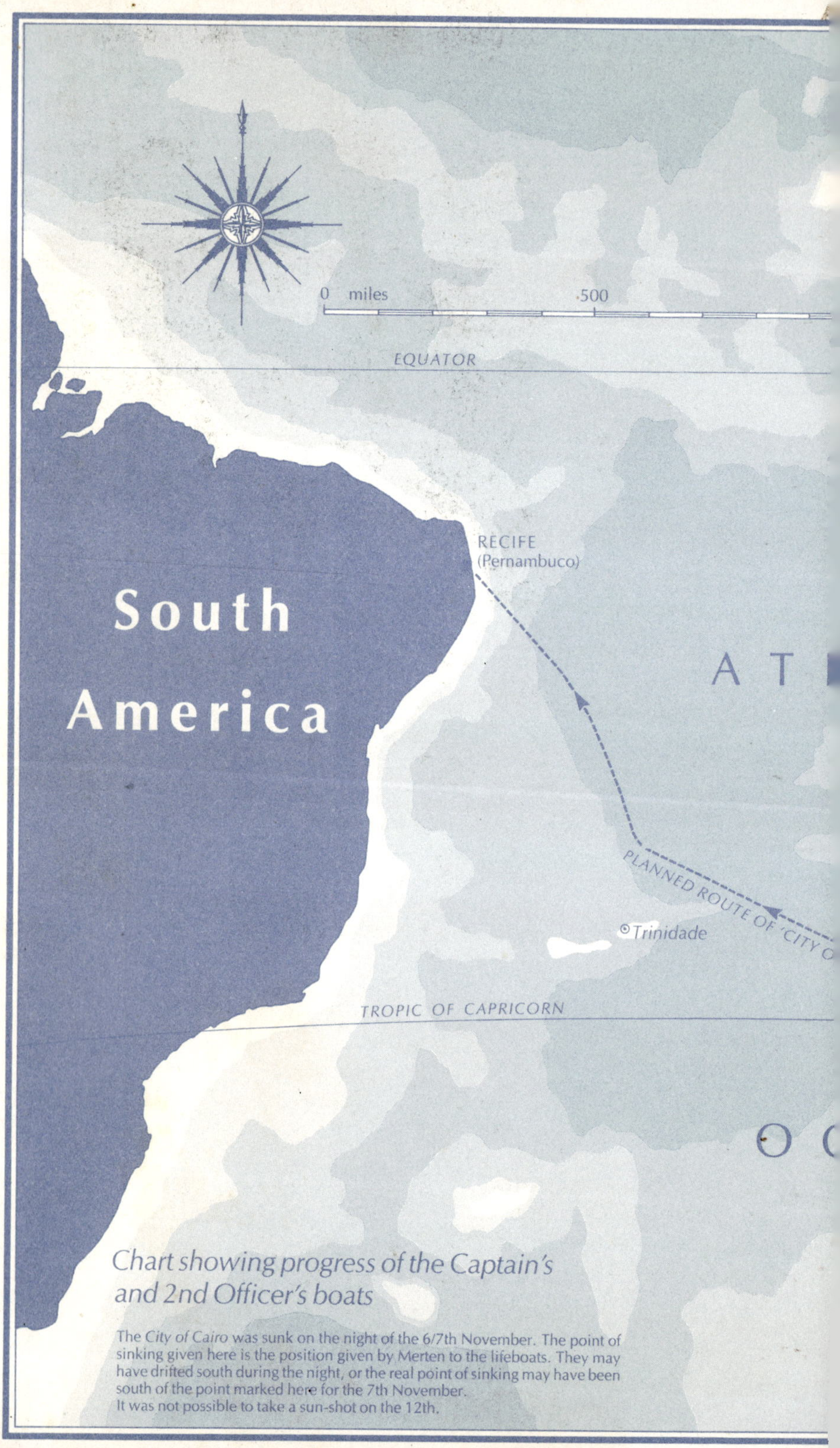

Chart showing progress of the Captain's and 2nd Officer's boats

The *City of Cairo* was sunk on the night of the 6/7th November. The point of sinking given here is the position given by Merten to the lifeboats. They may have drifted south during the night, or the real point of sinking may have been south of the point marked here for the 7th November.
It was not possible to take a sun-shot on the 12th.